COMMON
PEOPLE

COMMON PEOPLE

An anthology of working-class writers

EDITED BY
KIT DE WAAL

unbound

First published in 2019

Unbound
6th Floor Mutual House, 70 Conduit Street, London W1S 2GF
www.unbound.com

Lines on pages 100–01, 104 from 'The Thought Fox' by Ted Hughes, from the
collection *The Hawk in the Rain* by Ted Hughes, Faber and Faber Ltd., used with
permission from the publishers.

Text design by PDQ

A CIP record for this book is available from the British Library

ISBN 978-1-78352-745-8 (trade pbk)
ISBN 978-1-78352-747-2 (ebook)
ISBN 978-1-78352-746-5 (limited edition)

Printed in Great Britain by CPI Group (UK)

For everyone who finds their lives written in these stories

With special thanks to Paula Hawkins for generously supporting this book

Contents

Foreword

I started this foreword a dozen times. I thought I'd start off with something witty and literary to show that common people can quote the classics and should be taken seriously.

Then I decided, no. Be yourself. So I began a riff about what it's like to be working class. How, when all the world wants the same thing – a long life with enough to eat and a sound roof, a good education, meaningful, paid employment on safe streets and a reason to laugh from time to time – working-class people have to pick a few things off the list and do without the others. Bleak, I thought. Too bleak.

Context is where I went next. Facts and figures. Dazzle them with data. I was going to spend 500 words on how many of us there are, how much we live on or can't live on, by what horrendous percentage living standards have declined and poverty has increased, and the precarious nature of working-class life today. I would demonstrate, with a graph or preferably a Venn diagram, the grim intersection of class, race, disability and gender. But there's already an academic in this book who does that better than I can, so I thought I'd better leave the numbers to the expert.

I wanted to throw in an amusing anecdote about the editors and agents who took me aside at book launches and whispered, 'I'm working class too, you know,' and I heard in their confession a pride and nostalgia for the lives they had left behind or had to hide. I also heard relief that, at last, someone on these pages might tell their story and say it's OK to be working class, you can step out of the closet (or broom cupboard). But I'm not a comedian and the anecdotes weren't that funny.

In the end, fittingly, this foreword is an opportunity to thank everyone who has supported this book, this cause, this telling of untold stories. To all the writer-development agencies (New Writing North, Literature Works, Spread the Word, Writing East Midlands, Writing West Midlands and the National Centre for Writing in Norwich): thank you for the massively difficult task of sifting through so many submissions and providing us with the seventeen excellent memoirs by brilliant new writers whose lives demonstrate such resilience, humour, solidarity and courage. To all the published writers who leapt on board at the first opportunity, lending their names and their stories to this book of common people: thank you for your generosity and faith in this project and for standing alongside us.

And to you, you who have pledged good money and time, who have tweeted and liked and cheered from the sidelines, thank you from all of us, sincerely.

Most of all, these memoirs, written in celebration and not apology, are dedicated to everyone who has yearned to see their life on the page, who has hoped one day to read about working-class lives told by the working-class people who lived them. Today's the day. Enjoy.

Kit de Waal

Tough

Tony Walsh (aka Longfella)

They don't like it when we make it despite all their ifs and cuts
They don't like it when we take it as our right to shake
things up
They don't like it when rough voices start demanding
better choices
But it's tough, we've had enough and we are coming

They don't like it when our stories rise above the kitchen sink
They don't like it when we learn, remember, organise or think
They don't like it when we've knowledge so they price us out
of college
But it's tough, we've had enough and we are coming

They don't like it when we're standing on our own, on our
own terms
They don't like it when our candle lights another so it burns
They don't like it when we're spotted in a slot they've
not allotted
But it's tough, we've had enough and we are coming

They don't like it when we're uppity and throw a ladder down
They don't like it when we've sussed it and we grow and
gather round
They don't like it when we minions have articulate opinions
But it's tough, we've had enough and we are coming

They don't like it when our pens begin to join up all the dots
They don't like it when we send back what we've learned to
the have-nots
They don't like it when our writers can ignite us into fighters
But it's tough, we've had enough and we are coming

They don't like it when the common people sing a single song
They don't like it when forgotten people realise we're strong
They don't like when race and gender join with class as
one agenda
But it's tough, we've had enough and we are coming

They don't like it when our classes are not cowered
but empowered
They don't like it when the masses clock the power that
is ours
They don't like it when their victims will not suck their
fucking dictums
But it's tough, we've had enough and we are coming
Millions strong!
Yes, it's tough, we've had enough.

And we are coming.

Working Class:
An Escape Manual

Lisa McInerney

Of the various social classes, working class is the most slippery. If, like me, you were born into a working-class family or community, do not be concerned about being labelled in perpetuity. The world is lousy with people who will happily erase your identity, and you don't even have to pay them.

This is a big statement to make; after all, is it not that social class exists in all of its impermeability for a reason? If social class was an unsettled state, then surely it wouldn't be social class at all; it would be called 'current circumstances' and we'd all be flinging it on and off like modish headwear. But, alarmed by alarmist reports that membership numbers are shrinking, the middle classes seem to have taken the drastic measure of attempting to induct as many wretches as possible. And, wearing otherness as though it's a suit of armour, the working classes seem to have adopted adoption as a viable method of dealing with the successful. Whatever about median income and the evolution of Marxist theory, if you've got a pair of chinos or a third-level education, prepare for assimilation.

I write about working-class characters. I do so not because I want to redress the balance in English-language literature, where characters seem to be comfortably middle class by default, but because it's my default.

No car, no holidays, no opinion on Joyce; a council house, a cynic's caution, an army of cousins.

I have highfalutin ideas about storytellers' responsibility; there are certain stories that are yours to tell ('This task was appointed to you, Frodo of the Squalor, and if you do not find a way, no one will'). Still, it surprises me when I am asked questions about my supposedly noble motives, or referenced as a writer who writes about lives that are not often featured front and centre in literature. It shouldn't surprise me, because we're all very worried about the homogenisation of literary fiction, but it does, because if I'm working class why wouldn't I write about working-class lives? It's not as if I'm doing it as court-ordered community service.

A potential explanation is that writers, like characters, are assumed to be comfortably middle class by default, and because no one likes cognitive dissonance, the working-class writer will be encouraged towards redefinition. It's quite rude to say to a working-class writer, 'I am experiencing cognitive dissonance, so if you wouldn't mind warping into something more manageable?' so attempted erasures tend to be a little more subtle. But don't worry. I'm doggy-wide, and I've identified a few and outlined them for you.

Bonus points if your assimilation discredits the working class as a whole!

Competence is a foot out the door

There exists this canard that aptitude is something you pay for, that talent, hard work and tenacity are part of a success story only when they're moulded into a useful whole by an expensive education, one-on-one tuition, mentorships agreed on golf courses, or good old, pre-Reformation-style nepotism. Being first-rate at something that isn't drinking tins, childbearing or bare-knuckle boxing is a sure-fire tell that the subject was only tentatively working-class in the first place. So handy that a person's entire background, upbringing and personal philosophy can be peeled off like a purifying face mask if they make good, for the past is something to be overcome and not celebrated.

I spoke not so long ago to a broadcaster who asked whether published writers could still be working class, as if aesthetics is all that separate the social classes. We got a little further into the conversation and it came out that his partner had suggested he wasn't working class any more because he had become a broadcaster. Farewell to all that built your character, bucko, you're a bourgeois boy now. In this scenario, accomplishment mutates not only your present circumstances but all of your past experiences. In this scenario, class is simplified so as to be about money, and, occasionally, moral fortitude; its parameters don't really exist unless you're inept, in which case adversity is just deserts.

All a working-class person needs to do to become middle class is be good at something. Those who benefit from a class system – they are few but they are powerful – will ensure the class system is maintained. Ergo, we cannot have the idea that working-class people are just as talented, hard-working or tenacious as anyone else, otherwise 'class' could revert to its Marxist definitions and all and sundry will be wondering how, exactly, one seizes the means of production. So the lesson is: pick a skill and work on it, and you'll be courted by mortgage providers before you know it.

Working for the man means being his emissary
For a time I worked for a company that manufactured and fitted

windows and doors. I was hired to answer the phone and to answer emails, and in order to be all right at both I developed a clear phone voice and took care with my grammar and punctuation. Also I ironed my clothes before I came to work in them.

One day I answered the phone to a local councillor, who proceeded to eat the head off me over a delayed repair for a constituent's windows. We had not repaired the windows because the required part had not yet come in, but the client lived in a council estate and had assumed we were dragging our heels because the company was staffed with moonlighting nobs who hated the poor. She had contacted the local councillor, who hoped one day very soon to be a local TD, so he got on his high horse (stoned donkey, if he'd been committed to his theme) and charged into battle. I explained to him the problem was a lack of casement hinges and not snobbery, but he was still muttering darkly as he hung up. The main thing was that he assumed the building company I worked for represented Opulent Ireland, despite the fact that we were a motley bunch of white van men and incompetent typists. 'Working for the man' had become 'endorsing the nefarious plotting of the ruling class'. The only problem was that my wages didn't match the job title.

The other thing was that now that I had a full-time job it was assumed that I would be sending my child to a private school. I felt utterly transformed when a colleague expressed confusion at my plans – if you could call them plans and not lackadaisical assumptions – to send them to the local community school. 'Not into town?' she said, 'town' meaning the city eight miles up the road. 'You haven't put their name down *anywhere*?' This colleague was a job-sharer. She worked one week on, one week off, and though she had a large and beautiful home it seemed that she worked to keep her considerable brain active rather than out of financial necessity.

'No,' I said, calmly, but that evening I went out and bought a Lexus NX and *Debrett's A–Z of Modern Manners*.

Long words make magic spells

'Moratorium' is a common enough word in Ireland, because it refers to that blessed practice not every country can take for granted: the cessation of all election coverage in the media from 2 p.m. the day before voting. Ostensibly this gives the electorate a chance to reflect before heading to the polls; in Ireland we usually reflect on how aggravating and wrong the politicians are. So perhaps the word 'moratorium' is not so commonly used in other English-speaking countries, but it gets fair use in Ireland, and my character Ryan Cusack, who appears in my novels *The Glorious Heresies* and *The Blood Miracles*, is Irish, and on one occasion he uses it. Thereafter were raised little red flags. How would Ryan, being working class, know a word like 'moratorium'? Was the question not how would his author, being working class, know the word 'moratorium'? She learned it from the telly, as it happens.

Another reader said that for the sake of realism she had wished that even one of the *Miracles* characters had been a moron. If this was simply because she prized intellectual variety in a novel's cast, that would have been fine, but I suspect there was a little more to it, because it's rare that readers cry out for more simpletons in books about horny academics or the disorders of the gentry. Working-class people, know your place! But do not know your 'vicinity' or 'domicile', because they're big words for middle-class people.

I've gone on about this before, because I am loquacious and pugnacious and a bunch of other things working-class people are but can't spell. About a year before I wrote this essay, I wrote an article for the *Guardian* about how one's use of language is not a class signifier, because language is not a catapult to take you from plebeian to toff. However, no one ever listens to me, so the upwardly mobile should make use of this language scepticism. Club Middle Class? A thesaurus and a lozenge and you're in, mate.

Feminism is for ladies of leisure, socialism is for dandies

One thing I've learned from watching those of us on the left tear each other to shreds on social media is that there's no such thing as a working-class feminist. This was news to me, and news I'm sure to a lot of engaged, enraged and activist women. Surely the desire to see gender parity across all strata of society is not particular to the moneyed intelligentsia? Surely, my arse. Idealism and empathy, once traits associated with revolutionaries or mothers with an awful lot of sons, are in contemporary terms but fleeting fits of bourgeois conscience. Feminism is a sewing circle for the upper crust and socialism has something to do with champagne.

This is particularly confusing when you consider that the people most likely to benefit from feminist or socialist policies are the disadvantaged, and for feminism or socialism to triumph there would have to be a dismantling of the class system. It seems a pernicious trick to insist that asking for social change is an activity for the people who are least likely to want social change, but there you go. Out yourself as a feminist or a socialist and you will immediately be awarded your middle-class citizenship and expelled from the terraces, which, for some reason in this scenario, are peopled by Conservative voters and Men's Rights Activists.

If you think champagne's a signifier, wait till you eat this avocado

Avocados are for wankers. Yes, they are delicious and good for you, and are reasonably priced in Aldi, but they are symbols of affluence, and mashing one to go on a slice of wholegrain toast will immediately raise the market value of every house in a half-mile radius, which no

Millennial will ever be able to buy because they're too busy wasting their wages on avocados. The salt of the earth don't eat avocados! They're for privileged types who have nothing better to do than worship shiny-toothed food writers and Fitstagram celebs.

I really like avocados and until I became a published writer, and therefore indubitably middle class, I used to only eat them under cover of darkness. Working-class people are not supposed to like avocados. In order to extricate yourself from the working classes, you do not even need to enjoy the eating of avocados. Just public mention of a nice ripe Hass should do the trick.

Writing? Well, law-di-daw!

And so where is the working-class writer? In my experience she's found on social media, complaining that all of the other writers are blue-bloods whose work is of dubious quality and who'd topple from their pedestals in a true meritocracy, the rules for which she's drafted a dozen times in her head. All a working-class writer needs to do to become middle class is be published and *pff*! Ascended!

Tongues extracted from cheeks, now let's take a crabbier look. What's irritating about this last one is that when we assume that writers are middle class by default, we can so easily absolve ourselves of any responsibility to counteract. It is true that writers are more likely to come from comfortably middle-class backgrounds for a number of reasons, not least that it's prudent to have a safety net because there's balls-all money in writing. But when we assume that the working-class writers aren't there – that they're neither in situ nor emerging – how can we support them? How do we go along to their readings, choose their works for our curricula, or, for the love of God, buy their bloody books? The contemporary class system is a capitalist conceit and, as we are still a long way from being able to dismantle it, we must use its tools. Why aren't there more working-class writers? Why aren't there more working-class stories? Because not enough people clamour for them, and too many have accepted alternatives as replacements.

Middle classes inducting former wretches, working classes adopting out their successful. This moving of the goalposts may seem a fine thing, if its conclusion is a newly mutable class divide. I am not convinced. Inducting former wretches and wearing otherness has the same result: downplaying structural inequality in favour of the pretty hoax that social class involves no limitations that can't be overcome with integrity, hard work and humility.

In particular, the self-othering performed by working-class people, either by those who wish to reject the label and proclaim that they achieved what they achieved independently (meaning that if you don't excel, the only reason is your own moral failures), or those who wish to disown the ambitious (meaning that if you do excel, the only reason is your own deviousness), does nothing but sell out its fellows.

The truth is that systems that benefit the rich cannot exist without fevered maintenance carried out by the rest of us: *divide et impera*, and have each sub-class police the behaviour of the one below it. We're encouraged to believe that there are few working-class artists, few working-class idealists. That creativity is the privilege of the rich because the rich have nothing else to do. So what's more demeaned? Working-class people, or art itself?

There's a word for it in Ireland: notions. 'Notions' of course is a synonym for 'ideas', but in this context they're ideas of an unwholesome kind: ideas above your station. Irish people – particularly Irish working-class people – live in terror of being accused of having 'notions'. What sort of patience would a community need for a member intrigued by shiny things like poetry, fashion, radical politics or avocados? These are whims to be indulged, not enterprises to be implemented; they are not for people at the coalface. 'Notions' is the class divide seen through the lens of working-class experience; 'notions' is the fear of being labelled middle class. It's a struggle no less clandestine than 'keeping up with the Joneses'. Instead of worrying people will judge your modest means, you worry that people will assume you to be a haughty class traitor, pretentious, a phoney. Or worse, that they will annul the challenges you've overcome or invalidate the challenges you face. What's more indicative of 'notions' than making art? What, are you too good to work for a living?

Let no mistake be made. Discouraging 'notions' does not defend earthy, wholesome working-class mores. It's just another way of keeping you in your box.

So what's the state of the working-class writer? The state of this one is intermittent irascibility, the constant need to feel out role and place and be OK with it, the rejection of capitalist power structures alongside the paradoxical need to be defined by roots. Class is a construct, but a construct in the same way that our roots are a construct; those aspects of ourselves we feel connect us to our families, our communities or our countries are no less indistinct and no less meaningful. Like the broadcaster deemed 'evolved' by his partner, my experiences will not be written over, all of those events and words and challenges and joys that informed my personality whitewashed by my decision to attempt a career in the arts. I reject the idea that culture is defined by the cultured. Of course I do: the idea is profoundly stupid.

Slippery thing, though, working-class identity. Particularly if you want to scribble for a living. Worth keeping an eye on it. I'm only saying.

Don't Mention Class!

Katy Massey

I *am* working class, I am sure, but I am struggling to explain myself. It doesn't help that the 'me' I am trying to describe keeps being redefined, and it is not my doing. You see, when I was growing up in Leeds in the 1970s, I was the illegitimate half-caste child of a single-parent prostitute. Today, the only part of that description that is still meaningful is 'single parent'. As for the rest, it has mostly been reconstructed, and re-understood.

For instance, the words polite society uses to describe my ethnic origins have graduated from 'half-caste' to 'black' to 'multiple heritage' and, currently, I am 'mixed race' and/or 'a woman of colour' (or perhaps person of colour?). Of course, all these reinventions happened without my permission. I didn't get to change my subscription to any particular *identity*, I simply got on with growing up and older. British society and the blunt instrument of time took care of it.

But, while language around race constantly evolves, provoked by social anxieties about difference – there are few terms for 'illegitimate' heard in everyday life today. 'Love child' still appears in some newspapers, usually related to extramarital scandal, but I can't think of any new ones. It's as if the idea of illegitimacy itself has atrophied and is now almost dead, as the perceived stigma of being born 'out of wedlock' has decreased. New words, fresh vocabulary to hide or alleviate the pain of shame are simply not needed.

Even my mother's former job has been dignified by resignification. She would now be called a 'sex worker' not a 'prossie', or a 'brass', or... but our ages-long apprehensions about sex have produced more euphemisms for members of the oldest profession than I can list here. My mother is no different from anyone else, and though in her late eighties now, she still has opinions about nomenclature. This is what she would like you to know: 'Don't use "brass", love. Say "working girl" or "madam". "Brass" sounds like we were rough, and we weren't.'

Were we a bit, um, rough? Perhaps. But all of the elements that go to make up a person's social class – income, locality, race, education, parents' profession, etc. – are impossible to separate, meaning considerations of class that limit themselves to one or two of these characteristics are horribly unreliable when applied to the individual. My first definition of my childhood circumstances may beg a different conclusion, but I know what my mother means. We weren't rough, not really, especially if respect for education, good food and common decency mean anything.

Perhaps I could use a points system to establish my social class? I am no statistician, so forgive the vagueness of this notion, but don't some countries use this method to judge who is a desirable (versus non-desirable) citizen? Let's see:

I grew up in the city of Leeds, and am therefore a northerner – minus 10 points.

I went to boarding school between the ages of twelve and sixteen – plus 15 points.

My mother paid for my education via prostitution – minus
10 points.

I make a living as a writer and arts producer – plus 15 points.

I have brown skin – but it's caramel-coloured, so not *too* dark
– minus 8 points (it could have been 15).

I am overweight by more than twenty pounds – minus 6 points
(but minus 12 if present at a supper party where talk turns to
the diners' sports-related injuries or comparing their 'PBs').

And so on. But I am writing about the past, and this list speaks
to the present. I think my mother maintains that we weren't rough
because she was never a street prostitute – more of an escort. She
even ran a successful brothel for a while, opening Aristotle's in the
mid-1980s, when the country was high on money and strong women.
Two in particular showed her the way: Margaret Thatcher and,
madame par excellence, Cynthia Payne. Later, a Crown Court judge
would pompously comment: 'I'm sure Aristotle would be spinning in
his grave had he known his name was to become synonymous with
a massage parlour.' I give him more credit. I was only just a teenager
then, but I was seriously impressed with what she achieved.

Actually, my mother wasn't new to running her own operation.
She'd had a café, called the Wheel, and an ice-cream van with a
name nobody can remember, and a marriage bureau, as dating
agencies were called in the sixties. But Aristotle's was the first of her
businesses I remember clearly. And its existence was, though not the
first lie of my life, certainly the biggest.

Because nobody was 'out' about selling sex thirty-five years ago –
decades before the *Belle de Jour* blog and reality shows set in escort
agencies. It was also before sex trafficking and the exploitation of
women and girls was a widespread moral concern, so it was a very
hidden world. The environment Aristotle's emerged from was a

tough one. Only a couple of years before my mother opened the doors, the Yorkshire Ripper – a prolific client of Leeds' prostitutes – was convicted of twelve murders, mostly of working girls. He is still suspected of having committed many more. Women mostly had to protect each other and police themselves.

In the same decade, but down in London, Cynthia Payne had turned the selling of sex into something that was more naughtily suburban than urban seedy. In her leafy Streatham street Cynthia serviced a desire for sex and strong discipline with humour and charm. Like Thatcher, she had a bit of a 'sexy matron' persona, freeze-dried hair and instinctive respect for entrepreneurship. The collision of harlotry and industry was all around, and my mother, in early middle age with an apprenticeship of cottage-industry prostitution behind her, was perfectly placed to exploit it.

Following Payne's example, she sought to make the place as respectable as possible. The location helped: next door was, handily, a sandwich shop. Opposite was quite a smart pub, one of those new ones just starting to call themselves 'wine bars', and a little way down the street was an advertising firm that had produced a series of iconic ads for Porsche. As a result, there was a string of tulip-red Porsches parked along the road. The location was perfect for the purposes of selling sex: classy, close to the market but not in anyone's backyard.

The outside looked as smart as the interior. Above the front door, Mam had invested in a smart, tan-coloured awning, with *Aristotle's* writ large in curly font. There was a reception and waiting room, from which stairs took clients up to the first floor. Here were two 'treatment rooms', a hand-built Scandinavian pine sauna and a shower. It was all very tastefully done, with white walls and heavy, gilt-framed prints of romantic paintings. It was also spotlessly clean and very well organised.

Aristotle's opened around 10 a.m. and closed some twelve hours later, and it quickly became the centre of my world when I wasn't at boarding school. On duty were two sex workers and they needed a receptionist. When Mam offered to pay me £5 a time to work as the receptionist on a strictly casual basis, I jumped at the chance. This role required little of me: I would tell the punters who was working that day, as most had their favourites, take their money as they came in through the door and direct them upstairs. The rest of the time I would sit and talk to the girls. It was a free education.

Aristotle's taught me that selling sex is as sophisticated a process as selling any other product. Sex needs branding and Aristotle's, if not the Selfridges of the sex trade, could easily have claimed to be its John Lewis: honest value reliably supplied. Sex is not simply sex: it has to be branded so that the consumer knows exactly what they are buying. Street trade was visible then in Spencer Place, a few miles away in Chapeltown and the centre of Leeds' red-light district. Sex was more available there and cheaper, so Aristotle's had to offer something more, and it did. Privacy, cleanliness and safety from robbery and attack. It provided these things as much for the girls who worked there as it did for the punters who quickly began to seek the place out.

Mam soon found that the key to staffing Aristotle's was variety. There were fat women and thin women, big-breasted and small, black, brown and white, older and younger (the lower age limit was early twenties and the upper late forties). Each had their own rules about the services they offered, and this was negotiated between them and their clients. In the time-honoured tradition they split their earnings with my mother. Punters were also charged an entry fee.

Though they may have been busy in the evening and perhaps had a mini-rush at lunchtime, there were long days to fill when there were few customers. So, 'the girls' (as everyone called them) talked and talked. Not many of them worked more than a couple of days a week, and in their own time the majority were mothers and grandmothers, as well as wives and girlfriends, so there was plenty to talk about.

It is difficult to describe just how normal everyday life at Aristotle's was for me as a teenager. With little else to do but talk, smoke and eat, we set sail on rivers of words. Pamela talked for hours about other places she had worked, jobs she had had, and about her wonderfully camp little boy Richard, for whom I babysat. Rose told me about working in London and Glasgow from a shared flat with other girls or on the streets – far from home, and far from judging neighbours and her huge Catholic family. One girl, Ada, whose boyfriend was a writer whom she worked to keep, would bring his poetry in for us to read. I was sometimes goggle-eyed at their tales, but I at least had the sense to shut up and listen, especially when conversations took a more surreal turn.

'You know him has the newsagent's at the back of Morrisons?'

'I don't know him. Go on, though.'

'You do! Big fat man. Swaps the dodgy videos.'

'I don't. Go on!'

'You do... Anyway, you know he's selling soiled knickers for four pounds a pair?'

'Why? Can't you just buy them in a shop?'

'No, these are worn. "Soiled" is what he calls them in the ad.'

'No!'

'Well, I went into the shop the other day and nobody's behind the counter. I wander up to the stockroom door, and there he his, hunched in the corner like Rumpelstiltskin, rubbing Gorgonzola cheese into the gusset of some pound-shop pants.'

'God! What did you do?'

'I asked him what he was doing. He knows I do this, so I suppose he isn't bothered about telling me. So he says, "I'm rubbing cheese into these knickers." Then he stops, looks up at me and says, "You won't tell anyone though, will you?"'

We had a good laugh, but really it was characters like this who peopled the day there. There were so many men and women on the fringes of the sex industry, keeping their heads down, breaking bread with their families, and buying the *Daily Mail* while living off immoral earnings. There are the strictly legit types: the accountants, landlords and suppliers that come with any business (stocks of baby oil, talcum powder and condoms need to be maintained). And there were people, mostly men, who just liked hanging around.

Men like Eddie the Spiv, who sold ludicrously overpriced 'contact' mags full of ads for gorgeous nymphomaniacs seeking discreet, adult fun. The adverts were entirely fictional. Nevertheless, his box numbers received plenty of mail, all containing hopeful stamped, addressed envelopes. This meant that Eddie, to avoid arrest or just a good beating, had to reply to at least some. He wrote many himself, but the risk of sending several similar letters in an identical hand to the same punter was ever-present. His solution was to take writing pads, pens and the SAEs down to his local pub and get the middle-aged alkies who propped up the bar to write the letters he needed in exchange for free drinks. More than once he gave me a bundle to post on the way back to boarding school so that the postmarks would show they had come from across the North, and not solely from East Leeds.

Aristotle's was something of a community and my mother was its matriarch. Thanks in large part to her judgement, there were no fights and almost no thieving (and I am willing to bet that the incidents of STIs, mental illness and addiction at the sauna were less than on the streets outside the door). The stigma of what the women did for a living meant that I heard many conversations I could only have heard in that back room, among people who understood the business. And I believe this inside perspective meant I saw Aristotle's for what it was: a place where good-looking, decent women who could hold a conversation offered various sexual services in exchange for money. They could work hours that fitted around childcare and earn enough to live well above the breadline. For the punters, Aristotle's was something forbidden, a trip to the edge of criminality and deceit, a sophisticated artifice, and perhaps the best brothel in Leeds for a while.

But it was hard work. My mother got up several times in the night to run hundreds of towels through the washing machine at home. She drove to wholesalers to buy industrial-sized bottles of bleach and tile cleaner. She continuously hired and, on occasion, had to fire a stream of women, many of whom thought that working in a sauna was easy money, then quickly discovered it wasn't. She booked adverts in the local paper; she kept accounts. In fact, Mam was an exemplary small businesswoman right up until the day Aristotle's was raided by the West Yorkshire vice squad.

On the day Aristotle's was raided it made the front page of the *Yorkshire Evening Post*. Ten policemen burst in simultaneously through the front door and an unused back door upstairs. An elderly doctor, a regular of Pamela's, got the shock of his life. He was allowed to dress and leave after giving his personal details. This is key to the role of police raids in shutting Mam down – after the raid and the publicity, the regular punters, who are the bread and butter of a business like Aristotle's, become too scared to come near the place.

The police took my mother to the police station and presented her with their evidence. They'd obtained this by sending two constables into the sauna to pose as punters in the preceding weeks.

'I'm sick of only getting handjobs – that's all they'll pay for,' one officer of the law complained of his employers.

Understandably, my mother had little sympathy.

They already had days, times, sums of money that had changed hands, but this didn't stop them questioning her for hours and dragging up everything they could, including a minute enquiry as to exactly why Pamela was wearing stockings at the time of the raid.

The worst part for her was when they put her in the cell.

'Get in there!' said one of the officers.

'I haven't killed anyone, you know!' she reminded him, but he ignored her and slammed the cell door shut. They had put her in one of the men's cells with an awful stench and only a wooden bed to sit on. She had had enough.

'What's she doing now?' she heard someone ask.

'Crying her eyes out,' came the anonymous reply.

And it was true.

It might have been the questioner who came and moved her to a woman's cell. A stainless-steel toilet and a woolly waffle blanket lent it an air of relative luxury. He brought her food too. Bread with Stork margarine on it and salad so bland it was like water on the plate. She just had time to reflect that the salad could have been improved no end by a spring onion or two, when one of the kinder officers came to tell her she was free to go.

'We don't usually get people like you in here,' said the young man who escorted her to the desk sergeant.

And that was the problem with the whole business, really, as Mam says now, 'We weren't the types to go to prison,' so a career as a criminal queen pin was never really on the cards. She opened up the next day, of course, but a fine of £2,000 and being raided for a second time shortly afterwards would eventually shut Aristotle's down for ever and force the good women who worked there in safety into other, less reputable establishments or out onto the streets.

Today, I exist in the world as an educated brown woman who makes a living in the arts. I am middle-aged and, perhaps, middle class. As such, it may seem as if I have 'overcome' the circumstances of my childhood, somehow outperformed appropriate expectations of a girlhood like mine. But I do not believe I have overcome it. In fact, I believe I was made by it. I was partly constructed by the good women of Aristotle's, and what small successes I have had in negotiating adulthood are because of what I learned from them. But still, I have found it difficult here to find the exact words to explain how this happened. I have tried to find a vocabulary that is specific, not slippery, words that are fixed in time, not so easily subject to resignification. I am hopeful, but not optimistic, that they won't mean one thing today then something quite different tomorrow.

Shy Bairns Get Nowt

Chris McCrudden

My mam and dad grew up half a mile from each other in Whiteleas. It was an estate built on the edge of South Shields in the housing boom of the 1950s, when the county council laid a utopia of modest working-class houses over what had been 'white leazes', or daisy-covered meadows. I imagine they were designed by a council architect. If so, they built with a child's eye. Every one of those houses, with their four windows, pitched roof and red brick is that archetypal shape you get when you hand a crayon to a five-year-old and bid them draw you a house. When they were built, they were a dream of progress for people who'd grown up in the slum terraces near Tyne Dock. They were new, clean, and, barring a bedroom here or a bigger garden there, uniform. The perfect setting, you'd think, for a working-class monoculture. Yet the truth was more complicated for us, because we were a family split down the middle by a single saying: 'Shy bairns[1] get nowt.'

It was my grandma Joan's maxim. If you didn't ask, you didn't get. My dad had heard it his whole life but my mam hated it. So

---

[1]   Bairns: a colloquial term in north-east England for children.

much that it became her favourite shorthand for how dad's family weren't quite as respectable as us. If they were respectable, my brothers and I wouldn't have come home from visits to Joan's house with fifty-pence pieces won on the horses, clothes smelling of cigarettes, bodies and voices thrumming from refined sugar.

Teas where my mam's mother – my gran Hilda – lived were a more Protestant affair. We got lemonade (in the north-east of the 1980s, drinking plain water was considered a bizarre fad), malted milk biscuits and brown-bread sandwiches that slaked the tinder-dryness of tinned tuna with malt vinegar and sunflower margarine. The hostess trolley in her sitting room housed the same bottle of Bristol Cream sherry and Malibu from one Christmas to the next. Money still exchanged hands, but usually as an act of aggressive generosity. I lost count of the number of times my mam pressed a tenner into my hands at the end of a visit and made me hide it behind the carriage clock. I was a guerrilla fighter in a war where mother and daughter were determined to do everything for each other, yet not owe each other a penny.

It took me a long time to realise that the two sets of grandparents might have lived three streets apart, but were from different wings of the working classes. They lived in the same houses and sent their children to the same schools, so asserted their differences in more subtle ways. Not that Hilda's attitude to my dad's side of the family was ever subtle. As a child in the 1930s, Hilda's nickname was 'Sarah Bernhardt'[2] and she maintained a Victorian tragedienne's sense of injured dignity well into her eighties. That her daughter Ann married my dad at all was chief among those indignities.

---

2   Sarah Bernhardt was a French actor active in late-nineteenth- and early-twentieth-century Paris and London. A great star of the melodramatic stage, she was most famous for creating tragic leading roles, such as Marguerite Gautier in Alexandre Dumas' *La Dame aux Camélias*.

Hers was a dislike born of proximity. Literally, because Dad's family also lived in Whiteleas. Figuratively, because the only distinguishing factor between their lives was Hilda's performance of superiority. While Joan fed us cream cakes bought at the local freezer centre, Hilda got the bus into town and bought Marks & Spencer's date-and-walnut loaf. It was a cake that none of us liked, but whose wholesome ingredients and 'St Michael' label meant we could feel good about ourselves while it went stale in the cellophane. Joan's cream cakes, things of airy nothing, felt wonderful at the time, but I remember little of them now. I do, however, have photographic recall of the dry crumb and gritty buttercream of the date-and-walnut loaf: a cake that begs you to enjoy yourself, but not too much.

This was because Hilda had aspirations but, like her favourite cake, not too many. She had wanted better things for Ann. For her to finish her A levels and train as a teacher, which was a secure and respectable thing to do until you were married. Ann, however, had wanted different things: to go to art college or be a nursery nurse, neither of which were respectable enough for Hilda. Too downwardly mobile, too louche, too insecure. Fast forward to the end of the 1990s and I would have the same disagreements with my parents about studying drama instead of their secure choice for me, which was law. The difference was that Ann knew from her own teenage experience that sometimes it was better to back down than break a relationship.

More or less the last thing my mam ever said to me before she died of cancer at the age of fifty-three was that she missed Hilda, who by that time was alive in body only, her mind curdled by Alzheimer's disease. Yet while they loved each other fiercely and lived in each other's lives in a way that I haven't been able to do with my own parents, I don't think Hilda and Ann ever liked each other much. There was a chasm in the middle of their relationship that dated right back to the time when Ann had tested the limits of Hilda's aspirations for her. And which had led, crabwise, as all major life decisions seem to proceed, to her walking down the aisle with my dad.

There was a story in the family about Hilda's horror when she found out Ann was going to marry my dad. Not so much because she disliked her future son-in-law, but because she realised she knew his mother. Joan was a regular customer in the shop Hilda served in, and a woman who committed the ultimate crime of asking, 'Do you take coupons, hinny?' To Hilda, who couldn't go into a shop without buying something for fear of offending the shopkeeper, this was unforgivable. So Joan and Hilda's ideological clash provided both the mood music of my childhood and the root of my confused relationship with class and aspiration ever since. It was Joan's maxim of 'shy bairns get nowt' against Hilda's leitmotif of social anxiety, 'What will people think?'

I sometimes wonder what our lives would have been like if Ann hadn't taken her mother's part against the sin of asking for what you want. It didn't stop her wanting things for me and my brothers, but it did make it impossible for us to articulate what we wanted without feeling like upstarts. Even now I think of success as being something you're invited to participate in. That was how Ann thought things were: you worked hard at school, you got good exam results, and that was how you got into university. Then you did the same thing all over again when you got a job, preferably in one of the classic professions. I think she believed that life had an external examinations board. If you got the right number of marks, then the light of recognition would shine down upon you and lift you up to the next level of achievement. I was in my early thirties before I realised that opportunity is rarely offered and mostly snatched. I am my mother's child: the shy bairn who waits their turn.

There was another problem with 'shy bairns get nowt'. Not only were we taught that it was vulgar, it was an entirely sensual creed. If aspiration (but not too much) accumulated on one side of the family, the other side was about pleasure, because Joan was a lotus eater. The priest at her funeral in 2016 (who never met her) spun a marvellous work of fiction out of Joan's life, which revolved around the pleasures of gossip, instant coffee, the TV and cigarettes. He turned her good-natured idleness into a lesson of a woman consumed in caring for her extended family. I know she cared: nobody at that funeral needed a priest to tell them that. But it was easier to understand her by how she consumed: indiscriminately, sensually, seated. One thing I've inherited from Joan is her grabby attitude towards gratifying the senses, yet I've often wished that was better directed. I have just enough front to take the last biscuit, but I've never been able to ask for a pay rise.

Since I became an adult and a reader, I've read a lot about the supposed poverty of ambition among working-class households in Britain. That doesn't quite match my experience. Ambition was never a dirty word in Joan's house, but it was an insubstantial concept. What hopes Joan did have for my dad had the same airy quality and flat aftertaste as her cream cakes. He could be a professional footballer, and if that didn't work out there was always the Coal Board. Ann, however, was a more practical woman. So when she left work, which you still did when you got married in 1977, she got a new job steering my dad, then her children out of their backgrounds on the Whiteleas estate. Because while Hilda idolised her friend Margaret, with her genteel flat full of porcelain figurines, Ann made a little shrine in her heart to Mrs Thatcher's ideas of self-help.

First came the flat – bought not rented, and not in Whiteleas – and then the houses when I and then my brothers came along. She manoeuvred my dad out of his dead-end job with the Coal Board and into the police force, where there was better pay, a final-salary pension and, most importantly, no prospect of Mrs Thatcher's handbag full of redundancies. It put Dad, whose family were coal miners, on the wrong side of the picket lines in 1984. But that just gave physical form to the ideological battle that had raged between the families since Joan asked Hilda if she took coupons.

I remember my childhood in the 1980s and early 1990s as a series of bubbles. Our progress bubble, symbolised by home ownership and reproduction mahogany furniture, had a tendency to pop. Sometimes we'd have good patches and go abroad for holidays. Other times, when interest rates or my dad's dreamy attitude towards money management exploded in our faces, we'd sell up and move to a different house with a bigger mortgage to cover the gaps. Between the crash of 1987 and 1994 we moved house five times. What we never moved out of, however, was that awkward, liminal space between classes. My parents' ambitions for their sons started to focus on things like university. Ann got Delia Smith's *Complete Cookery Course*, served pasta and binned her chip pan. Yet we were still perilously close to Whiteleas. We even moved back there for a few months between houses, my brothers, my dad and I disturbing the hallowed quietness of Hilda's home. Because even shy bairns make noise.

But Whiteleas was changing too. Across the estate, laid-off coal and shipyard workers spent Mrs Thatcher's redundancy payments on her Right-to-Buy scheme. First the privately owned front gardens grew fences and walls, then new doors and windows that swapped council utility for faux-Georgian moulding and stained glass. A few bohemian souls even stone-cladded their houses, before *Coronation Street* made a sly joke of the activity. And it was Right-to-Buy that tipped the balance in the families' fortunes. My dad and his sister talked Joan into buying her house. Hilda was immovable: she wanted no one's help. So she began her slow spiral downwards. She gave up the house, moving into a small flat in sheltered accommodation. Here she didn't have to worry about the heating bills, but was operatically scandalised by her neighbours, who enlivened their last years by having affairs with one another. Then came dementia, and the flat became a tiny room in a care home around the corner from Joan's house in Whiteleas, where Hilda died in 2010. She left enough behind her to cover her funeral.

Joan died more comfortably. She stayed in her house, which my dad redecorated for her, until Alzheimer's disease scrambled her mind as well and took her first to a (better) care home and from us in 2016. The house is still there. My granddad John lived on in it, cared for by my dad, until he died at the beginning of 2018, which was the last time I went to Whiteleas.

As we were waiting for the rest of the family to arrive before his funeral, my brothers and I laid out some snacks. I washed the teacups that were kept for best, so never used, and used them. My brother looked for a bowl for olives and cubes of Manchego cheese and I plated up sausage rolls. We served Nespresso coffee and Yorkshire tea. And I can't think of a better metaphor than that spread – in a privately owned council house, on an estate intended to give working families a better start in life than the slums – for our muddled position between the working and the middle classes.

If my relationship with class is so muddled, maybe that's because the patterns I have to describe it in are so uneven. In nearly forty years on the planet I've seen so many stories about the subtle permutations within middle-class life and about five or six for the working classes. We tend to flatten a whole spectrum of experiences into a few tired tropes: the boy or girl done good, the escape from poverty, the sink estate rife with drugs and teenage pregnancies. Since the 1980s an idea has taken hold, shaped by cliché and the

Benthamite cruelty of the current Conservative government, that to be working class is to be deprived. This wasn't my experience. The working class was never a monoculture. It just looked like that to observers who couldn't be bothered to unpick it. And even though the words 'working class' still conjure up images of grey terraces, flat caps and the dreaded whippet (in my whole childhood I do not remember a single whippet!), the values, aesthetics and aspirations of the working classes have changed utterly, even though our image of them ossified some time around the miners' strike.

I deal with demographics for a living now, and I know that the class my grandparents inhabited looks very different today. So much so that even defining it is a struggle. If we classify 'working class' as people who earn under the national average wage (£26,000 in 2018) and didn't go to university, I see a population of 4 million adults, which is around 7 per cent of the total UK population. Yet even these people display characteristics that would put them outside the flat-cap stereotype of the working class: 40 per cent own their homes, 25 per cent go on holidays abroad every year. When I look at what they do for work, yes, many of them still work in the manufacturing and engineering jobs we associate with Britain's industrial heritage, but far more work in care homes and hospitals, in shops, pubs, restaurants. The new working class serves things when the old working class made them.

Yet this is still a flat picture. When we look at the working classes in the twenty-first century, do we include the 1.7 million adults who earn under the national average wage despite having that golden ticket into the middle classes, the degree? Do we include the unemployed and the unable to work? Both groups expand the definition of 'working class' in interesting and problematic directions. Adding graduates blurs those aggressively policed boundaries between the upper reaches of the working classes and the lower rungs of the middle classes that my parents tap-danced between their whole adult lives. Lumping the unwaged in with the waged is another way to breed resentment. Not just because you get the kind of tensions over 'respectability' that meant Joan and Hilda snubbed each other in the street for twenty years, but because being working class doesn't and shouldn't have to mean living on the breadline. I remember how irrationally angry I felt a year ago when someone suggested to me you could define working-class people by looking at whose children received free school meals. Poverty is such an important issue within the working class, but it's not the only story we can tell about it.

The people who built the Whiteleas estate in the 1950s set out to break that link between working-class lives and poverty. It worked for a time, though perhaps not in the way they intended. Today the houses in Whiteleas are largely in private hands. What were homes for heroes are now the stuff of daytime DIY TV, with the odd 4x4 parked outside. They aspire to a new condition, and the snob in me judges them on their success in passing as middle class as we drive by to my last grandparent's funeral. I roll my eyes at those uPVC Georgian windows in exactly the same way that people I've met over the years have judged me when they heard a flat 'a' or that I went to a comprehensive school. Why try to change yourself at all, they imply, when you can't get the imitation quite right?

Because there are two ways of looking at class. For some people, class is a vector: a quantity that has direction. It admits the possibility that Hilda can become Ann and then Chris. For others it's a fixed point. Where you start out is where you stay. So for me, that would be Whiteleas.

The daisies are coming out again in the sidings and the green spaces of Whiteleas. Since the council can't afford to cut the grass any more, they're rewilding, and older, sturdier strains of daisies than

I remember have woken up. In summer they're thick enough to turn the leazes white again. Whiteleas is reverting to a time before social housing and the welfare state that hoisted first my grandparents, then my parents, then me out of our fixed point in the social order. And while I love the daisies, I hope the old times aren't coming back.

The Funeral and the Wedding

Jodie Russian-Red

The Funeral

I'd been trying to convince myself that it was all completely
normal, an everyday thing, just going to a funeral. It's one of only
two reasons the entire family gets together. Everybody said, 'Wear
something bright and sparkly – that's what she loved to see you in.'
When I say 'everybody said', my mum texted me saying 'everybody
said', so I had no idea if that's true or if it was just my auntie Jackie.
It was probably just my auntie Jackie. To play it safe, I wore a black
glittery dress. She *would* have liked to see me in something bright
and sparkly, but you never know who's going to try and moan for
the sake of moaning.

My mum came down wearing her best outfit and jewellery,
which was strange to see. My brother was standing on the edge
of the back step, arm outstretched as far outside as possible, with
a cigarette at the end of his nail-bitten fingers. The cigarette was
probably from the 'communal bacca tin', which as far as I'm aware,
only my mum has ever topped up and only my brother ever uses and
often makes me wonder how many other families have communal
tobacco tins in repurposed cream-cracker tubs. He was staring down

at the green jumper he was wearing and then at his crumpled shirt on the ironing pile. He kept exhaling smoke into the kitchen: 'Is everyone going smart?'

'No, Jodie's going sparkly.'

My dad came down the stairs wearing a cheap black suit he'd told me the night before he'd bought for £30 in the Next sale in the retail park.

'Your suit looks good, Dad.'

'Not bad for thirty quid, is it? I got it in the Next sale; you know, the one in Anlaby Retail Park?'

He looked just like a shop security guard. In fact, I'm pretty sure it's the exact suit the Next security guards wear. I don't think I've ever seen my dad wear a suit in my entire life, apart from in his wedding photos, which is why I said, 'Was your wedding the last time you wore a suit?'

'Err, I think it was. I didn't have a tie, though. Or socks, but that was down to Nabby on my stag do.' The story I've heard before about my dad's stag do is that his friends tied him up with rope, stole his socks and tried repeatedly to set fire to him. Whenever telling the story he usually laughs, 'Yep, I nearly died, what a laugh!' The other part of the story is that he apparently 'refused' to let them shave his eyebrows off, which makes the story bizarre, because it can only mean that he didn't protest to the burning.

It all felt so strange: what a surreally normal, sunny day it was.

My brother ironed his shirt from the pile and changed into it, my mum sat on the back step smoking, I triple-checked my speech. Five minutes later, my dad got the car started, I triple-checked my speech again, my mum dotted her cigarette and my brother changed out of the shirt and back into his green jumper. We all locked the door and left.

At the crematorium, we hung around the car park and put our sunglasses on because the day was still being surreally normal and

34

sunny. I kept thinking about the announcement in the newspaper the week before: *Service at 2 p.m., Chanterlands Ave Crematorium (small chapel).* I couldn't stop thinking about the brackets: *(small chapel).* I felt like doing one great, big sigh.

Cousin after cousin gathered in a haze of smoke and cherry vapour and wheezed about how small they were when they'd last seen the other, what a mad night they'd had that one summer and, 'Are you still doing car mapping then?'

'Nah, mate, I packed it in. I'm at the Briggston's pork abattoir now.'

'Oh, are you? What's that like, then?'

'Well, I'll tell you something, I'm pig sick of it!'

'Heyyy! Ha ha, nice one!'

My brother kept muttering and fretting about everyone wearing a shirt and do I think he should have worn one? I tried to listen, but I was just staring up at the big, long brick chimney.

My uncle Paul's ex-wife Trish turned up and no one knew how to act or what to say while Paul stood in the corner with his new wife Coleen and pretended not to notice Trish. She said to me, 'Hiya Jodie, I haven't seen you in a while! How's your mam?'

When the hearse arrived, everyone dotted their cigarettes, put their vapes in their handbags and I pretended not to notice the coffin.

The service started with the paid-for pastor saying things someone had written down for him about someone he'd never met.

'She spent three years working in the metal-box factory.' (Did she? She never told me that.)

'When she first met Bob, he was up a tree, or so Tracey tells me.' (Why was Tracey talking to the pastor? Why wasn't I invited to the talk with the pastor? Hang on, how come Tracey's sat in the front row?)

'She went on to have six children, who went on to give Betty a running total of thirty-six grandchildren and great-grandchildren. One of them, Jodie, is going to come up and read a poem she's written.' (I looked down at my speech and pretended to triple-check it.)

I wanted so desperately to say all the true things that were interesting and funny and sad. I wanted to mention all the unique and complicated and inimitable things that everyone would recognise, and do justice to this event the whole family had anticipated our whole lives. Instead, I read out the greeting-card soothing platitudes I'd written that morning and I knew it was the right thing to do because everyone smiled and was happy as they contentedly imagined a different, probably less interesting person. I finished and walked back to my seat and pretended not to notice the coffin.

As we were exiting, my auntie Jackie put a hand-embroidered pillow on the coffin and then my granddad found her in the car park.

'You didn't make that yourself, did you?'

'Yeah, I spent all last week making it.'

'Well, it's gonna bloody get burned up! You don't want it to get burned and waste it like that, do yer?'

'I made it for my mam. It's for her.'

'Well, you're mad, it's just gonna get all burned up. What a waste!'

Fifteen minutes later we were in the Red Lion pub, on part of the estate I never ventured to. I'd grown up with stories from my family of all the nights they'd spent in there. I'd seen them put on sequinned, batwing-sleeved jackets, unlock the Old Spice from the communal family bureau I was obsessed with, and stagger after winning the darts tournament. When my life was still in single figures and I stayed up late watching the home-taped Lily Savage videos my grandparents had sat me in front of in the back room, I loved hearing their Baileys-soaked stories about the karaoke, how everyone was miserable that night until Bob did 'My Way' and got everyone up. I loved the running joke that my nanna ruined every single Saturday with 'The White Cliffs of Dover' by Vera Lynn. I loved that she didn't see it as a running joke.

The Red Lion pub wake was the biggest shock and disappointment of my adult life. As I stood peeling cling film off a bizarre buffet, I looked around, and all the stories and what a glorious, raucous, heart-of-the-community place I'd imagined the Red Lion to be were changed for ever. There were no chairs. There was no till. The toilets didn't have lids; the rusty hand dryer was on a chair next to the sink with a bitty bath towel draped over it to dry your hands. The towel looked like the landlord had emerged out of the bath in it sixty years ago, draped it on the chair and built the pub toilets and pub around it.

I balanced ten Hula Hoops, two breadsticks and half a slice of white, marge-spread Sunblest on a paper plate and pretended to remember Paul's ex-wife Trish. The immediate moment after my mum shouted, 'Who wants a drink?' the landlord shouted, 'I'm not putting on the cider tap, Janis, tell 'em they can 'ave bottled!'

No one ate any of the buffet until they were too drunk to notice how disgusting it was, except for me, who ate all the Hula Hoops as I sought refuge by the trestle table and pretended to be hungry while my cousin Louise moaned to my mum about Uncle Paul not acknowledging her as his biological daughter while he's stood there at the bar with the daughter he did acknowledge. We were all there; it was just like old times.

When I say we were all there, well, we were nearly all there. All but one.

The next day I was stroking the cat on the patio set and my mum came down the steps with a coffee and a cigarette and said, 'God, what a night! Your dad passed out and Steve ripped his jacket falling off the stool – did you know he'd already done four lines of coke by the time we went in to the service?!'

The Wedding

It's one of only two reasons the entire family gets together. From what I'd seen on Facebook, Michelle was taking Kerrie's name, which is our name; she wanted to become one of us. That's what I shouted to my mum as she came down the stairs in her best outfit and jewellery. My brother was stood at the back door with his smoking arm outstretched, his eyes glancing between the Levi's jeans he was wearing and the crumpled suit trousers on the ironing pile.

My dad came down wearing a cheap, sheeny waistcoat he told me he'd bought for £7 from Matalan the night before and started painting his bald patch in the mirror.

'What do you think of this waistcoat? I got it from Matalan in Anlaby Retail Park. Not bad for seven quid, is it?'

My brother said, 'Is everyone going smart?'

I said, 'Will there be a buffet?' and my mum said, 'I can't believe we were only invited to the night do.'

My brother ironed his suit trousers and changed into them, my mum smoked a cigarette on the back step, I surreptitiously added my name to the wedding gift, the taxi came down the street and my brother changed back into his jeans.

Opposite a giant industrial estate was the wedding venue, an ex-servicemen's club. We'd been before, for Tracey's wedding and for Steve's surprise fortieth, but this time it was different because there were no bowls of crisps and someone had wheeled in a ye olde sweet cart in the entrance with *Kez 'n' Shell* handwritten on heart-shaped chalkboards. To elongate the gap between outside and everyone, I ate as many flying saucers as anyone would willingly choose to eat (two), and headed in to tell everyone how small they were when I'd last seen them and ask them if they were still doing PAT testing or whether they'd packed it in.

We were the last to arrive (we'd only been invited to the night do) so everyone was already there and halfway through the semi-sober conversation.

'Are you still at that abattoir, then?'

'Yeah, but I'll tell you something, I'm pig sick of it!'

As my cousin Kerrie, the biological daughter who Uncle Paul acknowledged, danced awkwardly with her new wife on an empty dance floor to a song they hadn't picked and didn't know, my cousin Louise cornered my mum to ask why she thinks Uncle Paul won't acknowledge her as his biological daughter.

More aunties and uncles arrived, and my mum stood at the bar shouting, 'Who wants a drink? Jackie? What you having?'

Now and again, people said things like, 'I think it's for the best she missed this, don't you? I don't think she would've got it,' or, 'Do you think she would've approved of it? It's sad, but I think it's for the best,' but this is something that was said to fill air: it wasn't true. I don't know if people knew it wasn't true.

After the cousin bride left early (she had to take her army uniform off and put it in a clothing-protection bag in case it got dirty or creased), I bumped into my mum in the toilets sink area, blotting her lipstick on a piece torn from what was probably an entire roll of toilet paper stuffed into her handbag, and in between blots, above the sound of some anonymous cousin violently vomiting in the cubicle behind, she said, 'Can you believe how much that round was? Sixty-eight fifty! For one round! It's absolutely disgusting.'

Just before I said, 'You shouldn't have offered to buy everyone a drink,' she blotted. 'I'm not offering to buy everyone a drink again.

You know why? It'll have been your auntie Jackie's gin and tonic.'

I steered the conversation away from there being any possible revelation that I hadn't actually taken my purse with me and we talked about how awkward it was when Paul's ex-wife Trish turned up. The non-related bride staggered in front of the sinks to peel off her eyelashes and thank us for coming and say how happy she was to be part of the family and to 'please help yourselves to the sweet cart because no one's touched it'.

Everyone was there. All but one.

The next day I sat in the garden swinging on the hammock that's been reconstructed with Gorilla Tape since my dad fell through it; I was watching the cat watching nothing. I was wondering about whether I should get married, whether or not I'd left it too late, whether there was any point, if anyone would come, if I'd ever own a house, if I'd ever have children, if I could picture myself living a normal life; the cat sat watching nothing.

My mum creaked across the kitchen wearing my brother's parka, leaned down to the hob to light the cigarette already in her mouth, inhaled, slipped on my dad's heel-flattened shoes, opened the back door and came down the patio steps before exhaling. 'I just cannot believe that round. Sixty-eight fifty; it was Jackie's gin and tonic that did it, you know.'

Eight weeks later Michelle put on a Facebook post that Kerrie had moved in with a 'boy from the barracks' and taken the dog. My mum texted me at midnight wanting me to read it, pointlessly speculate and pretend not to enjoy having something to text about at midnight on a Tuesday. I texted saying that I thought my nanna would've really liked Michelle, and my mum texted back, saying: *Yeah, maybe. How much money did we put in their card?*

Little Boxes

Stuart Maconie

I grew up amongst poets.

Keats Avenue, Eliot Drive, Blake Close, Milton Grove.

I was a kid, one of a large, rough and ready tribe, on the huge Worsley Mesnes council estate in Wigan, and the names of these great men (they were all men too; no Dickinson Avenue or Plath Place) were not to me a litany of English verse, but simply the rugged and dependable furniture of young life.

I navigated by these ageless names, as if they were stars. Keith Clegg, who gave me all his Beatles singles in a black leatherette wallet, lived in Dryden House flats. The insanely fanciable Anne Thomas could be 'bumped into' (if you were very lucky) between Browning Avenue and Coleridge Place. Gary Mason had half his face melted off one icy Bonfire Night down Masefield Drive, when kids from a rival estate threw a can full of red-hot ash at him. He'd worn a balaclava every day, summer and winter, since.

We lived among poets. We fought, drank and snogged amongst literary giants. Later, I would learn that some poets themselves, the Mitchells and McGoughs, were actually from streets like ours and would have felt a kinship with us. Even the Betjemans and Larkins envied us our easy sensuality and natural vigour, whilst sneering at our houses and our jobs and loathing our politics and our power. For we were powerful then; vast, grey, regimented council-house estates like mine were the citadels of ordinary men and women whose work conferred prestige and influence, the last of their kind to wield that kind of power. Posh men in blue suits, clipped of voice, plump of lip, would tell me nightly on the news that we were 'holding the country to ransom', we recalcitrant, treacherous workers. If so, it was ransom money that paid for my school blazer and Vesta Chow Mein and football boots, and so it seemed entirely reasonable to me, then and now.

I can see that there is a certain irony in adorning council estates like Worsley Mesnes with the names of grand versifiers of our mother tongue. The juxtaposition is too keen, too absurd surely, between the heady grandeur of *Paradise Lost* and the proletarian homeliness of Milton Grove. But compared to the first houses I had known, my two grannies' little terraces and cottages in Haydock and Poolstock, full of love and shadow, heavy with the relics of dead granddads and antimacassars and the occasional puff of soot, this new brutalist estate, thrown up on the last great wave of sixties expansive council-house development, was gorgeous. In his book *Raw Concrete*, Barnabas Calder said of brutalism – stark, tough, primitive – that it was 'widely seen as the architectural style of the welfare state – a cheap way of building quickly, on a large scale, for housing, hospitals, comprehensive schools and massive university expansion'. This implies the cost-conscious, the purpose-built, the merely functional. But to me, who'd come into a world of coal fires and larders, and houses built in the Edwardian era, my new home was not brutal but clean. It was stark, elegant, the future. I hadn't a clue who Le Corbusier or Ernő Goldfinger were, but they had an architectural ally in the ten-year-old me, who loved having his own room and squares of grass to kick about on, and underpasses and arcades and balconies to run free on. I didn't regard Eliot Drive as a Waste Land. I didn't think Milton Grove was Paradise Lost. I thought it was paradise.

In the photographic archive of the Wigan World website, there's a picture taken in 1985 by one Alan Dalgleish from the fifteenth floor of Masefield House. This was the tower block we lived in briefly before moving to a more 'normal' life in the sprawling estate below. Amongst the more homely, touching pics of long-dead darts teams from the Bold Hotel and old 'Walking Day' parades, this image is straight from a Joy Division album sleeve or a Factory Records poster; streaks of light from cars below smudge and blur along bleak, nocturnal *strasse* that look more like East Germany than west Lancashire. Alan clearly saw the artistic potential in this moody study of alienation by night (photographed using a ten-second exposure from a 35 mm Nikon SLR camera fixed on a tripod, notes Alan). And I see, too, the chilly dystopian vibe the shot intends to evoke. But looking at it now, I also think, there's the Fine Fare minimart with *Apocalypse Now!* painted in disturbingly huge letters on the wall and there's the house where Brownie got off with the girl from the chip shop and Quinny set fire to his pubic hair. It works well as a symbol of a depersonalised urban aesthetic, but it was also home. It was my domain, from the giant substation at Westwood to the slag heaps of Goose Green. They were good times to be working class. We had jobs, we had power, joy, fun, even seasons in the sun... in Blackpool and Butlin's Skegness, in Torremolinos and Famagusta if you'd put in the overtime.

When we dropped like nervous fledglings from our briefly held eyrie in Masefield House – my mum didn't like the heights or the clanking, ghostly lift – we found a ground nest in Fisher Close. It was home to me from the age of about eight when we left my nan's on Poolstock Lane to leaving for college aged eighteen. By the way, if you're feeling embarrassed about your woeful lack of knowledge of the great British poet Thingy Fisher, don't be. For some reason, on my new corner of the estate, just where it abuts the Red Pond and the railway line, the nomenclature changes to commemorate local aldermen and councillors: Fisher Close, Baucher Road, Tyrer Avenue. Even as a child, this struck me as fatuous and pumped up, and it still does. I wonder if any of these grandees ever took a stroll, in waistcoat with fob watch, to admire their names on the signage and find them liberally augmented with stylised male genitalia and *WAFC Rules*.

Worsley Mesnes. The second word is pronounced in a curious and vaguely francophone way ('Manes'), making it sound like the fiefdom of a feudal lord in the Domesday Book or a Norman baronet. Before modern expansion and development, before about 1965, even when my estate was built to house Wigan's growing working population and to take them from the dark, huddled back-to-backs of Miry Lane, this area, a mile and a half south-west of Wigan town centre, was farmland, scrub and coal mines. It belonged to the recusant Catholic Downes family of Wardley Hall, still the seat of the Bishop of Salford. Wardley Hall was in Worsley, much nearer to Manchester, which perhaps explains my estate's name. Though I wouldn't have known it then, and indeed wouldn't know it now if I hadn't read two definitive books on the subject – John Boughton's *Municipal Dreams* and Lynsey Hanley's *Estates* – my sprawling estate was part of the last wave of large-scale social housing development.

Of all the five 'giant evils' (squalor, ignorance, want, idleness and disease) that Beveridge had identified in his famous report on the state of the nation that led to the creation of the Welfare State, and that the incoming 1945 Labour government pledged to defeat, none was as immediately fearsome and grave as 'squalor'. Britain's housing situation had been patchy, impoverished and squalid for many even before the Luftwaffe had wreaked havoc on our towns and cities. Now the situation was even more dire and pressing, and 'winning the peace' meant building a great many 'homes for heroes'. Tellingly, in the post-war Labour administration, the departments for housing and health were combined; decent housing was not just a matter of 'lifestyle', it was a crucial battleground for public health for the many.

Social housing was as much a part of Aneurin Bevan's crusading zeal as the fledgling National Health Service was. Bevan, Minister for Health from 1945 to 1951, felt that council housing should be so good that people of all incomes would want to live in it and the very need for private housing would melt away. Speaking to the Commons in 1949, Bevan said, 'These new estates should not just be for the poor. It is entirely undesirable that on modern housing estates only one type of citizen should live. If we are to enable citizens to lead a full life, if they are each to be aware of the problems of their neighbours, then they should be drawn from all sections of the community. We should try to introduce what was always the lovely feature of English and Welsh villages, where the doctor, the grocer, the butcher and the farm labourer all lived in the same street.'

It's a beautiful May evening in 2018 and I'm sitting in the front room of my mum and dad's flat on the outskirts of the old and much changed Worsley Mesnes estate. I'm tucking into my mum's home-made chips with her slow-cooked steak and onions from a tray on my lap and we are watching a teatime TV quiz show. (There is no point telling working-class mums that you 'had a nice lunch' or 'will grab something light' later. They will not let you sit in the house without eating; food equals love in houses where hugs and kisses are still awkward currency.) The TV show is *Pointless* rather than *Blockbusters,* but otherwise this is a scenario you could have found me very much part of most teatimes in the mid-1980s. *Plus ça change, plus c'est la même chose...*

But they do change. My auntie Mollie has just died in a home for dementia patients and the family is phoning around, trying to establish funeral arrangements. I end up chatting with my uncle John and auntie Kathleen, the Westhoughton branch of the family (Westhoughton is about four miles from Wigan, but when I was a child, this staggering relocation was discussed as if Uncle John had moved to Anchorage or Ulaanbaatar). Kathleen, now in her early eighties, has had a fall and broken her hip. She says that she's 'been a bit low but your Uncle John's been marvellous'. They praise a snazzy overcoat I wore on a recent TV show, and before I go, Uncle John says, 'Don't forget to send me tha' new book, lad.' Because of all this, I feel oddly emotional even before I set out to tour the estate I grew up in, this time for a new book ('Not another!'), and my loins are girded against the tidal Proustian rush that I am fully expecting to knock me off my feet this golden evening.

A broad, grey river of Tarmac winds like an asphalt Amazon through my old urban jungle. Long and winding, it curves from west to east, and back in the 1970s, I navigated it daily. It was the limits of the known world, and I was Magellan in shorts and a snake belt. You could take it and follow it from its source in Poolstock to where it met the sea at Newtown, as long as by sea you mean the A49, Warrington Road. The poetry falls down quickly here, and the road is called, prosaically, Worsley Mesnes Drive. But it is not long before things become more highfalutin, more literary, as I stroll down Eliot Drive and Huxley Close (T. H. or Aldous, I'm not sure, more likely the latter, as it was a Brave New World here in 1965).

Shakespeare Grove, Blake Close, Longfellow Close. Here is

where the tower blocks – Dryden, Thackeray and Masefield – once loomed until they were pulled down in a wave of demolition and 'improvement' in the early eighties. This is when Alan Dalgleish's picture was taken and when the area was semi-affectionately nicknamed Beirut. Now there are small, neat houses; each has a car, and rather smart cars in a few cases. It isn't St Albans or Wells. But neither is it the feral swamp of underprivilege that you might fear and that the TV commissioning editors love to demonise. On its nicer, newer fringe, now tower-less, it is essentially a homely suburban estate, with Previas and Focuses and satellite dishes tilted to catch the warm, golden honey of the evening sun.

I have never been to Radburn, New Jersey. But if I did, I'd feel at home. It was designed and built in 1929 as 'a town for the motor age'; cars were kept away from the house fronts of the tidy, squat Besser-block houses, which face each other across shared spaces and communal areas. The style became hugely influential across certain areas of the world, especially Canada, which is why I now realise my part of Worsley Mesnes was sometimes referred to as 'the Canadian houses', which again made me feel pioneering and exotic. There were Dutch houses too, characterised by their flat roofs, perhaps for clog dancing or the rolling of cheeses. Thus my mum would talk of workmates who 'lived in the Canadian houses' or the council 'doing work on the Dutch houses' and again I would feel that I had been liberated from the sooty Lancashire of my grannies' houses, all *Saturday Night and Sunday Morning* and *Kes*, and moved into a stateless international sphere, a world citizen – no, an interplanetary citizen, more *Space 1999* and silver wigs than *Coronation Street* and curlers.

There was an idealistic impulse to the Radburn idea: Walt Disney was a big fan, modelling much of EPCOT and Disneyland on

47

Radburn lines. 'Children going to and from schools and playgrounds will use these paths, always completely safe and separated from the automobile' was part of the Radburn ideal that was exported to the world. Clusters of houses in closes and groves were linked by pedestrianised zones, grassed areas, walkways and entries. The result, in a sense, albeit in a fairly odd sense, is reminiscent of Venice without the canals and palazzos.

Like Venice too, Worsley Mesnes was an easy place to get lost unless you were a denizen of its ginnels, corners and walkways. Far away from passing traffic and cop cars, those alleys were also ideal hidden venues for various illicit and nefarious activities, some more innocent than others. Radburn developments were felt by some to isolate communities from the flow of normal town or city life and to encourage insularity, problem behaviour and crime. In the Sydney suburb of Villawood, even the architect who designed the Radburn-style project there said, 'Everything that could go wrong in a society went wrong... It became the centre of drugs, it became the centre of violence and, eventually, the police refused to go into it. It was hell.'

Unlike its more famed counterparts in Hull, and the Meadows in Nottingham, Worsley Mesnes doesn't get into many of the histories of planning or the architectural treatises, but it is classic Radburn. And it was certainly not hell if you were an adolescent lad. The original 1920s poster for Radburn shows smiling kids on bikes or clutching football helmets with the slogan *Radburn; Safe For Children*. I don't know about safe, but what with Anne Thomas, nocturnal street football on electric-lit concourses and all the cans of red-hot ash being lobbed around, it was certainly thrilling.

There are some pop songs that I loathe for their stance or meaning rather than any musical shortcomings. Peter Sarstedt's 'Where Do You Go To (My Lovely)?' is one, a horrible attempt to drag a woman (thought to be modelled on Sophia Loren) down by a weak, petty man who cannot bear that she has become a star and doesn't hang out with him any more. But apparently, with the certainty exhibited by most jerks, he knows where she goes to when she's alone in her bed, and challenges her to go and forget him, adding creepily that he knows she still bears the scars, presumably of her early-life poverty and their dalliance. Yeah, right. She is just so over you, actually, and she isn't 'your lovely' either.

Equally hateful is 'Little Boxes' by Pete Seeger, a hit in 1963 and written by his friend Malvina Reynolds. The target in this rotten little song is the people of Daly City, California, a modern suburban estate. Pete sneers at Daly City's inhabitants, their taste, their attitudes and their opinions, which somehow he seems to have divined from a distance. But mainly he hates them for their houses. Unlike Pete, who presumably lived in a tepee, these saps live in the titular Little Boxes, which were all made out of something called ticky tacky and looked identical, exhibiting none of the daring defiance of convention that Pete put into his beard and little hat. Well, that's your opinion and you are entitled to it, but then again not everyone fancies growing a beard and wearing a little cap, singing dreary songs round a campfire, telling people what to think, Pete, you old blowhard. Tom Lehrer, a satirist who picked more deserving targets, said that it was 'the most sanctimonious song ever written'. I'm inclined to agree.

In common with all people with taste, no one listened to Pete Seeger on my estate. Not when I lived there. Depending on our age, we listened to Motown, Black Sabbath, T. Rex, Glen Campbell, Northern Soul, David Essex and Can. Unlike Pete, Malvina and their unlikely ally Margaret Thatcher, we had no issue with living in similar houses, living collectively cheek by jowl. They were not little boxes. They were fine little houses. Not as large or well constructed as the ones that Bevan decreed after the Second World War, but clean, modern and interesting. People could still show their individuality in their little gardens, with their décor, and in how they lived. They did not think having a different-coloured door than their neighbours was a privilege worth dismantling a decent social housing structure and system for. My mates all lived in them, and I knew their layouts as I knew mine, as they were largely identical. (This was handy at darkened parties.)

I once spoke to Irvine Welsh about this. We both grew up little mischief-makers on council estates, he in Edinburgh, me in Wigan, and now we sat like the Four Yorkshiremen, reminiscing about our childhoods over a bottle of very drinkable red at a literary festival. 'All your mates lived in the same kind of house. I mean, some people were richer than others, some cleverer, some cleaner. But you get that anywhere. It didn't occur to us that we had to live in a bigger house in order to prove ourselves. We liked living in the same way. We had more important things to do with our lives than fret about moving up the property ladder.'

Away with Pete and Malvina's smug, creepy 'Little Boxes', then. There's a far better song by the Australian band Triffids, called 'Hometown Farewell Kiss'. It's not exactly a hymn of praise to estate living. In fact, it's about a crazed arsonist returning to his old stamping ground, bent on fiery revenge, but it is about knowing a particular patch so well it is seared into the memory, into the muscles and the senses, knowing every corner, every back road, knowing where to turn.

Even after all these decades, I still know where to turn, guided by old desire-lines grooved into the heart. I turn at where the Crooked Wheel once stood, a purpose-built estate pub that geometrically resembled its picturesque, Constable-ish name, but only when seen from the highest storeys of Thackeray, Dryden or Masefield Houses, and even then only with keen eyes and a dreamy imagination that could overlook the pigeon shit and security rows of jagged bottles. It's gone now, not burned down, just swept away when Beirut began to smarten up – which it definitely did – in the eighties.

So the Crooked Wheel has gone, but one of the two chip shops on the estate is still there, and a few customers are queuing for their 'chippy teas', still perhaps the ultimate working-class comfort food despite the arrival of Nando's and Maccy D's. I remember that when I was a very small boy, some people would arrive with bowls from home to collect their chips in, thus ensuring a larger portion. We never did this, as it was thought slightly common and needy, I fancy, but even the detail feels more reminiscent of wartime than the era of *Blake's 7* and Brian Clough. The old world gave way to the new slowly, and old habits die hard, and maybe somewhere in the North, someone is standing in a chippy queue with a white porcelain mixing bowl in one hand, and an iPhone 9 hooked up to the cloud in the other.

I stroll down Eliot Drive, hoping that the other chip shop is still there. This was the one I'd walk to from my nana's in Poolstock during the school holidays, fetching chips, steak pudding and curry sauce ('small fish, little batter' for Nana) to eat in front of *Crown Court* or *The Sullivans*. The woman who would serve these to me had green eyes, freckles and red hair, was, I guess, about thirty, and engendered the same slightly painful, confused feelings in me that Agnetha from Abba did. I wonder if she noticed. Maybe all eleven-year-old boys look that tense and awkward, especially when being asked if they 'want a mambo with that, sweetheart'. But not only is she gone, so is the chip shop, which makes me a little sad, even though I'm not hungry.

'What are you looking for, love?'

The voice comes from a woman of indeterminate age leaning in her doorway. She is chatting to her neighbour, of equally mysterious age, who leans on his. They are both tattooed but whereas once that would have been the mark of the ageing Teddy boy, the ex-squaddie or naval rating, or perhaps the extremely lively and free-spirited woman, now it means nothing. I imagine the Duchess of Cambridge has a tattoo, and possibly the Archbishop of Canterbury. It is as classless and empty of significance as liking *Bake Off* or the World Cup or sending out for pizza.

'Shops went years ago,' the man says, in a voice like sandpaper on raw brick, when I tell him vaguely my business. 'I used to live here,' I say, at which they look me up and down and I become very aware of my brogues and manbag and my lack of tattoos. I am not particularly better dressed than the people I meet on my old estate tonight, just differently. For all I know, their authentic trackie bottoms, Superdry tops and trainers cost more than my get-up. It says more about my old habits and prejudices and mod/soul boy sensibilities that their clothes are part of a pan-generational trend of all classes that has missed me. I still assume that grown men who wear sportswear of an evening are some form of PE teacher and may well ask me to do squat thrusts or lunges at a moment's notice. From an open window nearby, I hear what I assume at first is an argument and my heart sinks at this reinforcement of clichés about 'us'. Then I realise that this is simply a warm, teatime family conversation, but this being Wigan, conducted at the tops of our voices in loud, challenging accents, like the Chinese.

I move into the heart of the estate, headed for my old house. My surroundings look smart and fresh and not at all dilapidated. The grass has just been cut, perhaps by the council, although it occurs to me that many of these houses now will be owner occupied, bought under Thatcher's relentless, hungry, almost vindictive drive to privatise the country, starting with its housing stock. Toddlers on bikes wobble around the grassy squares, and I realise that the designers of Radburn may well have had their hearts in the right place when they put kids first rather than cars.

There are grannies, and toddlers swinging on gates, and girls still in their ties and blue pleated skirts from school, skipping and chatting. Two young couples are making plans. 'We'll sithee at weekend and go and have some food.' In contrast to the typical image of a council estate, that of a cacophony of screaming kids and red-faced shouting adults direct from *Jeremy Kyle* and the squealing tyres of hot-wired cars, there is birdsong and the musical tinkle of children's laughter. It is just like where the nice, ordinary people live. Because these are nice, ordinary people.

I know these streets, I know where to turn. I get a weird emotional charge when I round the corner into Fisher Close. There is my old house. The house where my uncle Cliff passed out behind the front door one Christmas Day in the late 1970s and I couldn't get back in after skulking out with some mates to escape the trifle and relatives and depressing late-period *Morecambe and Wise*. There is the little patch of grass where I slipped in the cold, wet mud and sprained my wrist dashing away from an errant jumping jack one Bonfire Night. There is the little visitors' car park where we replayed every game of the 1974 World Cup, me always Johnny Rep after my new dashing hero of the swashbuckling Dutch national team. Here's where I first heard 'Floy Joy' by the Supremes on Mike Tyrer's transistor radio in the company of Brownie and Nidge and Clegg, Gary with his burned face and my next-door neighbours, Richard and George.

I walk away past a children's playground that is full and noisy at 7 p.m. and I remember the deserted, forlorn one I saw in Poundbury, Prince Charles's model village in Dorset, a lifeless experiment in ersatz architecture and fake community. I was mulling a passage in Lynsey Hanley's brilliant *Estates* that chimed perfectly with how I felt. 'Even though I have lived away from home for a third of my life now, it continues to shape the way I think about the world outside it. Rather like rappers who continue to talk about the ghetto experience long after they have moved out and to their country ranches, it's a state of mind.'

Walking through them again, I realise that these little houses are in my blood. These streets made me. I know these streets. I know where to turn. And I turn up the main road toward Wigan as I have a thousand times before, to the Latics ground, to the Wigan Casino, to school, to the John Bull, to the gas showrooms to get the coach to London or the Free Trade Hall. The cliché that leapt to mind was that growing up here didn't do me any harm. Except that, viewed objectively, it did, when you compare the life chances of the kids who grow up on these estates, compared to those who go to Eton or live in the Home Counties. But I don't feel that way, and even framing that thought seems mean and disloyal and treacherous.

P. J. O'Rourke, the American humorist, enraged by some mewling, whey-faced loon from one of our posh broadsheets, was inspired to write a fabulous piece of invective – worth looking up in full – that ended 'I'd rather be a junkie in a New York City jail than king, queen, and jack of all you Europeans'. I wouldn't go along with that, but I feel his bristling ire against the well-behaved, well-brought-up, well-heeled commentariat who sit in judgement on the urban working class. I'd rather have grown up pretending to be Johnny Rep with a plastic football, drinking illicit Pernod with Anne Thomas and listening to 'Floy Joy' in a car park than to have ever set foot in the dining room of the Bullingdon Club. You had to watch out for the odd flying can of hot ash. But it was worth it.

Which Floor?

Loretta Ramkissoon

No one ever tells you that, however you die in our tower block, you will leave this world upright. It's impossible to fit a stretcher horizontally in the lift. When the paramedics come to transport the body down, they have to take the lift, just like everyone else. They wait at the door and when the lift's trusty ping signals its arrival, the stretcher is carried across. Then they stand in the lift with the dead body. When unlucky enough to not be able to put the lift out of service, you run the risk of the door opening on another floor, the bemused faces of the people on the landing staring until the penny drops and all eyes fall to the floor out of respect and awkwardness. The CCTV captures the entire ritual. There's no dignity in dying in a tower block. My grandfather always tells me that when he dies, he doesn't want to die upright. He wants to be carried out lying down, preferably out of a house. 'Always have your own front door,' he says.

The two lifts are situated in the middle of the building. They are our root and our core. They bring people down when they die and up when they're born. If the block is the tree, then the flats are the branches. When a diagnosis is made and a funeral booked, we all mourn the tree's loss. When one floor hurts, we all hurt; when one branch falls, we all feel the pain.

Braithwaite Tower began construction in 1965 and was completed in 1967. It mainly consists of concrete, steel, glass and bricks. It has twenty-two floors, twenty of which are habitable. The original lift shafts are still in place, though the lifts themselves have been upgraded once. In the last fifty-one years, the lifts have carried people up and down an estimated 13,292,640 times.

My grandparents were thirty years old when they moved in in April 1967. For the first time in their lives, after ten years of living in one room with two small children, they had their own place to call home. My mum and uncle were ten and nine years old respectively, and for the first time in their lives they had a room each to sleep in. In fact, I still sleep in my mum's old room. It was her childhood bedroom and then it became mine. I wonder if we used to lie in bed at night dreaming of the same things growing up; of best friends and passing exams, travelling far and wide, first loves and finding jobs, home ownership and lasting marriages.

My grandparents were one of the original families that moved in. Let's call them one of the founding families. Out of the eighty flats, they are one of the few founding families still there. My grandparents care about our estate; they witness the number of founders decrease every year as members move on and pass away. But they are never forgotten. Their stories continue to live on in these walls, even when new families have taken their place. One day there will be no founding families left, which fills me with sadness. Who will be left to tell our story when the lift shafts are all that remain?

We know when a new family moves in. Word spreads through the vines and we become aware that the lifts are straining under the transportation of new furniture emanating from the removal vans parked outside. New families are often encountered in the lifts. They are analysed, and established residents later speak about them on the landings by the bin chutes. Once these families have proven their commitment to the block, they are accepted, welcomed as members.

My family has seen many people pass into the afterlife over the years and we have been to countless funerals of people in our block, covering almost every religion, or none at all. We become known by our floor numbers, our personal identification numbers, as if we were all different regiments within the same army. Mrs Poole on our floor, Mrs Miah on the seventh, Mr Girgis on the fourth, Mr Jiménez on the nineteenth, the drugs overdose on the twelfth, the cardiac arrest on the second. We have visited Muslim burial areas; we have eaten hummus and kebabs with the Coptic Egyptians; we have been to Spanish churches, Filipino masses, Jewish synagogues, Greek Orthodox parishes, Hindu temples, Christian cremations and have attended many wakes in Irish pubs on the way back from Kensal Green Cemetery. The cuisines we've sampled have all varied, but there is one constant… Grief brings people together. Whoever we are in Braithwaite Tower, we all take the same vessel to our resting place and we all go to meet our makers when the lift reaches the ground floor.

The lifts themselves are small, silver, mirrorless rectangles, cold and uninviting. In a way they are coffins in themselves and sometimes even they die. There are a few rare occasions where both lifts break down at the same time. A mass panic ensues. People crawl out of their flats like woodworm; everyone congregates on the landing to discuss how terrible it is. It makes us appreciate the value of the lifts in our lives. Our community comes together when this happens. We meet people en route as they race up and down the twenty flights of stairs. Children are sent out to carry the Tesco shopping bags upstairs for the elderly. People stop to catch their breath and are overtaken by others. The groups of youths smoking weed on the stairs have their habits disrupted. (The stairs are usually forbidden territory, only used to do something illegal, or when one doesn't want to encounter anyone. The lifts are too transparent for anything like that.)

Newborns, too, get their first taste of tower life via the lifts. Babies are carried over the communal threshold and welcomed into their new home. For the young, the lift is a fun plaything. It was for me too. A vehicle that generated envy, as few other school friends had to use one to get home. Children grasp no concept of wealth.

I don't remember the first time entering Braithwaite Tower. But I do remember being a four-year-old and looking up at the main entrance. Hearing the buzz of the intercom, pressing the lift button (it used to make a clicking sound, then light up yellow, not the sleek blue digital button that was recently fitted). The excitement I would feel getting into that rickety, sterile old lift was second to none as I watched the red LED numbers counting down (or up), getting closer to the sixteenth floor. Of course, the main excitement wasn't the lift itself (although that was thrilling), but the thought of getting off at my grandparents' floor and seeing their familiar green door open up to a home full of warmth and love. I would cry and scream when it was time to leave and beg my mum to let me stay the weekend.

When my mum's illness took over, Braithwaite Tower became my permanent home. I slowly went from child to adolescent and my feelings evolved in parallel. I started to hate it. My eyes were opened to a world of wealth as I went from school to university. Houses with gardens worthy of bringing friends over, huge double beds perfect for sleepovers, living rooms capable of hosting movie nights. When I lived at home throughout university, one of only two students with a state education in my entire course, I omitted

Braithwaite Tower when talking about my life, and I'm ashamed of that now.

I saw country manors with Land Rovers in the drive, horses in stables and riding boots in conservatories. This new world became my focus, and I resented where I was from and what I had to compete against in order to survive in my surroundings. My generation in Braithwaite Tower is almost all still living at home, still in our box rooms, in our single beds at thirty. We age both slowly and rapidly here. Our lives are fragmented, told in brief glimpses up and down in lifts. The encounters here leave no room for hiding. The lift traps you. We meet, we greet, we depart, we repeat. I have seen people grow up through snapshots in the lift. From being a seed in the womb, a bump in the stomach, a baby in a pram, to a schoolchild coming home in their sports kit who now leaves the house every morning in a suit and shirt, ready for office life. Then some disappear... to university, to go abroad, to get married, to have children of their own. But they usually all come back. Some to bring their children to visit grandparents, some when romances abroad end or marriages disintegrate. Sometimes when someone dies upright. They come back for another snippet of their story. Other factors may change: grey tiles on the walls, new carpet in the reception, new stickers on the bin chutes, new placards outside warning people not to feed the pigeons or to play ball games (usually knocked down and replaced after a heavy football match).

On average you will see the same person in the lift twice a year. It's quite possible to only see someone once a year. This is the case with Gianni on the eighteenth floor. We have an annual catch-up that lasts sixteen floors and approximately forty-five seconds. It's enough to update on the snapshots of our lives. Ours is a community that builds relationships in a silver vessel, a community that develops attachments when we pile into the lift and ask each other: 'Which floor?'

When you get into the lift with someone from your peer group, there's an unspoken exchange that takes place in your head:

'So you're still at home too. Of course you are, guess it makes sense.'

'Yeah, but I have a good job – look at my handbag, I hope you've noticed my handbag/car keys/watch.'

'How are you able to afford a Mercedes? Guess we can: not paying market rent has its perks.'

Conversation that actually takes place:

'Hey, how are you?'

'All good thanks, how are you? Haven't seen your grandmother in a while – is she OK?'

'Too cold for her to go out at the moment. I'm doing OK. Your mum told me your sister moved to New Zealand?'

'Yeah, she did. Didn't work out though, so she's back now.'

'Must have been a good experience. Any plans to move out?'

'Nah, can't afford it.'

'Same.'

'This is my floor, take care.'

'See you soon, bye.'

One year later the same encounter is likely to take place.

'Hey, how are you doing?'

'I'm good. Work's taken over my life; so tiring… How are you?'

'I'm good, finally moving out next week.'

'Wow, good luck. Freedom!'

The following year:

'Hey, long time no see.'

'I know. I moved out for a bit. I'm back home now, though.'

(Nodding) 'Cool. How's work?'

'Not bad. I'm retraining at college at the moment; hopefully will become an electrician soon.'

'Amazing. I'm really sorry to hear about your dad…'

'Yeah… thanks. Mum's not taking it too well. We'll be OK, though.'

We have a bond in the tower. We know what it's like to be the Rapunzels *and* the princes of our own fate. No princes or princesses come to rescue us here; we can only save ourselves. There's nothing in life like having your own front door, my grandfather says. I still have hope that maybe one day I'll have that, but for now I appreciate Braithwaite Tower more than ever. The shame I felt is now pride.

Some residents have a regular routine. My grandfather leaves every morning at 8 a.m. to get milk and the newspaper. The school run between 8.30 and 8.45 a.m. is the slot to avoid when you need to go to work in a hurry (the lift is usually full of prams and children, so you'll have to take the next one). Paul from the eleventh floor always goes down to the betting shop at 11 a.m. on Saturday mornings, singing in patois for good luck. Darragh gets the lift at 8.55 a.m. every weekday for his morning walk. We usually meet in the lift (I get the lift at 8.55 a.m. every morning too). He's on the twentieth floor, so it picks him up first. I watch the lift pop up to the twentieth to collect him before coming down for me. We discuss the weather, films, his grandchildren, my grandparents.

One morning I got into the lift at my normal time, but Darragh wasn't there. I guessed he was away or feeling under the weather. That evening I returned home and my grandparents said: 'Darragh died last night.' Cancer. The news had slowly filtered down through the floors. We soaked it up and collectively grieved. He had known how long he had left but chose not to tell anyone. Now when I take the lift in the morning, I watch as the little blue LED lights blink and hover on sixteen, then open their doors. They pick me up first now.

Our winning feature was that we stood above the rest of the world, gazing down at the worker ants, cars stuck in traffic, aeroplanes disappearing into the horizon, umbrellas blossoming in the rain. We used to be one of a kind. We used to watch the world from above. No one wanted to live in such an ugly construction. 'Who would want to live in a place like that?' they chanted.

But they don't see the sky ablaze with fireworks on Bonfire Night. They don't see the sunset turn London peachy pink and reveal its kinder, more empathetic side. They don't see the double rainbows that dissolve through the clouds. When people remark at how high up we live – 'Sixteenth floor, please' – my grandmother always responds with a smile and says, 'Closer to the angels.' Until now... They are even blocking us from getting to them.

With every day that passes there are glossy constructions rising above us in droves. A new range of vocabulary: thirty floors, forty floors, sixty floors, luxury apartments, Manhattans starting from £750,000, first phase sold out off plan. We watch as the towers no one wanted to live in become the most desirable properties on the market. Yet we remain strong, even though the new towers' lifts may be classier, their look glossier, mirrors of fame and glory, we know we were the originals. I now stand on my balcony and watch the cranes and skyscrapers scrape past us. We may be neighbours, but their starting prices are four times the worth of ours.

With each year that passes, our views decrease. Now our sunsets are slowly disappearing, our views blocked, but we do have the privilege of looking across into the curtainless, characterless Tupperware boxes that house those who have made it in society. These flats aren't affordable and they aren't social. They are investment pieces, bringing alien currencies into our boroughs. These blocks look at mine and say: '*No, we don't really want you here; you don't really fit in here any more. You're old-fashioned, out of date. Can't you see? This is what we look like now; these are the people we house now...*'

But in reality they're no different from us. They still stand upright in their silver coffins.

When that news alert woke me up, 'Huge fire engulfs tower block in west London', I jumped out of bed thinking surely this couldn't be the way I would hear about my own death. But as I looked out of my window, I saw another tree fall. We wept for our sister tree and exchanged whispers in the lifts, wondering how an entire tree could go to bed one night and be cut down by the next morning. The letters fell through our letterboxes, telling us the block would be inspected, reassuring us we were safe. As a community we questioned. 'Do we have sprinklers?' we asked. 'No,' we were told. 'And if there's a fire, what should we do?' 'Stay in your flats,' we were told. Our branches may be scarred, but from the scab, beauty is formed. Our communities grow closer, stronger.

The council spews words ending in –tion: innovation, demolition, regeneration, which can all be translated into G E N T R I F I C A T I O N. But we hold strong; this tree will not fall. My grandparents always tell me: 'Have your own front door; there is nothing more valuable than that.' Here we all enter through the same door, we don't own it. We don't own the building that holds our homes any more than the birds own the tree they choose to nest on. Only we aren't as free as those birds. In a land where money talks, we are rendered speechless. But like the others, something will always bring me back to Braithwaite Tower. We were here before these glasshouses that dodge all the stones thrown up at them.

I used to think we died wrong, unnaturally. But now I see that maybe we die stronger. Standing, ready to walk out of this world and into the next on our feet. The same way we walked into Braithwaite Tower when it became our home. I wonder if, when my time comes, I too will stand in the lift as I prepare to meet my maker. We may live tall and straight, we may be elevated and fall, but when the wind blows we don't sway, because when us tower people die, we rest in peace upright.

Misspent Youth

Emma Purshouse

With me, pool's the thing. A thing that started when I was twelve, in the caravan-site games room where there was the *Space Invaders* machine with the cracked screen, and that beautiful green lawn of a table.

I'd sit away from it, parked on the metal chair by the window, underneath the poster of Spain. Somebody had put a wine bottle on the windowsill with a candle in it. I'd pretend to be picking off the stalactites of wax that had dribbled down the bottle neck, but really I was sneaky-peeking at the players. I liked the way they moved round the table, and their banter.

There was a skinhead, much older than me, camo trousers, twenty-hole oxbloods, wouldn't have looked out of place kicking shit out of other skinheads on the terraces. I'd seen that kind of thing at the Wolves games, all these fired-up lads raging. I'd also seen a copper on an 'oss corral a lad against a wall, and then lean in off his saddle to smash his fist down into the kid's face. Yeah, I'd seen that too. Before I was even ten. Put me off coppers. Been brought up to respect them, but that made me question it... proper question it.

Anyway, on one of the days of the holiday, I'd gone in the caravan-park games room and the skinhead with the oxbloods was in there playing against himself, potting the balls, getting low over the cue. After a bit he looked over to where I was working on my wax-picking and said, 'Wanna game?' I looked behind me at the bull on the poster, sure the skinhead must be talking to someone else. No way on God's green earth he could have been talking to me, the uncool, fat, goofy kid wearing an Elvis T-shirt. Yeah, an Elvis T-shirt back in the 1970s. I know. Perhaps I've always liked to live on the edge. Dangerous.

Unlikely as it seemed, he *was* looking at me. The skinhead was looking at me! He had to be. There was no one else in the room.

His head was shaved to a grade two. He had a hard face. A scary face. I wasn't sure what to do. He looked like he was reading me, head on one side. 'Can show you...' His voice didn't match his look. I probably shrugged. I probably wanted to run. But there was something about the way he said it. I must have nodded. I don't remember speaking. I'm sure he did all the speaking. Just sort of talked through the game. Showed me how to hold the cue. To be honest, it felt natural. I was hitting balls straight away. 'Lean further over your cue... hold it in to your side... look down the length of it...' I started potting a few balls. He looked surprised. 'You played before?' Shake of my head. No way I was speaking. I might have squeaked or something. No way I wanted my Black Country accent getting out and sharing the air with his cool, cocky cockney. I don't remember what he showed me with regard to rules. I don't remember much else about that first day at all, other than the sound of the balls when they were hit, and the way they ran through the table once pocketed.

After that day I went to the games room every day of the holiday, waiting for him to come in. And when he did, we'd play.

And then the holidays ended. And we went home. My parents weren't drinkers, didn't go down the club or up the pub, like other parents in the street, so there was no access to be had to a table.

Then school restarted. And that was shit. Even though school days were broken up with the light relief of midweek and weekend Wolves matches (so keen I even went to watch the reserves), it was still shit. Some might question the notion of footie being light relief. I was watching Wolves in the seventies, after all. I can assure you it was. The terraces had nothing to offer that the playground couldn't match and double. Kickings before I'd even got through the school gate, the name-calling, the gobbing. All year I got my head down in the middle of the class and tried to avoid the attention of teachers and kids, sharpening and resharpening my pencils. Dealing with the broken leads, smashed protractors, the school bags that went out of the back of bus windows, the shoes lobbed up trees. And all that year through, between the crap school and the crap football, I thought about the pool table at the caravan site, and I played it in my head.

The next summer I was back, two weeks in Tal-y-bont near Barmouth, in a caravan. The same caravan, of course – creatures of habit, our sort. Well, you knew what you'd be getting. Rain on the roof mostly, and a variety pack of cereals.

In previous years I would have been mithering to swim, build sandcastles with my dad, but now I beached myself in the games room, sunbathed in the glow of the light above that table. And I played anybody that came in. The little kids, the kids my age, the old men with Stoke, or Brummie, or Liverpudlian accents, who gave out sweets and tips on what to do and where to put the white. And I sucked it all up: the sweets, the pool, the accents. I loved it. And at the end of the holiday it was back home, back to school, back to the grind, and the never-ending 'you are shit' of a comprehensive education.

I carried on with the same old routines, but introduced a new element to the week. I started watching *Pot Black*. Every week. It wasn't pool, but it was the closest thing I could find in the interim between the once-a-year seaside holidays. Cliff Thorburn and his cowboy swagger, Hurricane Higgins and his sniff-and-stalk style. I wanted a piece of that confidence. They oozed something I wasn't.

I left school at fifteen. Walked out after the last exam and never went back. Some of the people in my year 'stayed on'. I didn't even know what that meant. Just couldn't quite comprehend why anybody would go back when they didn't have to. I wasn't even sure what they did. I'd seen prefects swanning round. They had a common room, but it never occurred to me to ask why or what it was for. Or what they were for. It didn't seem to be any of my business. And nobody seemed to think it worth explaining. Occasionally, in the couple of years after I'd left school, kids out of my year would reappear in Wolverhampton from places that might as well have been the other end of the world... like Preston. And their voices would have changed, and they'd be talking posh.

Me, I got on a scheme when I eventually turned sixteen. Exploitation! That's what a lot of folk said. Maybe, but I had £25 a week and once I'd paid my board out to my parents I could spend what was left on what I liked, and what I liked was pool.

They all had pool tables then, the pubs. Not like now. And I chose the Tavern in the Town to hone my craft. A biker pub. It was over the way from where my scheme happened, and not as busy in the daytime as it was at weekends. I could go over on my lunch break and have a few games. Sometimes I would just watch. I wasn't so fat now. Grown taller. The Elvis T-shirt had been replaced by denims, a Scorpions T-shirt. The pub was dark and you could lose time in there. And I did sometimes, running back late to work.

It was winner stops on in the Tavern. Chalk up your name, wait your go. I could pot. No doubt I could pot. Positioning the white was a bit hit and miss, but getting better. In my memory the song that's always playing when I think of the Tavern is Tina Turner's 'Nutbush City Limits', ramped up to full volume.

Like a lot of things in life, pool is all about knowing that you can. And I'll never forget the first time I knew. When it all came together. When it all just clicked. Bonner had just walked into the Tavern. Leather hat. Not a Cliff Thorburn, cowboy-cool sort of hat, but a grizzled, sweat-stained, light-brown affair that looked like he'd fished it out from down the back of his maroon Draylon sofa before leaving his flat (it had to be a flat, not a house). As wide as he was tall, Bonner. And he was pretty fucking wide. He was like Lemmy's older, rougher-looking brother. He didn't so much speak as growl. He had obviously woken up one morning and decided he was going to go for the walking cliché look and he'd hit the mark.

Yep, look at him standing there. He's definitely hit the mark. When he chalks up his name the chalk snaps.

I've just won the previous game by default. The other guy has potted the black, and the white has dropped. Bonner walks up to the table. 'You can set 'em up, our kid.' This is bad form. The winner doesn't set them up, the newcomer does. Everybody knows that. I take a swig from my cider, but even with a sip of Dutch courage I'm not going to argue, not with that. I do as I'm told... I've always done as I'm told. But today as I do as I'm told something loosens up inside me. Something... something shifts, and the music and the light and the mood all tunnels together and I focus... and there is this voice in my head telling me... telling me the moves... telling me what needs to be done.

Money in slot. The push and the drop. The rack and the clack. The balls triangulated. Flip of a coin. Tails never fails. I'll break.

Slide of a cue. Crack of the pack. Two yellows gone. Game on. And this is a stage. A green-baize stage. Spotlit. Arch of a bridge. Thwack and the smack.

Pause for chalk. Cocky walk. Thwack. Smack. Smack. Thwack. Smack. Brush? Final yellow. Hush. No rush. Tap. Fine cut. Slows up. Jaws and... drops. Black. Bottom bag. Long shot.

Bang. Shake of his hand. You are on fire, girl. Smile.

Next.

I've hit the zone. Dammit, I'm on a roll.

Apparently the 'Next' might not have been in my head. It might have come out loud. And Bonner? Bonner is a pissed-off, fruitloopy, badass biker. He is the walking cliché who is not taking 'Next' well. He froths at the mouth. He is incandescent with rage. Can't speak for incandescent rage... and froth. And he looks at me, and he carries on looking at me and I know he wants to smash me into pieces and I know he wants to knock me into the middle of next week. I know he wants to pick me up like a bar-room barstool and fling me at something. And the pub knows it, and it goes quiet. And Tina Turner knows it, and she stops wailing. And the interested spectators know it, and look the other way. But I hold my ground, I tell you. I stand cue in hand, with all the bob of Cliff Thorburn, and all the sniff and swagger of Hurricane Higgins, and all the new-found in-the-zone confidence that is within me. And I say it again: 'Next.' I look him straight in his eyes, and he throws his pool cue down so hard onto the table, the slate bed shakes. He clenches his fists, reaches to grab the white ball off the table and then slings it against the wall. My ground holds, and my look says, 'You lost, Bonner. You fuckin' lost.' I give it a perfectly timed beat, and allow my eyes to add, '... to a woman.' And then I watch him walk out of the pub.

I like to think he went home and sobbed into a misogynistic bag of chips, but I don't know. In my remembered pub the jukebox restarts and the chatter picks back up, and the glasses begin clinking again. And, truthfully, that day I didn't care about anything else, because I was in the fuckin' zone. Adrenaline pumping and nobody was taking me off that table that afternoon and yes, I probably should've gone back to work, but hey, I was being exploited, everyone said so, and the government could go fuck themselves. I was playing pool. And I wasn't just equal. I was better, better than equal. And all those biker blokes knew it. And it was glorious.

Of course, pool, like life, isn't always about being on a roll. Sometimes there are the days when it doesn't work out and you don't feel it. There were other Bonners that came later. The ones who 'let me win because I was a woman'. The ones who had 'bad backs', or were 'a bit too pissed'. The ones who thought a girl shouldn't be out in a pub on their own without a man. There was the bloke who got me round the throat and pushed me up against the wall because I beat him. That night I managed to strangle out a laugh and hold his eyes with my fearless Bonner stare, and he let me go. And then there were those stuff-of-legend days, when I drubbed the former England pool player, who went home in a sulk. Oh God, the rounds of beers the barman bought me that night, in his sheer delight of 'that knob finally being put in his place'.

And there were those many, many nights when good blokes shook my hand and said 'good match'. Two players playing for the love of a game, gender not mattering.

And nowadays? I don't play so much. Well, a lot of the pubs don't have tables any more, and there is other stuff to do. But occasionally, when I glimpse a pool table through a window of a pub, I can't let it be. And I walk in and put down my quid and wait my turn, and then for an afternoon there's banter and craic and nothing else matters. And sometimes I hit the zone again… it all comes back… flooding back. For an afternoon I'm calling the shots.

I'm stalking round that table and the years drop away, and pool's the only thing that matters. Back in the zone. Better than equal.

Darts

Cathy Rentzenbrink

I won the Snaith and District Ladies' Darts Championship when I was seventeen. I was the youngest-ever winner. There was a presentation evening where a newsreader from *Look North* handed out trophies and I got an extra one for getting a 180 during the match. The presentation evening was at Drax Club, and I had to leave my sixth-form college in Scunthorpe early so that I could get there in time. I explained to my English teacher, whose class I'd miss. 'Darts?' he said. 'How unusual.' I didn't get the impression he thought it was unusual in a good way. Still, he let me go. I was an eager student and had recently got a very good mark for my essay on *The Bell Jar*.

You don't get much about darts in literature. Martin Amis is a fan. There's a lot of darts in his novel *London Fields*. In one of Sylvia Plath's letters to her mother she writes about her and Ted Hughes having a game in a pub when they are staying with his parents in Yorkshire. I wonder what they were playing and who won. Around the clock? 501? Maybe Ted got stuck on double one. Maybe Sylvia offered advice: 'Think it's a field.' Maybe they both got stuck on double one. That's called being in the madhouse and can go on for ages. Maybe they got bored and decided to settle it by going up for bull. It doesn't feel like a realistic scene, does it? Darts and literature go together like... not much, really.

My dad remembers his first-ever game of darts. He was in the Prince of Wales in Falmouth. He was eighteen. His parents were both dead and he'd run off to sea from his aunt's house in Cork City three years earlier. When he'd get signed off a ship he'd go ashore and find a nice-looking pub and make some friends. Once he got into it, darts was a great way to get to know people. He decided to get his own set. He saw some he liked in Woolworths – they had a dartboard up and you could practise – but they cost £17 and he only had £7. Later that day he went into the working-men's club for a pint and told one of his new friends how disappointed he was that he couldn't afford the darts. The friend asked him to describe them, went off, and came back a few minutes later. 'Here you go,' he said. 'Give me the seven quid.'

The darts lasted for years. Dad met my mother. She was a grammar-school girl, so it raised a few eyebrows that she'd hooked up with a tattooed Irish sailor who could hardly read and write. My mum once heard herself being discussed by her teachers: 'She comes from a working-class family but they have middle-class values.' What did that mean? My granddad was a bus driver who'd had to leave school at fourteen, but he loved reading, believed in education and wanted his three children to have the opportunities that he hadn't. He bought them a set of encyclopaedias on hire purchase. We still have them; they are called *The Books of Knowledge*. Everything else in their house was home-grown and home-made. They were not exactly poor, my mum says, but there was never quite enough of anything. She used to swap her pudding for her sister's meat. My granddad was a dab hand at carving a tin of Spam into five equal portions. He liked darts, too. There was a dartboard on the wall of the sitting room. They'd untie the washing line my granny had hung up over the Rayburn and use it to direct the ceiling light at the board.

My dad was earning well by this time. It was an era where you didn't have to be able to read and write if you could do difficult, dirty and dangerous things and organise other men to do them, too. Dad wanted to take Mum and her parents out for a meal. It wasn't something any of them were used to. He chose the Fox and Hounds at Scorrier and dressed up in his white denim suit, which he had professionally cleaned every week. Dropping the suit off and picking it up would always remind him of standing in the pawn-shop queue with his mother. That too was a weekly process. When his father was paid, his mother would redeem his suit so he could go to the pub in it. After the weekend she'd be putting it back in so they could eat for the rest of the week. Each time my dad paid for his cleaning he felt he'd come a long way from the poverty of his childhood, and he loved having money in his pocket. He was looking forward to spending some of it when he walked into the lounge bar of the Fox and Hounds, but there was a flurry of concern among the staff. The landlord came up to him: 'We don't serve the likes of you in here,' he said. 'You'll have to go in the public bar.' They didn't. They went back to the Stag Hunt in their own village and played darts instead.

My parents got married the day after Mum's last A-level exam and she did Open University while my brother Matty and I were small. There are still some of her books knocking around with our scribbles in them. Dad became a tin miner and we used to go to the working-men's club on Friday nights. One of my earliest memories is being put down to sleep with Matty in a corner under a pile of coats. Another is running out to meet Dad when he came in off night shift. I slipped in the snow and bashed my cheek into the step. I still have a little scar.

By the time the stolen darts finally fell apart we were living in Yorkshire. The tin mines had closed down and we'd moved north for Selby coalfield. Now when Dad came home from work he had coal dust round his eyes that would never quite wash off, so he always looked as though he was wearing mascara. It took him a long time to find a set of darts he liked as much as the old ones. When he did, he bought two sets, so he'd always have a replacement. He got me some, too. We had a dartboard up in our house and we'd play when I got home from school and before he went off on night shift. He'd give me a one-hundred start and the off, which meant I could sometimes win. When he was on day shift and had his evenings free, he'd go down to the pub in the next village, the Bell and Crown, where he played for the team. On weekends we'd go off to tournaments, big knockouts that smelled of ale and fags.

When I was sixteen the Bell and Crown came up for sale. Dad felt he'd had enough of doing difficult, dirty and dangerous work underground. My parents had always saved most of what they earned, and they borrowed from the bank and from breweries so that we could buy it. Moving in was highly exciting and I loved working behind the bar, listening to the jokes and the stories. Weekends were manic and it was a matter of getting drink to people as efficiently as possible, but the weeknights were all about games and chat. Men's darts on Mondays and Thursdays, dominoes on Tuesdays, ladies' darts on Wednesdays. I signed up for the ladies' team and so it was that a few months later I won my two trophies, one of which had a little gold figure on the top, in a skirt, with an outstretched arm poised to throw a dart.

I am sadly out of practice at darts. Rusty. You have to play a lot to keep the hand and eye in. I don't look like the type of person who plays darts. There's a lot going on in that sentence, isn't there? What does the type of person who plays darts look like and why don't I? I don't think I did at the time, either. There weren't lots of seventeen-year-old bookworms competing. Most of the ladies were at least twice my age, and often more. That's what I liked about it. The conversation. Hints about the menopause and difficult husbands. She's the landlord's daughter, they'd say about me, when we visited the neighbouring pubs. A couple of years later, after I'd gone to university and made lots of posh friends, they'd make up little rhymes about me: 'She was only the landlord's daughter, but she lay on the bar and said "pump".' I'd laugh and smoke another cigarette. I'd switched from Regal King Size to Marlboro Lights in my first week. I was rebranding myself along with my choice of fags.

I mentioned darts in my first book *The Last Act of Love*. It's not a book about darts, it's about my brother Matty and the horrible way that he died, but the backdrop is the pub, so there's lots of darts and dominoes and the tug of war on Boxing Day gets a mention. There's much more of this in the final version than there was in my first draft. I'd rather glossed over it. Perhaps I thought that none of that stuff really belonged in a book. That's the problem with education, wonderful though it is. It shows you what has already been done. It's easy to jump from the fact that there's not much darts in literature to the idea that darts don't belong in literature, and that people who play darts don't belong in literature, and that people who play darts certainly can't have a crack at trying to write literature.

In the same letter as she describes playing darts with Ted Hughes, Sylvia Plath mentions a trip to Whitby. There is, she explains, something depressingly mucky about English seaside resorts. The sand is muddy and dirty. The working class, too, is dirty, strewing candy papers, gum and cigarette wrappers. We used to go to Whitby for a treat. I don't remember it as dirty, but then I've never seen the New England beaches that Plath longs for. My dad used to organise an annual trip to Whitby for the men's darts teams. All year long there would be a raffle on darts night for which we'd provide the prize – a mixed grill – and the proceeds would be saved up to pay for the coach and give every player a little brown envelope of beer money.

My dad remembers stopping off at the Spotted Cow in Malton on the way back one year. He went to the bar and asked for twenty-eight pints of bitter and a pint of dry cider. 'Who's the dry cider for?' asked the barmaid. At that moment, all six feet four of the cider drinker fell through the front door. 'Him,' said my dad. They both looked at him for a moment. 'He's not as drunk as he looks,' said my dad. I can't imagine Sylvia Plath would have been impressed if she'd bumped into them all barrelling down the road. I liked being on the bar when they came back, full of jokes and stories and ready for yet more drink. One year, one of them had brought a live lobster as a pet and then let it free on the bus.

I was always encouraged by my parents, but I do remember that whenever I said to anyone outside my family that I wanted to be a writer, they told me not to be daft. Teachers told me that if I worked very hard I might be able to become a teacher. Friends told me to be careful not to show myself up. Customers in our pub told me that I sounded as if I'd swallowed a dictionary, that I was so sharp I'd cut myself, and that book learning wouldn't get me a husband. I don't think I'd ever have written anything if I hadn't left the pub and the village. I'd still be pulling pints and playing darts and reading books but thinking that people like me didn't write them. University was my Narnia. I found a door to another world. Getting a job in a bookshop was another big moment. I started looking after authors when they came in to do book signings. I began to see that there wasn't anything all that different about them. They were only people; they weren't that unlike me.

Books tend to be about children who go to boarding school, not about children who play darts with their dad, but you have to not let that stop you. I've found class to be far more navigable than other bits of my identity. I can choose whether or not to think about it, which I don't feel is the case with my gender or my race, or the fact that I am a mother. I feel lucky. The longer I am alive, the more I learn that the greatest possible gift and advantage in life is to have loving parents. The perspective I get from working in prisons, where so many people have been neglectfully or cruelly parented, means I don't feel inclined to moan or feel sorry for myself about anything. I try not to succumb to envy of those people born with a different type of spoon in their mouths, who seem to have an instinctive knowledge of how to go on. What I most envy about posh people is their confidence. There's a sense of entitlement that I lack. I know I'm generalising here, but they do seem to like the sound of their own voice. Whenever I write a piece or get on a stage, I have to work so hard to overcome a chorus of jeers from my childhood: 'Oooh, look at her, she thinks she's someone. She likes the sound of her own voice, doesn't she? Look at her, showing herself up again. Too clever for her own good, that's what she is. Too clever by half.' Sometimes I fear I'll be on my deathbed, trying to think about all the love I have known, and instead, a sharp-featured nurse will bend over me and say in a Yorkshire accent: 'What's the matter with you? Did you swallow a dictionary?'

I have multitudinous insecurities but I try not to let them stop me doing things. I may not always know what the rules are, I tell myself, but nor did my dad when he was first off the boat, nor do lots of people. I do wonder what I might achieve if I didn't have to expend so much energy on fear management. Back in Yorkshire, we had a practice dartboard called a champion's choice board. The treble and double segments were all smaller than they were on a matchboard. The idea was that if you practised in tougher conditions, then when you came to a match it would be much easier: the trebles would look massive, the green of the double one really would look like a big field. It worked then and made me a better darts player, and it works for me now as a metaphor. Whenever I do anything that seems like a huge stretch, I calm myself down by thinking of the champion's choice board and reminding myself that if I can do this, if I can cope with whatever is scaring me now, then in the future everything will feel easier.

People conflate class and intelligence. These days people assume I'm middle class precisely because I write books and can string a sentence together. I talk about books on Radio 4, so I must be middle class, surely? How could I be anything else? *The Times* recently put my book in a list called 'Middle-Class Misery Memoirs'. 'But didn't you notice the darts?' I wanted to say. Sometimes I get 'accused' of being middle class. 'Typical middle-class whining,' some man tweeted at me about an article I wrote about motherhood. I ignored him, which was probably the best thing to do, though if I'd channelled my Yorkshire barmaid self, the girl who used to keep very good order in the Bell and Crown, I'd have told him to fuck off. I do think I've become a bit soft, sometimes, a bit too well-behaved. I had to learn table manners along the way so I knew what to do at lunches and dinners. Maybe I picked up an excess of civility at the same time as I was learning that you wait for everyone else to get their food before you tuck in. And you don't eat or drink the contents of the finger bowl – but I already knew that from reading *The Bell Jar.* Books are very helpful when it comes to social mobility.

The Snaith and District Ladies' Darts Championship is still the only thing I've ever won. I've been shortlisted for a few bookish things but have never walked away with the trophy. If I ever do win anything I think I'll mention the darts. It will be a strange thing for a literary type to say, 'This is the first thing I've won since the Snaith and District Ladies' Darts Championship.' Writers tend not to have grown up playing darts because they didn't grow up in the sort of houses where there was a dartboard on the wall. Good that I'll say it, I think. Good that I'm allowing myself to think I might win something book-related one day. People like me can write books. People like anyone can write books. You have to learn to like the sound of your own voice; you have to trust that your perspective is interesting because it is yours, that you are seeing the world through your own eyes and can use your own words to describe it. It doesn't matter what came before: it matters that you are here now and have something to say. And, while writing might be hard and can often feel like a madhouse, you don't get coal dust lodged in your eyelashes and you never have the indignity of getting stuck on double one.

This Place Is Going to the Dogs

Louise Powell

While other children went to Florida, I went flapping. To the uninitiated, going 'flapping' might sound like travelling to a holiday camp where 'The Birdie Song' is constantly on repeat, meals consist of millet, and the signature dance involves waving the arms up and down all night. As exciting as that prospect is, the truth is even better.

'Flapping' has nothing to do with birds and everything to do with dogs – more specifically greyhounds. When you go 'flapping', you visit one of the unlicensed greyhound tracks that operate around the country, where every man and our mam can race their dogs with hardly any questions asked. There are few rules, even fewer regulations, and better still, you can even bet on the outcome of each race.

It's the greyhound equivalent of the Wild West, tinged with the same lure of freedom and big rewards. The people flock to flapping tracks in their hundreds to pan for the little nuggets of gold from deep within the bookies' satchels. They climb out of their battered five-door saloons with a fistful of coins jangling in their tracksuit pockets, ready to duel to the death with the men standing by the rails who shout out odds like threats. There's cigarette smoke rather than gun smoke, but the fight is just as fierce: it could be the night that they win enough money to get the family through Christmas, but that prospect could just as easily turn out to be a mirage.

It might not seem like the ideal place to take a little girl of six, but my parents couldn't afford to be picky about our family outings. Holidays were like drinking wine and buying new cars, mythical things that other families did, not us. Before you start feeling sorry for me, I was extremely proud that we were so different. If anyone had offered six-year-old me a choice between going to Disney World in Florida and going flapping, I'd have thought that you were taking the mickey: who would want to spend their time in a theme park meeting humans dressed up as dogs when they could go flapping and see the real thing for themselves? Greyhound racing flowed through my veins and warmed my little heart right through.

Good job too, because Easington Greyhound Stadium felt like the coldest place on earth between November and March. Lying on the outskirts of the ex-pit village of the same name, it was an independently owned flapping track bordered by open land that stretched west towards the A19 and east to meet the North Sea. The blunt brick building hunkered down into the sloping land, desperately seeking warmth from the scant grass it offered. There was a sandy oval to the front and a car park of loose stony chips to the back; when vehicles pulled in on winter nights, their headlights caught the dust from the stones as it streamed upwards, as if the land itself were exhaling.

We breathed a sigh of relief ourselves when we reached the track in our clapped-out C-reg car. Braving the cold for the dogs was part of the fun, but a breakdown in this weather was the stuff of nightmares. Easington Greyhound Stadium was a sanctuary from the horror of the hard shoulder, the fear of breakdown and its unpayable expense. As the car door squeaked open, the noise coming from the track was profane. Hot-blooded howls from the hyped-up greyhounds punctured the air as sharply as the frost, while men and women greeted each other in lower, louder tones. Geordie, Mackem, Smoggie and Sand-dancer voices intermingled, so that only the occasional word could be made out, and underpinning the cacophony was the crackling, static-filled sound of the track tannoy doing its usual pre-race check. With the wind wailing at our backs and friends hailing us, we half ran, half sauntered to the turnstiles, where I was lifted over the clanking monster and into relative tranquillity.

To my childish eyes, my parents and brothers emerged from their battle with the turnstiles clutching the true marker of adulthood: a white race card with an oval photograph of a greyhound on its front. It was only three or four pieces of A4 paper folded in half, a thing so basic that it wasn't even considered worthy of a staple, yet I adored it all the same. I had a pocket dictionary at home, but encyclopaedias were expensive, and this little booklet was the closest I could get to one. With two races spread over half of each A4 sheet, it was a mine of information. There were race times, lists of data about previous performances that everyone called the 'form', and names of owners, but I was most entranced by the race names of the greyhounds who were running that night.

In a world populated by Rovers, Tysons and Busters, a race name was something of a necessary evil. It was supposed to be reflective of the dog's abilities or the owner's personality, so of course there were grand-sounding names like King Kong and Diamond Girl. But when King Kong's only rampage came at feeding time and Diamond Girl showed no sparkle on the track, the race card bearing the dog's name and form made the joke crystal clear to all. I could read the form as well as the names, and I enjoyed these little ironies more than a six-year-old child probably should. But what I loved more were the race names that made images in my mind, ones like Money Tree and Bird of Paradise. I would show my approval of such monikers by drawing tiny pictures next to them in our mam's card, until the night when one of my brothers grabbed it suddenly in astonishment.

'Every dog that you've drawn a picture next to has won tonight,' he gasped, and my artwork was circulated around the family to cries of surprise. When he eventually passed the card back to me, envy tinged his voice. 'That's eight out of eight races. How did you do that?'

'I don't know,' I replied, spooked. Scared that I was having some preternatural influence over the dogs that were running, I decided from then on to wait until a race had passed before I judged the names of the greyhounds. And no, I didn't always vote in favour of the victor.

It might seem harsh of my brother, but really he had every right to be put out. He was winless despite scrutinising each variable of the form, and all I did was draw a picture to choose a winner. And therein lay the frustration and the attraction of a flapping track: when the form worked out, you were in clover, but when it didn't, you were knee-deep in something much less pleasant.

In theory, greyhound racing is a simple premise: six dogs emerge from wooden and metal boxes called 'traps', chase after a mechanical 'hare', which looks more like a sock than a rabbit, and the one who gets to the line first is the winner. Most of the races at Easington were 'handicaps', which meant that the traps could be moved closer or further away from the winning line, depending upon each dog's level of ability. To give each dog an equal chance, the best runners go to the back, and the worst ones to the front. So far, so straightforward.

Until, of course, you realise that the six greyhounds have six different owner-trainers, all of whom are desperate to land a gamble. The training of greyhounds at Easington was completely unregulated: the most complex check involved matching a dog's earmark (a three-letter tattoo of identification) to their race name. They could be trained anyhow and fed anything, so you could never truly know that the 'best' dog really was at the back, or the 'worst' dog was ten metres closer to the line until the race was over. You might look at each dog's previous runs, but how could you be sure that they reflected their true abilities? The dogs might have been unfit, unwell, unable to produce the speed or stamina that the distance of the race required. All the form did was tell you how the race *should* pan out; how it *would* do so was another matter entirely.

The little white race card that I so adored, then, could barely be worth the paper it was written on. But even as their fingers flicked through it and their betting-shop pens made notes in the margins, my family kept their eyes peeled and ears open for something far more valuable than form: the indication that someone was *trying*.

Not for a baby, of course, but for an event that was just as precious: a successful gamble. When the form could mislead you and people deceive you, it was time to study real figures instead of printed ones. The smallest details could be an indication that someone was running their dog with the intention of winning tonight. The lass who normally kept well away from her brother was sitting with him for the quarter of an hour between the first race and the second. That was funny – she had a dog running in the third. The lad with stout enough bowels to cope with the track café's burgers kept making pungent trips to the bog as if he had a bug. Maybe he did, but he also had a dog running off top in the sixth race. These quirks could be completely innocent, but when they coincided with a sudden, unexplained decline in the dog's performance, alarm bells rang.

'I'm sure they're trying tonight,' our dad would murmur. We'd all lean forward like conspirators. 'Their dog's in trap five. They've ran him in sprints but he hasn't got the pace. He's over a longer distance and he's only got the six to beat to the corner. If he gets round that first bend in front, it's goodnight Vienna.'

And so it proved to be a good night, for us and for the dog's owners. I was far too young to be allowed near the betting ring, a line of four bookmakers' boards that stank of sweat and smoke, but I always watched the process with fascination. A crowd of men would gather round the bookies, chatting casually as they waited for the prices to be chalked up.

'What d'you reckon?'

'I'd say 6/4 the six dog, 3/1 the one, 4/1 bar. The five'll probably be the outsider, no form at all.'

A nod of agreement, a drag of a rolled-up fag.

Then: '*6/4 the field!*'

Like soldiers in battle, the men shot forward at the cry. I was always impressed to see our dad and my brothers courteously let the gambled-on dog's owners get their money on before they placed their bets. But when the five dog strolled to the line, their cheers rang out first.

'Get in there!'

'Ea-*sy*! Ea-*sy*! Ea-*sy*!'

'Take 'em round again! He'd still win!'

They kept cheering as they dashed off to stretch out their palms before the abashed bookies.

For the most part, people took it with good grace when their selection was beaten by a gamble. The fault was with them, not the dog's owners: they should have realised that it was a stayer rather than a sprinter, and besides, they were planning their own coup themselves. But, in the words of our mam, 'There's always one.'

This 'one' was a brooding bruiser of a man who had thought that backing the six dog to win was 'like taking a Dime bar off a bairn'. The bairn must have turned out to be a right little tough nut, because there was the six dog, a valiant but well beaten second, and here he was, penniless. He stood there, eyes fixed on the panting six dog walking alongside the lass who owned him, as noiseless as a dormant volcano. But when they came into earshot, he blew his top.

'Your dog's dodgy.'

More potent than a punch, more wounding than a weapon, these three white-hot words stunned the crowd and the dog's owner. To tell someone that their dog was 'dodgy' was the ultimate blow. 'Dodgy' was short for 'dodgepot', a term reserved for aberrant creatures who showed no interest in reaching the hare and refused to pass other dogs. When dodgepots turned up on the track, as they did from time to time, they would be identified as such in low tones, well out of earshot of their owner. As shameful as it was to own a dodgepot, it was even worse to have your dog accused of being one when all it wanted to do was win.

So when the six dog's owner straightened up, squared her shoulders, and snarled, 'If I didn't have my dog on this lead, son, I'd wrap it straight round your neck,' no one protested. And even as our mam hurried me away from the scene in case it all kicked off, I was proud of the woman and aggrieved at the man who had insulted her.

It was inevitable that skirmishes arose in the charged atmosphere of Easington Greyhound Stadium: there was pride at stake as well as money. I was six years old and I knew it as well as if I'd been through it myself. Like women of the factories, the once-proud men of the pits had suddenly been forced to endure the spine-shrivelling abasement of having to sign on the dole. 'Just one' visit to the Jobcentre grew into ten, twenty, thirty, in sync with the rejection letters that politely told them they were useless. Pitch in jibes from the neighbours, taunts from relatives, tears from children, and was it any wonder that the spectacle of a greyhound desperately chasing after a hare it would never catch had such a great appeal? Getting one over on the bookies or your fellow punters was the only measure of success left; of course people were going to disagree and, occasionally, fight. But if you were away by nine, as we always were, a war of words was the worst you'd see.

Going flapping was, for the most part, like being a member of a slightly dysfunctional extended family. When someone overstepped the line, there was always someone else to fight your corner and share your sweets. That same someone might spoil your planned gamble with one of their own, but we all came into this world with nothing anyway, so we were used to it. Next time might be your time, or the time after that.

Your life was going to the dogs, but that was a reason to smile, not cry.

Underdogs

Helen Wilber

Do you know the best thing about football? It's the getting there. Nothing compares to marching in the same direction as 30,000 other human beings. Together we are an army on the move, a sea of denim and cheap blue nylon. We are average people with average aspirations. Some of us go without holidays, nights out, clothes, to be here, walking as one.

And this year, for sure, is *our* year.

I'd never been to the football until you took me. Everyone remembers their first time: the smell of processed meat, the salivating sniffer dogs, the mechanical click of the turnstiles. On the steaming concourse, we fought through the queues for pies and lager, the row of outlets resembling a twilit underground shopping centre. I followed you up the concrete stairs, resisting the urge to run. But what I remember most is the blast of cold air as we peered over the cliff edge at the bright green sea below. And then, the noise...

I wheel my bike down High Street, looking in the charity shops and the dingy pub windows adorned with blue flags and crepe-paper trimmings. The baying cars on the ring road are backed up for miles. It feels like Christmas Eve. Behind the clock tower posters of the team are displayed on railings like towels over hotel balconies. I continue down towards Primark. Some homeless people sit with their backs to the shoe-shop window. The ones who are awake turn their faces towards the spring sunshine.

I lock up my bike and go into Superdrug. The shop is crowded, even for a Saturday. But this is no ordinary bank holiday. If Leicester beat Manchester United tomorrow, the biggest gift in English football is ours. The girl in front of me is told by the shop assistant that that the hairspray in her basket is on two for one. 'It's a sign!' hisses her dad.

That first match you took me to was brilliant. How could it have been anything less? I remember it was cold; near Christmas. A lacklustre Millwall were the perfect pantomime villains, every kick drawing boos and hisses from the jubilant crowd. 'Is every game like this?' I shouted in your good ear (the one that wasn't damaged by meningitis) as City banged in their fourth goal. 'No, every game isn't like this!' you laughed.

I leave Superdrug and I stand in the sunshine, looking at the flags with the life-sized images of City players. I launch a silent prayer, 'Dear God, even though I don't believe in you, please let Leicester City win the League.' I can't remember wanting anything more than this, not even a bike as a child.

In the Buddhist Centre café the orange walls are adorned with blue-and-white trimmings. Even the Buddhists are backing the Blues. Lucy and I order lunch and talk excitedly about the football.

After lunch we head to the pound shop. Brucciani's are selling blue cobs (that's bread cakes, baps or rolls to you) that look like pebbles from an alien beach. The straw-headed dummies in the school-shop window are draped in Leicester City scarves.

In the evening there is a party. High on alcohol, adrenaline and hope, we eat the birthday cake, sodden with sickly blue-and-white icing. Every conversation is about the football. Will tomorrow be the day? Or will we have to wait until next week, when City play Everton at home?

I miss you most when there's a party, a gig, New Year's Eve. A Friday night could flash by in seconds when we were together, talking intensely in our huddle, ignoring everyone else. We were always the last to leave any party. There was always so much to say.

The next day I wake up early. Will today be *the* day? The local and national press have been carping about how City will always be the bridesmaid, never the bride. But what do *they* know? I text my friends to arrange a rendezvous, wondering how I will make it through to kick-off time.

Opening the pub door it is like stepping off a plane somewhere hot. There is no air, and the heat from the sweating bodies is stifling. The place is dangerously crowded, eight deep at the bar. Scenes from Hillsborough flash through my mind; the terrified faces from a time when fences penned in fans as if they were dogs.

I have no chance of fighting my way into the pub, so I leave. Hipsters in tight jeans and Vardy T-shirts are walking six abreast and City fans are queuing outside every pub. The city is awash with blue and white.

There was no reason for us to become friends except for the fact that we liked each other. You were nearly twenty years older than me when I wandered into the office next door, looking for work.

'I don't believe in volunteering,' you told me, grumpily. 'Why on earth do you want to be a volunteer?'

'I need work experience,' I said. 'Nobody will take me on without experience and I can't get experience unless someone takes me on.'

'I'll think about it,' you said.

I ring Jack and persuade him to watch the match with me in a pub near home. I cycle to his house amid the blaring commentaries of pub TVs and car radios, panicking about the ticking clock. I must see this match. When I get to Jack's, he is listening to Five Live and while he is lacing his baseball boots, Manchester United score.

The moment we walk through the door, City score the equaliser and the pub erupts in ecstatic cheers and fist pumps. We laugh; this run of luck of ours is ridiculous. Nothing will stop us now. I go to the bar and order two pints of lager.

'Sorry, I don't know much about politics,' I said, that first night when we went out. I was drinking pints and you were on the Bacardi, moaning about the measly British measures. You told me that you didn't drink much; you had always preferred drugs.

'All I know about politics is that a very small number of people have got more or less all of the wealth,' I said.

'Well then, you do know about politics!' you said.

You had been part of many left-wing causes, from supporting the miners to fighting running battles with fascist groups in the eighties. You told me about the hunger strikers in Northern Ireland, how they took it in turns, the next man starting his strike after the death of the last.

'They wanted to be treated as political prisoners,' you explained.

Your real heroes were always the people closer to home, though, the ones that you knew from up North. There was Yvette, the first female bus driver in your home town. But the characters from the shipyards were the ones who stood out, the ones who had inhabited the vast hangars where giant, whale-like vessels were nestled in intricate cat's cradles of scaffold and walkways. You told me about the cross-dresser you knew, how she came to work every day in high heels and full make-up, waving cheerily at the cat-callers and bigots until eventually they got bored and their disdain was replaced by grudging admiration. Now that takes real guts, you said.

Jack and I find a place to stand in front of one of the TVs, trying not to get in anyone's way. This is a pub where it's best to blend in. Having a bloke at my side makes me feel safe, though I resent the fact. The mood is charged, boisterous, combustible. A tracksuited man shouts almost constantly at the TV, swearing at the other team and abusing the ref. I look around for other women because I don't want to be the only one. The few that I see are dressed to impress, in high heels and short leather jackets that skim their tiny waists. The men, glassy-eyed with drink, are casual, their bellies sagging over tracksuit bottoms or jeans. In the corner I spy the skinny one with the blond hair. The one I know, though he doesn't know me; the one who hits first and asks questions later.

When you told me about how you came to live in Leicester, I didn't know whether to believe you.

'Really, you stuck a pin in a map?' I said.

'It was time to get out,' you said. 'The police had had enough of us. They were getting heavy.'

A raid had taken place, something to do with an abandoned caravan that you were using to take drugs. Unspeakable things were happening to your female friends while in police custody. When the pin came down slap-bang in the middle of Leicester, you found out whether you could study here, and when you knew that you could, you applied to the poly. After the interview, you dropped some acid and wandered into one of the city's parks. You decided that you liked it here. There seemed to be loads of nice places to take drugs, you said.

Manchester United is playing dirty and we are no better. The game is full of yellow cards, hair-pulling and weaponised elbows. We watch, urging Leicester on. At half time, I buy more lager.

Jack is out of work. His last job was delivering oxygen cylinders for medical use to the homes of people who were sick, sometimes dying. The houses were chaotic; sometimes there were vicious dogs, squalor and dysfunctionality. One house was entirely filled, floor to ceiling, with rotting oranges. Jack's employer hated it if employees wasted time chatting with the patients as they hooked them up to the ugly brown cans.

Sometimes I wish my friends would ask me about my job, but they're not that interested; I'm barely interested myself. There's nothing much to say about admin, and Tuesday will come knocking soon enough, brutal as a bailiff. Good friends like Jack are as precious as bank holidays, and just as rare. For now, the lager is flowing and we are on the brink of greatness.

The second half is as good as the first. Manchester United look like scoring, but our Kasper is fantastic, parrying blows like Zorro, and the equaliser doesn't come. The din in the pub gets louder as the clock shows seventy-five, then eighty minutes played. Suddenly we are all chanting, 'We're going to win the League.' Everyone is on their feet, banging beer glasses deafeningly on the wooden tables.

I'm not sure when you decided to give up drugs, but it was years before we met. 'The hardest thing is sacking your friends off,' you told me. 'Stopping seeing the people you usually see, avoiding all the places you usually go, you know?' (I didn't.) You rented a cheap cottage in the country for a month especially for the task in hand. You said, 'People talk all kinds of bullshit about giving up drugs.'

'But doesn't it make you feel really ill?' I asked.

'It's no worse than the flu,' you replied.

Your childhood wasn't up to much. Perhaps that's why you chose social work. You didn't know your dad, and your mum sounded challenged, at best. You didn't attend school much. The house where you lived had a big hole in the floor. You left home at sixteen to live in a student house with your older brother. He moved out on the day you moved in.

The match ends in a one-all draw. If Spurs draw tomorrow, we will win the League. If Spurs win, we still only need one win or two draws. Surely it must happen now? I cycle home in the rain and I tipsily make dinner. I haven't felt this happy in ages.

Dear You,

A lot has happened since you died. There is some crazy, exciting news, but I will fill you in on the other stuff first. I saw one of our friends the other day, the one who had the party where we stayed until everyone else had left and then walked home in the snow. We were talking about you. She asked me how you and I became such good friends. I reminded her that we met through work.

It's been a terrible couple of years. We've had a referendum and Britain has voted to leave the EU. The country is divided between those in favour and those against. In London, a tower block burned down, killing seventy-two people, because it was covered in cheap, flammable cladding. And I daren't tell you who is in the White House; it would give you (another) heart attack.

They've knocked down our pub, the one where the bar staff used to shout, 'You've just missed him,' if I got there after you'd left. The land was needed for student accommodation. Vice chancellors earn megabucks nowadays and some say that they get more perks than bent coppers. The students don't live in grubby housing any more, like we did when university was an escape hatch for working-class kids. They pay through the nose for wipe-clean apartments and leave forty grand in debt. Don't worry; most of them never pay it back.

I'm still a bit annoyed with you for dying. I know you couldn't help it, but you told me that you were going to live to be at least 140, and I believed you. I miss talking to you. I still do it in my head – not all the time like I did at the start, just sometimes.

We all miss you.

In other news, Leicester City won the League!

The Dark Hole of the Head

Jill Dawson

Robert McCrum, literary editor of the *Observer* at the time, once broke off from a conversation to ask me, out of nowhere, 'Which school did you go to?'

'Boston Spa Comprehensive,' I said.

He looked embarrassed. 'Yes, well – and you did OK, didn't you?' he added, turning back to his phone. He was apparently in the middle of an agitated discussion with his daughter about her entrance exam to somewhere or other. It was only later that I figured out that McCrum, whose father had been headmaster at Eton, had expected me to name a private school. One he'd actually heard of. I don't know which – Bedales? Marlborough? (Those – and Eton – are the only names I know.)

I have come across these assumptions often in the literary world. McCrum had probably not read any of my books: novels set on council estates in Hackney, or about domestic violence in America; about women who grow up in the 1950s as skilled thieves; of maids who work for famous poets, or peasant women for famous doctors, or social climbers who long to learn French; or about eighteenth-century rural agitators, boys who give up their hearts after suffering in love, and school exclusion.

But he's right – I did do OK and I *loved* my Yorkshire comprehensive school. My older sister passed her eleven-plus and went to Tadcaster Grammar and I think I was the luckier of the two of us. When I was in the sixth form we were taken on a school visit to see Ted Hughes at the Yorkshire Playhouse. I remember sitting in the front row and tittering as the tall man stepped out from the curtain and strode towards the one stool on the stage. He was not the commanding figure we'd expected. 'His flies are undone!' Vicky Stables whispered beside me. Hughes didn't look like a poet should, we girls thought. We didn't approve of the dark green raincoat he wore loosely around his shoulders, the sort a 'dirty old man' would wear.

But then he sat on the stool and began reading. He had a Yorkshire accent, to our surprise, and a voice of rolling warmth and power. He began reading 'The Thought Fox' and it was as if someone had turned a key in my back. 'I imagine this midnight moment's forest...'

I sat up straight. We'd read the poem many times in our brand new sixth-form classrooms at our local comprehensive. 'Yeah yeah,' we said, 'we get it,' when Mr Foggin laboriously explained that it wasn't just about the real fox but about the writing of the poem, about imagination, memory, creation and recreation.

'Two eyes serve a movement, that now,/And again now, and now, and now...'

Over thirty years later and I can hear Hughes's voice, intonation, and the impact of those words on me. He didn't read in the modern drone that poets like Simon Armitage use. He practically shouted the line: 'with a sudden hot sharp stink of fox'. Vicky Stables jumped out of her skin. She was too mesmerised to titter this time.

The words had entered 'the dark hole' of *my* head. Poetry had me in its snare. You could say I was, perhaps more than other girls from Boston Spa Comprehensive who sat in the front row of the Playhouse that day, a ready candidate. I was anorexic. I weighed around six stone and had lately begun to notice a downy hair growing on my forearms. I was having a relationship with a bullying, needy boy a couple of years older than me who worked in the carpet store at Thorp Arch Trading Estate and bought me giant bars of chocolate to try and 'feed me up'. But I found it hard to fathom the ways his moods flipped towards me: one minute I was a bitch and worse; the next he begged me to marry him. This young man later told me he was being sexually abused by his older brother at this time. This might have gone some way to explain his frightening behaviour towards me. But I was a girl of sixteen and I didn't know that then.

Our school trip to see Hughes changed my life. I wanted to be a writer. I think I knew this already but in that badly lit theatre, listening to Hughes murmuring, 'The window is starless still, the clock ticks,/The page is printed,' I knew it with a dreadful certainty. I want to make people feel things; I want to enter the dark hole of others' heads. The problem was that being a poet, or a writer of any kind, was an impossible, ridiculous ambition for a girl from my background. What did my parents hope for? My mum thought a teacher would be nice. (She was in awe of teachers. In my teenage eyes it was a lowly profession.) Neither parent had gone to university themselves. There was a vague hope that I might, but no clear plan for how this miraculous thing would happen.

I had already had a poem published in a women's magazine, but I didn't tell teachers or parents that. I'd been so embarrassed on seeing it there in the newsagent that I shut the pages and left the magazine behind. The poem was about my anorexia and contained the strange truth I could only articulate as a poem – that if I carried on not eating like this I would surely die.

Poetry and embarrassment were bedfellows to me. My dad had once said to me that he couldn't see the point of any books that weren't practical or instructional (our house had an entire set of encyclopaedias with red hardback covers that were not often disturbed, and many books on gardening and golf, which were). When I dig around now, trying to find the reason for the source of both the fierce obstinacy and the utter hopelessness about my desire to write, all I can find is a weird feeling of shame. Seeing Hughes – *who had an accent like mine* – made something shift, made something preposterous at last just a tiny bit possible.

Our English teacher, Mr Foggin, also introduced me to a book and a writer who had a lasting effect on me: *Akenfield* by Ronald Blythe. Blythe appears – with his permission! – as a mischievous character in my novel *The Crime Writer* thirty years later, such is my indebtedness to him. The idea of vernacular voices, the lack of a neutral storytelling authority (implicitly from the educated classes) is what I got from Blythe, aged sixteen, and it was revelatory.

By the time I was in my mid-twenties I was visiting schools as a published writer too, to offer workshops and readings. Over about a decade of doing this I visited young offenders' institutes, a school in Chicago for pregnant teenagers, a school in the Chicago projects, libraries, literacy projects, schools in Hackney and Tower Hamlets, and south London comprehensives much tougher than my own. I was reading books by African American women writers – Toni Morrison, Maya Angelou, Toni Cade Bambara, Ntozake Shange, Alice Walker. I felt more affinity with their writing – they had bodies, they wrote about sex and giving birth and raising children (I had my first son aged twenty-six), they wrote in astonishing lyrical voices about experiences they deemed important. Many of the admired writers in the English canon felt to me like disembodied intellectual heads compared to the sensuous, living writing I was reading.

I think I was looking for a mirror of some kind – which is odd, since I was a white girl from Yorkshire. But I often got the impression that lurking in my workshop group was a girl or boy who felt how I felt when I read Maya Angelou, or Ronald Blythe, or heard Ted Hughes. Ah, so that's what a writer sounds like. Here is their voice. Not so posh, after all. Not overeducated. Not dead. Someone like me.

Once, a sixteen-year-old boy in the secure unit I was visiting wrote me a short story and begged me not to read it in class but afterwards, after I'd left. 'I don't want to see your face when you read it,' he said, handing me the paper. I read it on the train going home: the story of a boy in a secure unit who is about to go out to sixth-form college after several years inside and who has been having workshops with a visiting writer – a woman, he writes, who reminds him of his long-dead mother. 'Mum believed in him; she was the only one, until now.' I knew this boy was inside the institution for arson. But he told me in this 'true story' what he couldn't do in class: his father had killed his mother and then committed suicide when he was seven years old. He had been in care for a long time; this was not deemed relevant to the arson, committed at fourteen. So therefore no one had mentioned this in his defence and he simply wanted to tell me about it so I would think better of him.

The following week, on my last visit, he didn't want to talk about the story, though we both acknowledged that I had read it. We talked about the fact that Dwayne (as I'll call him) was about to leave the secure unit and go out in the world, and was thrilled about his place at a college. We talked about the future, and I asked him how he imagined his life outside. 'Different?' he suggested, with hesitation. Then, more confidently: '*Different.*' The officer who had arranged my visits and helped Dwayne with his college application beamed. Sometimes a young person – especially a troubled or unhappy one –

can only picture more of the same. Nature abhors a vacuum and so does the future. It will grow to fit the shape we hold for it.

Back to 'The Thought Fox' again, and the power of what we imagine and how it creates reality. 'Brilliantly, concentratedly,/ Coming about its own business.' Writers' visits to schools should never be a luxury, an add-on, only for well-off schools that can afford them. The arts are as essential a subject as any we have. Sometimes a visiting artist or writer, a trip to the theatre, can change lives. I am grateful to Hughes and Blythe and poetry for saving mine.

Domus Operandi

Riley Rockford

20:00 When we are shown to the table, it is already two hours later than my family would have eaten at home. Somehow I have made it onto a programme at a famous graduate school, and here I am at the birthday dinner of one of my classmates. People are ordering water that you pay for, and I don't dare to ask for tap water. So if I'm going to have to pay for water, I'm definitely going to get bubbles in it. I'll take that air over getting nothing extra for my money. 'Sparkling,' I say, and then, moments later, hear someone else ask for tap water anyway. Around me they begin to speak of summer houses, and skiing trips. My classmates are crystals, casting rainbows across the table, as generations of their families radiate from them, fanning wide.

20:12 I am finally at one of those bright, swirling dinner parties, and I don't know if I have any of the right things to say. And these are nice people too, so sooner or later one of them is going to ask me something directly. Across from me, the guy who grew up by 'the Heath' (which is a lot posher than it sounds: it's in Hampstead) is explaining that in the 1950s his grandfather crossed a continent with only a backpack and a camera, and next summer he will retrace those steps and make a 'documentary feature' about it. I wonder what my granddad was doing then. Working in the laundry, I guess. Slipping notes to the girl who would become my gran, notes that sometimes were without words, just a stick boy and girl holding hands. They only went twenty miles down the road for their honeymoon, and it rained most of the week, but that didn't matter at all. They would wait forty years before getting on a plane. And ten years after that, I would get on a plane, because they had saved money to give me a holiday for working so hard in school. But I don't think I can use these stories here. I need something else.

20:17 Unfortunately I am seated on the corner, and the waiter asks me if I'd like to try the wine.

20:21 While I am smiling and passing the butter, I slip out of the restaurant and run back home. I will have to be quick. I don't have long to find something I can use.

At university, I had been introduced to the globe artichoke. A thistle you can eat. Thistles are from where we are from, so I thought it would be a nice thing to take when I went home for the first time. The artichoke flower head is an inflorescence – a cluster of many budding small flowers. I cooked one for each of us. I brought real butter instead of marg to have on them too. I laid it all out, and I explained that the good stuff is inside all the little compartments. The edible parts are the fleshy bits – the heart. They lifted their eyebrows. Expensive, fiddly, and not even that nice. After, they were still hungry, so they made a quick stew from corned beef and it smelled great, but I didn't say so. Once the buds in an artichoke bloom, the structure changes to a coarse, barely edible form. I sat staring at the ugly grey-green flower heads lying broken on the kitchen counter.

20:25 Someone is describing their unpaid internship with a tech company as I turn my key in the lock. In the front room, the time is February 1968. Dad, a boy of eight, is on the settee eating a bowl of cornflakes with the milk warmed up. His face is a bloom of freckles and in his mouth big teeth stand waiting for a big body to catch up with them. Through the television, he watches the Winter Olympics in Grenoble, which are being transmitted to the world for the first time in colour. Dad watches on a black-and-white set, but still the glistening snow crystals tumble before him like jewels from a pirate's treasure chest, and the alpine sun shines out onto his face.

I try to cross the room to get to him, but the floor is covered in bottles and pint glasses. The ones at his feet are those he will first taste six years from now. Hundreds more, from the late 1970s and through the 1980s stretch across the carpet and are stacked up by the window, bending and slowing the light coming through. More are appearing at my feet, as he continues to drink them in the present, which is rock bottom. Some fall and make such a cold, screeching sound, but it doesn't reach him. He is watching Schranz, the Austrian superstar, in the men's slalom race, sailing across the mountain and then skidding to a halt, to the consternation of the crowds. Dad holds his spoon in mid-air, and from it falls a drop of milk, like a first tear – heavy, so hard to surrender – onto his pyjamas, which are just beginning to be too small. Schranz will claim a mysterious man dressed in black had crossed his path out of nowhere.

20:29 Here is my uncle coming in from his job at the Wrangler factory. As he climbs the stairs, I see he has brought another haul with him today. He is slight, with a twenty-six-inch waist. In the stockroom he puts a pair of size twenty-eight jeans on over his own. Later he slips another pair, a thirty, on top. By the end of the day he is also sporting a thirty-two and a thirty-four. Wearing his bomber jacket, his shape doesn't look conspicuous, and he walks coolly out of the front gates. The plant makes a million pairs a week – these four are nothing. But he can get £8 a pop for them in the pub which, added up, will go a long way, this being 1985, and it will pay for a bus ticket down south to see his new baby niece. Walking home through the timorous air of early evening, buried beneath the many layers he has pulled on over himself, he watches something, Sputnik maybe, passing overhead. It is a reminder that we will not be here for a long time, so we might as well be here for a good time. At any moment, the job could go away, your girlfriend could leave, we could all be gone if some bigwig decides to make it so.

20:35 The group has ordered lots of small plates to share before the mains. When they arrive, I see that one is the fancy-pants, show-off, too-big-for-your-boots, more-money-than-sense edible thistle. It is a gremlin crouched in a bowl, staring at me, teeth bared, drooling. A classmate offers to show me how to eat it, and as she speaks I realise hesitation will look like ignorance here, especially if you have already demonstrated that there are indeed many things about which you know nothing.

20:39 Upstairs, in the summer of 1990, Gran and Granddad sit in bed, with a crossie and the *Daily Record* respectively. I come to stay every holiday, and I am sitting between them, with a bumper puzzle book. Before sleep, Granddad tells me stories from his head. Tonight, he says that once upon a time there was a magic sweet shop where we went to buy a bag of sweets. I ate them walking down the street, and as we walked through the forest, and over the hills, and at home, after I'd had my tea. Soon a week had passed and I still hadn't finished them. And that's when we realised – it was a never-ending sweetie bag! We reached down inside it, and saw there was no bottom – it was just sweeties, all the way down. Each night, he goes back downstairs to sleep on the couch so I can share the bed with Gran. And then she tells me stories too, but real ones, about when a couple of GIs came down their street, and how one of them drew her portrait on the back of a cigarette box. She tells me how her dad had come across the water to find work in the mills. When she was a child, they all played outside their tenement building, and one day someone from one of the houses opposite had put a bath out in the street. Neither she nor any of the other children had seen a bath before, so they just assumed it was for coal and dragged it round the back for their parents. She tells me how she and Granddad waited six years to have my uncle, by which time they had given up. And then, another six years after that, along came my dad! So, you never know.

During the night, I listen to her snoring, to the clock marking the wearing away of our summer, to the gulls outside calling to one another over the estuary. The little holy-water font hangs on the wall above us, a tiny clasp holding on to the promise of blessings, a still, quiet pool, the idea that all of us pilgrims might find a place to rest.

20:50 We will soon be an hour into dinner and I haven't said anything yet. I will start to look like a weirdo soon. Upstairs on the landing, the loft hatch is open, and on the floor is Dad's box of birds' eggs, safely stored for the last twenty years. Each egg is nestled in its own little space. One – Dad's favourite, and now mine – is pale blue. He would handle it so delicately, would never allow it to be broken. Downstairs, where he is now, the TV is smashed from when he got in a fight, and so are some of the bottles. He is smashed. I am too, in a different, invisible way.

20:59 Someone is announcing they have a book deal to write about their sailing trips. She grew up spending weekends at the marina on their boat, working hard under the sun. Setting out up the coast, lunch in inlets, camping on islands. I'll admit, these scenes are just like those in a book. I don't have places like this. So what would I write about, then? If I ever dare. Suddenly it goes dark on the landing. The meter must have run out. I feel my way downstairs and find Mum in the hallway, looking through her purse for coins. Her hands are not soft but are gentle. She left home at fifteen and went to the south coast to find work in the hotels there, where she met my dad. He made her laugh. She was still young when she had me. Now she goes into the cupboard under the stairs to give the meter what she has. We have put so many coins into that slot, heard them fall all the way down. Are they sitting below the house in a gleaming reservoir, waiting to come back to us? That stash of coins must be somewhere, but we don't have it. We have the fact we spent it, and had nothing left after. We spent it on heat and light, which cooled and faded, was always about to run out. Mum pauses in the dark cubby, waiting for more energy. She watches the dials turn. She has no control over which numbers are up. Then, yellow light floods the little room, a hum starts up again and the little wheel continues turning. Specks of food get warm, leap up and hit a ceiling.

Mum had a boyfriend who wanted to marry her. But he was not good, and he made her sad in a new way. He had a bit more money, though – he worked in computers and wore a tie to work. I didn't think this was a good trade-off, but Mum said he was someone we could count on.

Anything could make him hit the roof. Swearing, something on the telly, foolishness, childhood (specifically girlhood), energy, inexperience, and then experience. Mum did leave him in the end, but for three years, in the smallest bedroom, there was the possibility of a dead girl. Smoke curled slowly out of him, and at any moment she might do something to make his rage catch fire. And then they would both go to hell.

21:15 I open the bathroom door and there I am in the bath, age fifteen, a flannel over my face. Repeating that life is precious. You shouldn't waste it. But the thought of living might be more choking than the thought of death. Especially since you won't be going to heaven now – you'll only have seventy or eighty years max, so you'd really better make them count. You'd better achieve things to make up for what you wished you'd had, *and* what your parents don't, *and* what you've given up in the next life to feel free in this one. But being cautious, needing to make sure you do things right, checking around you for danger, taking care of yourself – this will look like weakness and immaturity here. Hurry up.

21:23 A little funny thing comes out of my mouth before I have time to screen it, and the others laugh. A big laugh, both because it was funny and kind of clever, and because my saying it surprised them. So now I have a little credit banked, at least.

I cross to the bedroom that Granny (Mum's mum) never leaves. All of the journeys she takes are in her mind. Her chosen menu is the same every day. Only two kinds of food – tinned mandarins and soft processed cheese. And these are paired with pills, two kinds. These pills have gone through everything. Through the 1980s, 70s, 60s, 50s – pills, all the way down. When she is awake, she sings to herself – songs from the 1940s. The walls in here are papered with pink and yellow flowers – she is surrounded by meadows. I leave her there, nightgown fluttering in the breeze as she waits for her sweetheart, and continue on.

21:34 I skip dessert. They are seven quid each. I walk into the kitchen and find a dead person. She's kneeling at the oven. She's the next generation up, the furthest point I know to go. She'd had enough. Or she didn't have enough. We don't know quite why she did it. She didn't talk about what she was feeling. None of us ever talk about what we are feeling.

21:49 Then, an opportunity! I actually have something to say. I could bring in the perfect reference here. But – I don't know how to say it. Do you pronounce the g or not? I try to find a memory of someone saying it aloud, but I don't have one.

I lie on the table, half in, half out of my shell. They prod me with their little forks, inspecting, coaxing. My body is whole, but from the outside I look grotesque, still emerging, and from the inside I seem to be trying to get away.

I had thought that if I could just get the degree, life would get incrementally easier, and all kinds of things would come into view. I had thought that then the possibilities would be as wide and bold as my desires. But it wasn't so, and now my desires are losing their nerve. Perhaps I should not have expected more than this shift, which is not inconsiderable, after all.

22:16 The bill comes, and of course we just split it equally amongst everyone, regardless of what you had, because that is the sophisticated way it is done. Granted, this is the easiest, breezy, carefree way.

I look out from the restaurant over to my house. Through the windows I can see them all turning in for the night.

I see my uncle, coming up the hill to home, a pirate ship laden with denim, a spacecraft protected by its payload shroud. A little person underneath proliferating layers piloting a big person. The view from the flight deck is vast, and full of nothing.

In the front room, I notice some of the bottles have rolled-up bits of paper inside them, with messages written on. Dad must have lost them in there along the way, and I didn't even think to look inside.

Gran and Granddad are playing dominoes. Her ruby wedding ring moves up and down in the space between them, a strong, skipping heart.

In the kitchen stands a young woman, who knows the war has been won now but fears she may be losing something inside of her, and that in this, she is without allies.

Mum is sitting quietly on the back step, sipping her favourite drink. I cannot tell you what she is thinking about, because I don't know. Perhaps she is looking back, perhaps she is looking forward; perhaps I will find a way to ask her.

The lights go out in each room. Except for Granny's. She keeps her light on all night. She is a crackling wireless, old now, ever in song.

Out the back, the whole family's clothes are on the line, rippling gently with the wind. Sometimes they puff up, swollen with energy from the atmosphere. Then, one breaks away, lifts upwards, but is caught moments later in the claw of the neighbour's tree. From there, that piece of moon-soaked, starlit cotton waves hesitantly at the sky.

This is just one of many little houses, but together we warm it, light it, stuff it full. We may be small, but we are budding all our lives, until we die. Things could change. Something new and surprising is always possible, right up until the very end.

Steve

Daljit Nagra

When I think of my schooling, which was a stone's throw away from
Heathrow Airport, I'm reminded of Allen Ginsberg's 'Howl': I too
saw the brightest minds of my age destroyed. Ginsberg's dramatic
words draw me close to so many of the pale faces of the kids from
the council estate next to our school. They were able, bright, some
even gifted, and they all succumbed to mediocrity by either leaving
school at fifteen, which was permitted back in the 1980s, or – those
who were more compliant – leaving after Year 11 with a clutch of
CSE grades, to end up in uninspiring jobs. In this sense, I think the
minds of my friends were not so much destroyed as intellectually
deprived. I'm sure a few of these friends fought their ways into
positions of employment that stretched their minds, or they went
on to advanced studies at a later stage, but these would have been
the exceptions.

When I think of my schooling, the best instance of neglected minds
for me is my fair-haired friend, Steve. He grew up in a household
with several siblings, his mum was a nurse and his dad was a school
caretaker. They'd already instilled in Steve a strong work ethic,
so in his teens he'd go on to hold down a part-time job in the DIY

store FADS. I met Steve in our early teens by chance; we'd take the same route to school and it wasn't long before we started walking together past the scary council blocks. What drew me to Steve were his abnormalities! He wasn't into football, or sports in general. He couldn't tell a Kevin Keegan from a Martina Navratilova. He wasn't into watching the idiot box, so no talk about last night's episode, say, of *The Sweeney* or *Starsky and Hutch*. Perhaps even more abnormal, he was a reader. What self-respecting male reads books? His ground-floor bedroom even had a bookshelf. It had books such as a tea-stained copy of *Kes*, jokes by Spike Milligan and the lyrics of Lennon and McCartney, all paraded proudly in alphabetical order. Weirder still, Steve had a compendious hardback of common laws. He'd walk to school muttering laws from his red tome about the rights appertaining to a citizen's arrest and so on. He was a rarity – an exotic breed around the breeze blocks – weaponised with the strictures. Don't mess, or be citizenly arrested by Steve and his lawful book.

I assumed he'd grow up to one day become a lawyer; being gently chubby, he might have taken shape as a Rumpole of the Bailey, or perhaps he'd be a keen-eyed sleuth, a Columbo. Yet when we reached our final years of schooling, when the stakes should have risen, when we should have felt an academic urgency, a grander ambition stirring our hormones to some noble purpose, Steve was struck by a disarming level of academic under-expectation. Not only did school hold us back by patronising us with meaningless qualifications, Steve's parents and our general social circle had all pinned their hopes on jobs at a local office or factory. This would have been fine, except that Steve was academically gifted. His general knowledge would have impressed Bamber Gascoigne (quizmaster on *University Challenge* at the time), he could weave narratives with a Dickensian flourish, and he could ascend the invisible steps of abstract thought and return to earth without a bump.

Surely he should have set his sights higher. We'd all known some students who'd gone on to sixth form, but this was often to retake exams. None of us knew anyone who'd been to university or who knew the consequences of such a preoccupation. I watched Steve's alarming detachment from academia with a migrant's beady perspective. I was born in England, in our town, Yiewsley, but my parents were from India. They'd expected me to become a doctor or a lawyer. I was driven by a migrant psychology to succeed to a status higher than that of my parents. I didn't know how to become a doctor or a lawyer. I hadn't enjoyed my careers interview where I was told – like all my friends, like Steve – to quit school at sixteen and get a job. I remained determined to suffer the edifying white of the classroom chalk for as long as I could, unlike Steve, who neglected revision and exams with impunity. He just stopped caring about his studies, and no one cared to stop him from not-caring.

I watched on, saddened, as he slowed his academic mind to accelerate his music ambitions. I didn't understand why he wouldn't want to keep both education and music equally on the burner. While still at school, he joined a band as a rhythm and lead guitarist, and rehearsed in a garage, performing for friends and family in a disused shop, and onwards to reach the popular heights of our school assembly, where his band strummed with aplomb 'Another Brick in the Wall', and 'Red Red Wine', along with other popular songs of the era. I watched, proud to be his friend. The assembly was a final confirmation that he'd traded in the schoolbook for the songbook, the mighty Bic had fallen and the Grattan-catalogue Hondo guitar was now God.

It was no surprise when Steve left school at sixteen. He gave up his various part-time jobs and took up a full-time position with a furniture company while performing in pubs around west London with his band, Standard Issue. Would he be showered by limelight?

Become a starman? Steve as the next Mick… Ronson. Steve playing with Paul… Weller. Steve… 'With or Without You'. I don't think he burned with ambition: perhaps he wasn't messed up enough; perhaps the tragic lack of guidance, of mentoring, of social connections held back the band from developing their own voice. Too many humble, gentle types in the same room don't make the ego blaze! Though I suspect he just enjoyed the camaraderie of playing in a band. He enjoyed the experience that nourished his need to enable others to smile, to put a smile on his own face. Happiness without the burden of fame and its spiralling expectations. Life in the band introduced him to the song of his life, his devoted wife, Lisa, and the music of love has played for them ever since.

He's now fifty-one and for the past decades he's worked for several businesses, at best in a lower management role. He hit the ceiling many moons ago, and he's watched countless youngsters with solid degrees from respectable universities float past him. Not that Steve ever saw himself bossing a large workforce; it's more that his ability to move around jobs that suit his skills has always been limited. Despite all this, he has been hugely successful and has always been valued at work. My main concern is that he would have found satisfying the academic fruits that I grabbed for myself. I went on to mess up my own life for a while, before studying A levels at evening classes then, at the age of twenty-one, I headed for university. Over time I built up enough self-belief to write poems with a serious purpose. I'm now a poet and an academic at a university. Why didn't Steve want what I wanted? The intellectually thrilling platform from which to spring? He had as much right as I had to seek platform, then spring! Perhaps he was held back by the narratives of entitlement for blue-collar workers constructed by the powers that be and by his family. Perhaps he was too strongly expected to toil, to seek economic gratification, to leave the nest and make immediate wingspan.

The white working classes are often cornered into a pejorative type, but Steve is also a kind of type and one that rarely takes the stage. Throughout the decades, I've never heard him express a bitter attitude towards those who've bypassed him in the workplace. An honest man who'll rarely blurt an expletive and has never been physically aggressive, who is politically correct and a moderate drinker, though I wish he'd have an extra pint when we're out! He accepts himself and lives with a beam of self-effacing delight, is replete with witty one-liners, and remains as curious as ever about broadsheet issues of the day. A soft-spoken and dignified man who starts the car for the hour-and-a-half journey to work, who is committed to his duties as parent and husband, who never rants politics and who quietly voted against Brexit.

I was never close to my family and I didn't expect them to visit me at university, Royal Holloway in Egham, Surrey. But even though I lived many miles from Steve, he'd visit me almost every week over the three years of my English degree. When we were younger, he'd knock for me on the way to school each morning, and now at university, he'd arrive straight from work in his shirt and tie, and drive us off to a country pub, or we'd go for a curry. He'd almost always insist on paying for the drink, the meal. However far we'd venture, however difficult my years at university, he was a mainstay who'd always drive me back to my room. I'd wave him off surprised and gratified to exist in this unusual friendship, this paternal attraction that came naturally and against the odds, a bond that neither of us felt inclined to cut from its cord and leave behind.

No Lay, No Pay

Paul Allen

'You fanny-tested it, boy?'

Sharker Harlock's face bore his usual arrogant smirk, mixed perhaps with just a dash of superciliousness and a smattering of outright bastardness.

A test involving fannies? On a barrow full of muck?

I should point out that in the building trade 'muck' is a mixture of sand, cement, water and plasticiser, used for laying bricks. And in September 1972, at twelve years old and having been working on-site with my dad all summer, it was me that had put this very barrowload that Sharker seemed to be questioning through the mixer.

I should *also* point out that at that age and time of my life, though completely in the dark about girls and sex (voluntarily as it happens; I was far more interested in motorbikes and roaming the fields with my dog), I did have at least two versions of what a 'fanny' might be bouncing around in my head, gleaned from overheard conversations:

1. A useless tradesman, i.e. one that 'farted and fannied about'.
2. Something to do with a lady's front bottom.

It sounds ridiculous in this day and age that that was the sum of my knowledge in this particular field of expertise, but they were far more innocent times, and I was very, very shy, to the point of being regarded by the girls at school as vaguely retarded. Also, there was no internet.

'Well... have you?'

God, I hated Sharker at times. He was my dad's best mate and, inexplicably, every now and then would be sporting a shiner my old man gave him the night before down the pub. They never seemed to fall out over it, and from what Mum said, Sharker would sometimes get a little too much when he had the drink in him, 'So your dad, being his mate, knocks him out before he upsets anybody.'

Yup, them were the days. We all looked out for each other on council estates.

'OY! GORMLESS!!'

Back then, I often wished I had been carrying more age and muscle so I could do him Dad's matey favour and knock him out myself. This was such a moment. I shook my head, miserably.

'Errr... I dunno... probably not... Do I have to?'

Sharker shook his head in a mix of disbelief and pity, sucking sharply through the roll-up that never left his lips.

'Ain't your dad taught you summat as simple as the fanny test? What the fuck sorta bricklayer you gonna be, boy?'

I might have known nothing about sex, but growing up where I lived, I knew plenty about standing my ground. Knew a reasonable amount about reciprocal swearing too.

'A fucking sight better one than you, Sharker Harlock! You want this fucking muck or wot?'

'Oooh, easy with that cursing, boy,' Sharker laughed. 'I'll be telling Hazel and you'll be getting your spotty arse tanned.'

Hazel was my mum. And yes, if she knew I had used the F-word,

I would indeed get a well-deserved hiding. She had crept up behind me once, over the playing field one summer's evening as I had been merrily shouting and swearing my six-year-old head off at some of the posh kids (that is to say, they lived in privately owned houses and as such were our mortal enemies) from over the field. Pulled my trousers and pants down in one quick move and slapped my arse so hard it echoed around the houses on the perimeter like a gunshot. Took me a coupla days for my bum to stop stinging and considerably longer (years, in fact) to stop feeling the burn of shame from that one.

And whilst Dad's mates were always loud, abrasive and heavy on the swears, he himself was a quiet man who rarely swore in front of me and my sisters.

Sharker sighed the sigh of an incredibly patient man, and I knew instantly that in an act of unimaginable generosity he was going to stop giving me grief, and instead revert to charitably bestowing a nugget of his impressive and hard-earned wisdom upon me.

'Muck's gotta be just right, innit, boy. Not too dry, not too wet, an' nice 'n' buttery to boot. Definitely not sloppy; you can't lay brick and block with soup. So, first thing, flatten the fucker out.'

He used the heel and bottom flat of his brick trowel to smooth over the shiny grey mixture in the barrow.

'Now, draw a fanny on it...'

This time it was the tip of the trowel, used like a scalpel to draw an upright, lemon-shaped outline, then a sharp flourish, to slice a vertical line straight down the middle from point to point, perfectly bisecting it.

'And now, if it's juuuuuuust right...'

He slid the trowel point first into the muck just below the pictogram, then eased it forward so it was running about an inch deep and parallel to the surface underneath it, until the point of the trowel was buried in its centre. Then, gently levering the heel of the trowel down and the tip up from underneath, the middle vertical slash opened upwards and outwards, looking disturbingly like the puckering lips of someone who had a mouth that ran from top to bottom instead of from side to side.

Sharker grunted his satisfaction. 'And there it is, all nice and ready for you to slip your old boy in. Or, in this case, lay two hundred of London Brick Company's finest commons with. That's a good mix, young Allen. And make the most of seeing that fanny; that's about as close to one as a fucking useless string of piss like you will ever get.'

Naïve and unworldly I was, stupid I wasn't. My fledgling sexual education took a giant leap forward as my scrambling mind tied in Sharker's impromptu vulvas-for-dummies lesson with the stuff the Scottish fella in *Living and Growing* (the grainy black-and-white sex-education film shown in school) had been banging on about. In truth, I stared at it in fascinated horror. All I could think was, 'Christ... is that what one looks like?

As it turned out, Sharker was right, and it *was* some years later before I got to see a real one. And aesthetically, to be fair to him again, he wasn't a million miles out on the basic workings of the thing. I did initially think, 'Ooh... I dunno, that don't look quite right, perhaps I should tell her to get that checked out or summat,' but luckily for me that sixth sense I've always had to warn me about stuff sometimes told me that:

A. A real one was bound to be a lot more realistic than a sand-and-cement-based one in a wheelbarrow; and
B. That sorta talk beforehand both spoils the moment and, more importantly, would result in an immediate cessation of proceedings.

So I kept schtum.

Dad, Sharker and his other building mates had worked together for years, been in the army before that together, and been friends as kids even before that.

They were a motley crew: Sharker Harlock, Whippet Edwards, Old Wongy, Young Wongy, Bull Stimpson and Pug Jones. Even today, I have no idea what their real names were. The only one who didn't have a nickname was Dad, though everyone called him by his second name, Roy. Sharker was the ladies' man, forever 'sharking' around the girls when they hit the pubs after work. Whippet was leaner than a blade of grass, all muscle and sinew, so I got that. Bull was thickset and solid – again, made sense. Pug was the ugliest man you could ever meet; there it is, *ipso facto*. But Young Wongy and Old Wongy? Gawd knows. On-site they were a law unto themselves, though they got away with it because, to a man, they all worked their arses off. And did they ever give each other grief.

'Bull, I stuck up for you in the pub last night... Sharker said, "Bull Stimpson ain't fit to live with pigs!" I said, "He fucking is."'

'Buggeration, Pug. If ugliness were bricks, you'd be the Great Wall of China.'

'Sharker, you'll find life a lot easier if you grease that brick trowel of yours up, 'cos if you leave it on my mortarboard again, I'm gonna shove it up your fucking arse!'

'Christ, Whippet, you're short... What's it like to be the last one to realise it's raining... AND have your hair smell of feet?'

'I see on the telly the other night we all spring from apes, Young Wongy. Shame your poor fucking mum didn't spring far enough.'

'Old Wongy, you fat fucker, I was shagging your missus last night and she told me being fucked by you was like having a big wardrobe fall on her with the key sticking out...'

They never let up or eased off each other, though I knew they all loved each other like brothers, which is kinda what they were. They had been kicking and punching as a unit for survival their whole lives, and humour is undoubtedly one of the soul's weapons in the fight for self-preservation. And though I didn't realise it at the time, Dad knew I would learn basic and important life lessons from being part of this unity and camaraderie.

He himself gave me advice sparingly. I mean like, hardly ever. I'm fairly certain his way of thinking was this: 'Gotta let Paul make his own mistakes and then, when he's picked himself up, he'll probably do it again, pick himself up again, then do it a few more times till he has had the shit completely knocked out of him, then one more time, then finally learn from it and *perhaps* not do it any more. Perhaps.'

Sometimes what little advice he gave was cryptic, at least to my ears. In my mid-twenties I was married and working all the hours God sent to pay the mortgage off before we tried for a baby. My then wife went to see a pregnant friend of hers and when she came back it was: 'I want a baby.'

'You want a WHAT!?'

'You heard me. I WANT A BABY!!!'

Cue a big row and me schlepping my sorry self around to Dad's house, where sympathy and advice would hopefully be found. What was I thinking? As soon as I walked in, Dad saw I had a face like a smacked arse.

'What's up with you?'

'Dad, I just don't understand women...'

Dad shook his head in exasperation and mild anger.

'Fer Christ's sake, what?! Do you understand colour telly?'

My turn to shake my head, though in my case from confusion.

'Errrm... no?'

'Well then, what's your problem? Now put the bloody kettle on...'

And there it was. My wife got pregnant, Dad got his cup of tea, and I got years of scratching my head, thinking, 'What the hell did that mean?'

Constructive criticism wasn't his forte either. I went through a stage, as a lanky, growing, beanpole kid, of falling over a lot. Dad's answer to that?

'Your problem is your feet are growing too big for your brain. You just gotta wait till it catches up. If it ever does.' Yup, not big on being all about the helpfulness. He had, however, given me some good advice that first day he started taking me out on-site with him. It went like this: 'Right, this is all you gotta remember. Building is just four things, and that's it.

1. Level.
2. Plumb.
3. Digging bastard holes.
4. Filling the buggers up again.'

And you know what? It is. You dig bastard holes (footings). You fill the buggers up again with concrete (foundations). You build (level and plumb). That's pretty much my whole working life described in full.

But there *was* actually a fifth element, something he hadn't told me, something essential to the soul and infrastructure of every building site I ever worked on. Something Sharker Harlock had given me a glimpse of right at the start of it all.

Sex.

I don't mean the physical act of it. In truth, I mean the exact opposite! What I actually mean is everything else to do with it *but* the physical act of it.

Talking about it. Endlessly.

Joking about it.

Teasing about it.

Moaning about the lack of it.

Relating every job we ever did in some way to it (if I had a quid for every time some twat said, 'Shame there ain't hair around it, you'd soon find your way in,' when I was struggling to locate something in a hole).

Declaring any mistake anyone ever made on-site to be proof of their undoubted uselessness in the bedroom department.

The list is endless. Hardly a day would pass without it rearing its head (ho ho), whether in acrimony, hilarity or just plain old general discussion.

I guess back in the day it was just one of the fundamental ways working-class men who had a very physical job to do, day in day out, dealt with keeping their nose to the grindstone and bringing home money for rent (these were the years before Maggie told us if we grafted we could buy our house instead of renting it off the council) and food. And in truth, I wouldn't have had it any other way. Life on-site was actually bloody good fun most of the time, back then.

Obviously, health and safety was pretty poor, and every now and then someone would get hurt badly or even die (I've witnessed three deaths on-site in my time, and been standing next to a bloke who got electrocuted so badly he wished he had died), but, according to Dad's mates, there was always a bright side.

'Poor old Ernie fell off the top lift of the scaffold on plot three. He's proper fucked. Still, give it a few weeks an' his missus is bound to be "hungry"; face like a bag of spanners but decent tits an' that...'

Every cloud, huh?

The only extremely vague mention Dad ever made about sex to me was when I was fifteen and he took me out of school ('CSEs ain't gonna do him any good, Hazel, he's gotta start paying his way') to go full time with him on the trowel.

'You know what a working girl is, right? They been plying their trade as long as we have. You'll always find builders got a certain respect for them. We got more in common than you might think. We call ourselves "self-employed", but we're not really, we're all somebody's whores and all dance to the tune of the man paying the wages. Brickies and working girls got summat else in common too. The common rule we live and work by, regardless of everything else that happens around us: "No lay, no pay".'

Whether it's scorching hot, freezing cold, whether you're ill, hung-over, or just plain dog-tired, you got to be on-site at seven every morning, that mixer's got to be fired up and loaded and you got to be putting bricks down by half past. You stop twice a day for dokky (farmers in our region used to dock workers' money when they stopped for food, hence that widespread local term for a break), but you don't stop long; you get back on the string line and you keep getting bricks down till fifteen minutes before the site shuts. Have the crack with your mates by all means, but keep that trowel working.

'No lay, no pay. It's that simple.'

All these years on, I remember that, word for word.

And sometimes, when I'm on the trowel, just for the fuck of it I'll draw Sharker's crude vulva into the muck, open it up and smile as I see his stupid, leering mush grinning and peering through it at me across the sands of time.

He's been dead, along with my dad, for many years now. Hard labour and building wore them both out, along with the drink and fags. But to me, he will always be immortalised, albeit in a barrow-load of mortar.

*

'Every encounter is a moment of another's becoming.'

— Dr Tim Gibson – friend, mentor
and one of the most human of human beings I ever met.

Any Relation?

Louise Doughty

In 2004, one cold spring afternoon, my father told me a secret. We were in his car at the time, driving back to the small East Midlands town where I had grown up and where he still lived with my mother. We had spent the day in Peterborough, the city where he had been raised, visiting elderly relatives.

It had been a long day of tea and stories, and we both fell silent on the drive home. It was early spring and the light began to slant across the fields. As dusk gathered, my father, still looking straight ahead as he drove, spoke a single sentence. 'If I tell you something, will you promise never to tell anyone else?'

My little writer's heart, dark as pickled walnut, began to constrict in my chest. What was my father about to say? 'You are not my daughter...' or, 'I have another family,' or, 'I once killed a man.' I was too excited to make the promise, but he continued anyway.

'I left school when I was thirteen.'

My disappointment was profound. I sort of knew that already. He had often talked of how he had won a place at grammar school but that when his mother saw the price of the blazer she had said, 'We can't afford that. You're not going.' He had gone to the rough school instead where, in the playground one day, a teacher had given him a backhander so hard it threw him against a wall. He had left early and worked as an apprentice – his own father was a painter and decorator.

For some reason, though, he had a bee in his bonnet about education. 'He was always the posh one, our Ken!' my Great-Aunt Lenda had remarked to me once, raucously, pushing at his shoulder while my father laughed. He did his lower and higher certificates at night school and, eventually, studied for an external degree in engineering at Nottingham University, while doing a full-time job to support his wife and three children. 'Your father was no help when you were all small,' my mother once said, in an uncharacteristic moment of disloyalty. 'He studied every evening and every weekend.' When I was twelve and he was well into his fifties, he finally got a PhD, the highest academic qualification anyone could get. Ever since, he had called himself 'Doctor Doughty'. He took great pride in explaining his PhD thesis in engineering to anyone who mistook him for a medical doctor.

My mother had left school at fifteen and gone to work as a secretary in the firm where she met my father. No night school or studying for her when we were small. She had the ironing to do.

'Don't you think, Dad,' I said quietly, as we drove, 'that actually, that's something to be proud of?' I was thinking how hard my father had worked: a full-time job, studying at night, he and our mother both giving everything to provide us with advantages they had never had. All three of us had gone on to higher education and it meant the world to him. The photos that took pride of place on the walls of the bungalow we were heading back to that day comprised a row of me and my brother and sister in our graduation gowns. 'You had none of those opportunities and yet we all went to university because of what you did for us.'

My father was not prone to talking things through quietly – he was a man who liked an argument – but on this occasion he said, thoughtfully, 'I suppose so, yes, OK, maybe you're right.'

I think of this conversation whenever I brag about my parents' humble origins. Like many a middle-class child of working-class parents, it's something I'm prone to doing when I feel embarrassed about how privileged my life is now (i.e. quite often). I thought about it in 2013, when I received a letter inviting me to prepare my entry for *Who's Who*. My father's own ancestors had been Romany Travellers on his mother's side; his grandfather on his father's side had grown up in a workhouse where he went by the name of Pauper 57. Back then, our family was not so much working class as underclass.

When I received that letter, my father had been dead for eighteen months. Knowing how much social status had meant to him, I got a little moist and sentimental. 'Look, Dad,' I whispered to myself, 'from Pauper 57 to *Who's Who* in three generations.'

The lynchpin of this Dickensian-sounding elevation was my father and his determination that his children would, above all else, be educated. Education was the key to everything.

After leaving school and his apprenticeship, my father had moved away from Peterborough, to work in the engineering firm in Melton Mowbray, Leicestershire, where he met our mother. He was a townie, she was more rural working class – her father worked in Dickinson & Morris bakery making Melton Mowbray pork pies. We ate D & M pork pies quite regularly and it was a family tradition to have one for breakfast on Christmas morning. As a result, I am a terrific pork pie snob and can bore for England on how to tell if a pie has been properly hand-raised and how the meat must always be grey, not pink, and peppery. The choices for girls like my mother were few: shop girl, nurse or secretary – and even then, only until you got married, when you gave up work and looked after your husband and your home.

Despite his achievements with night school and external studying, my father felt his lack of formal education acutely. He had taken elocution lessons in his youth, 'To learn how to talk proper,' as he joked. With neighbours and teachers at school, he affected an accent more upper crust than middle class – he would pronounce 'theatre' as 'the-ay-tre', although he lapsed into Fen dialect peppered with Romany when he was talking to one of our aunts or uncles. He had read the *Complete Works of Shakespeare* from cover to cover, because he thought that was what educated people did. 'I always say, *King Lear* is Shakespeare's greatest comedy!' As children, the swiftest way to earn a rebuke was if we did anything common. This included wanting to wear blue jeans, saying 'caff' when we meant 'café' and watching ITV. At my graduation ceremony at Leeds, he mortified me by saying loftily to one of my English Literature professors, 'Of course, George Eliot wasn't the only woman novelist to adopt a male pseudonym, George Sands was a woman as well, don't you know?'

Nonetheless, we didn't have a sitting room; we had a lounge. In the lounge we sat not on a sofa but on a settee. We had dinner at lunchtime and the evening meal was called tea. Holidays were the same each year – a two-week break in a caravan in Devon, spent mostly sitting on a windswept, pebbled beach watching the sea while huddled into towelling tops eating cheese-and-tomato-ketchup sandwiches from a Tupperware. After a few hours of this, we would be allowed an ice cream and sit eating it in the welcome fug of the car, before returning to the campsite for our mother to make something she called 'caravan hot pot' – a mixture of tinned vegetable soup, tinned new potatoes and corned beef. When I went to university at the age of eighteen, I had never holidayed in a hotel, flown on an aeroplane or eaten in a restaurant.

We were raised with the idea that thrift, hard work and sobriety were the routes to happiness. My parents were teetotal and never spent a penny they didn't have – for both of them, what had ruined working-class families when they were growing up were the twin evils of drink and debt. *Never drink* and *never get into debt* were the pillars we were raised by, although it's safe to say that at different phases in our lives, all three of us have blown it on both fronts.

We were also raised as exemplars of the phrase: *the world doesn't owe you a living*. Our father knew it was his duty to feed, clothe and educate us all – then we were on our own. After our local state primary school, our brother passed the eleven-plus to what was then a boys' grammar – by the time it came to my sister and I going, the school was co-educational and charging fees. Our mother went back to work as a secretary so they could afford to send us, whereupon we found it full of crusty male teachers who – with a couple of terrific exceptions – regarded girls as the barbarians at the gate and our admission as the end of a great school. My sister and I were both, for different reasons, incredibly miserable there, we all performed indifferently and it prejudiced me for life against fee-paying education and boy-heavy classes for girls. When it came to the next stage, though, we had one of the great privileges of our generation – we all went to university with our fees paid by Leicestershire County Council and on full maintenance grants.

When I moved to London in my mid-twenties, it astonished me to realise that some of my peers had parents who bought them fridges or holidays, or, most incredibly of all, *their own places to live*. For my first three years in the capital, I lived in a flat above a butcher's shop in Camberwell, south London. There were five official tenants who paid a peppercorn rent, but a large number of other residents – boyfriends, girlfriends, friends of friends – passed through and in practice it was basically a squat. The front of the flat overlooked the main road and one day one of the windowpanes fell clean out onto pedestrians below. The kitchen was on the ground floor at the back and looked out on to a small yard where the butcher brought the carcases through and had his outside toilet. We would see him occasionally, on his way there for his regular morning visit. He would wave cheerily with a bloodstained hand, clutching a pack of Marlborough.

I had one of the second-floor rooms, where tentacles of damp climbed down the wall from a top corner and I slept on a single mattress on the floor, using an upturned orange box as my bedside table. During this time, for a while, I dated a middle-class boyfriend who owned his own three-bedroom house in north London. The first time he came to my room in Camberwell he looked around and said, 'Where is all your stuff – at your parents' house?' Stuff? I didn't know what he meant. Later, the same boyfriend said to me, 'You've got a real chip on your shoulder about class.' 'Chip?' I thought. 'I've got a chip the size of Ben Nevis.'

When my first novel was published in 1995, I had, by then, got a journalism job. When one of my colleagues asked me what my novel was about, I said, 'It's about a group of office workers. It's based loosely but vengefully on my two years as a part-time secretary for London Transport.'

'Two years?' he replied, surprised. 'That's a long time to spend researching a book.'

I had always said I wanted to be a full-time writer by the time I was thirty. A week before my thirtieth birthday, I got my first book deal. The day before, I had a phone call from an editor for whom I had done some freelancing, inviting me to be the theatre critic of a national newspaper and naming a salary that was quadruple what

I was then earning as a part-time secretary who did the odd feature and book review. I had become a full-time writer with twenty-four hours to spare. When I told my father how much I was going to be earning, he drew a breath. It was twice the salary he was receiving when, at the age of sixty-two, he was told he was being made redundant and given twenty-four hours to pack up his desk after four decades with the same firm. He started to cry with happiness. He knew about the book deal and the other bits of freelance journalism, but this was a job. All that effort and sacrifice had paid off. His daughter was getting a proper job at last.

I left a flat-share off the Brixton Road and rented a bijou bedsit in Hampstead. I spent two and a half years going to the theatre for a living while writing my second novel. By the time it was published, I was pregnant by a BBC radio producer who had grown up in Surrey and we moved in together, into a maisonette on Tufnell Park Road. My journey from the East Midlands to full-blown member of the north London liberal elite was now complete.

In 2008, I was a judge on the Man Booker Prize for Fiction. During one of the discussions, one of the other judges said something I disagreed with. 'Bollocks to that!' I responded. A short silence fell, then the judge remarked, 'You can take the girl out of the East Midlands but you can't take the East Midlands out of the girl.'

He had a point. Geographically, I had migrated no further than one hundred miles south, but at times, it has felt like crossing continents. I have lost track of the number of occasions I have been asked whether I went to Oxford or Cambridge and the look I have got when I reply, 'Neither,' usually followed by a swift, 'Oh, but that's OK.'

I am still startled when I realise that the writer or journalist I am talking to is related to another writer or journalist I have heard about. 'Any relation to Charles Montagu Doughty?' I have been asked, several times. The author of *Travels in Arabia Deserta* is little known now, but he's the only Doughty literary types can call to mind. The last person to ask me this question was an elderly drama producer I met some years ago, when my first radio play was about to be broadcast on Radio 3. When I replied that no, I was no relation, he responded cheerily, 'Oh gosh, you know, I'm so old I remember when having a play on the Third Programme meant you were really something. Now they'll let anyone on!'

I find such small encounters funny – and take great pleasure, in my chippy, East Midlands way, in telling such people about my ancestors raised in workhouses, although sometimes I think about how my father would have been mortified by my talking publicly about it. He would have much preferred it if I was able to respond to the Charles Montagu Doughty question with a cheery, 'Oh yes, dear old Great-Uncle Charles!'

Few things make me more proud than not having those kinds of connections. And yet, chippiness aside, I have to concede one great and invaluable advantage, born directly from my parents' lack of material help or significant surnames. We were raised with the most stringent work ethic: a belief hammered into us all, on an almost daily business, that the world didn't owe us a living, that nothing would come to us unless we strived for it, that we would always have to press and push for what we wanted, because it wasn't coming any other way. My parents worked every day of their lives in the belief that their lives and ours could be bettered. Nothing irritates me more than the characterisation of working-class people as lazy or feckless. Hello? The clue is in the title.

Nowhere is such a work ethic more useful than in the field of novel-writing: because yes, you may have been born with a modicum of talent and/or a significant surname, but unless you sit down and churn out those words, again and again, for year after year, you ain't producing anything. This is surely true for all forms of artistic expression. And so, despite my inverted snobbery, there is this that I inherited: my father's and mother's sense that hard work was everything and there was no sitting back to be done, no time to be wasted.

I was also lucky enough to have been born at a time when that kind of work seemed to be rewarded, when social mobility felt possible for people like my mother and father. Our bungalow was built in the sixties. When our parents wanted to house their growing family, they, as a working-class couple with one income, were able to buy a plot of land on the edge of a town and get a local builder to build it. My father once told me they were terrified at the prospect of taking on a mortgage of £4,386. Because of the size of the plots, that same road is now considered posh, suburban, way beyond the means of my parents' present-day equivalent. The same mortgage today would be around £80,000. That wouldn't even get you a one-bed flat in the same town now, let alone a family bungalow with a large garden.

I grew up with a bunch of kids like myself – the children of aspirational families. We all played together on the waste ground at the end of our road, where more houses had yet to be built. There are no young families on that housing estate now, only retired couples who bought their homes decades ago. Above all, my parents were able to send all three of their children to university on full grants – given their anxiety about debt, we were exactly the kind of family that would have been heavily discouraged from higher education under the current system.

So for all my showing off about our backgrounds, not only did I inherit my parents' sense that you work for what you want, I inherited it at a time when the possibilities that work might be rewarded were much more firmly embedded in our social structures than they are now. They were certain – and they were right – that their children would grow up more advantaged than them in every respect, because that was the way it worked. This is my bequest from them, and it is invaluable, but my generation is the first generation that knows its children are likely to be worse off than themselves. My parents would be horrified, and baffled, by that idea – something has gone wrong, they would have thought. And they'd be right.

I Am Not Your Tituba

Eva Verde

'Without libraries what have we? We have no past and no future.'

— Ray Bradbury

I was born in 1980 in Newham, one of the most impoverished boroughs of London. A girl. Father unknown and a teenage mum. Brown. Violins, please. I left the maternity ward on a snowy January night, wrapped in two stolen NHS blankets.

Our life was simple, yet it rarely occurred to me how much we financially struggled. Our permanent party of two meant I had privileges that kids with working parents and other siblings didn't – time.

Weeks were ordered, routine, peppered with visits to my nan, window shopping and hours lost in Forest Gate Branch Library, which was on the first floor of an old brick building tucked off the busy High Street. We'd push at the library's heavyweight doors in unison, our efforts granting us entry to a mammoth room of hushed silence and warm natural light, a full removal from real life outside, speeding noisily on without us. The snug, homely bookishness of the space was my personal version of heaven. By five or six I was a familiar face to the kind yet superior lady librarians nestled behind the front desk, their glasses hanging from necklaces, resting on knitwear-encased bosoms. If there was anything I wanted to be when I grew up (other than She-Ra) it was to become one of them. Stamping books and talking in intelligent whispers. For a small person, I had purpose.

I never gave my appearance much thought. My ethnicity less. Every other person in my world was one shade of brown or another; my classroom could have been the poster for diversity. In 1988 my school held a multicultural event, encouraging children from local schools to participate in an evening of sharing food, songs and dancing from around the world. An audience of proud parents watched us perform dances and poetry in the national costumes of their homelands. My class was selected to perform a Celtic dance; school shirts, borrowed maxi skirts, and garish scarves and shawls were our haphazard attempts at costumes. This Technicolor explosion, vivid African prints alongside the silks and sequins of saris, the unity and respect for others' beliefs, rituals and traditions has never been forgotten.

It can't be. I have it on VHS.

My mum married a lovely man, who became my dad and gave me sisters. We grew to a family of six and, with the lure of green spaces and cheaper housing, left London for Essex. In November 1990, I enrolled in my new school, and was first shocked then rather alarmed to find myself the sole brown child there.

Chelmsford was alien territory, learning a different world all over again. Regular words and phrases took on new meanings; both 'up town' and 'down the town' referred to the modest shopping centre, where the buildings sat flat and unremarkable with not even a double-decker bus passing by for a fleeting hot splash of colour.

My 'up town' had been impromptu visits to Parliament Square with my nan and uncle, plum skies hugging an illuminated Big Ben as I dragged my fingers along the black iron fencing, admiring it. I clung to these memories, the old life's events, as my new life felt ever more a wilderness.

And the shame started.

In my Letts page-a-day diary, because the ten-year-old me had much to say, I wrote: *I'm hung like a picture. It's like I got off a spaceship. You move for the better but nothing's better and I don't count.*

I'd been in Chelmsford three weeks. A month later the shame grew spores: *I feel stupid. Asked Mum if I was adopted. She said why would she adopt a kid, being a kid herself. I don't feel belonging inside me, though. Not even to my family. I don't remember feeling it before, but I don't and everywhere I go there's eyes like nasty question marks on us.*

Being the only brown face in my white family meant outside of the home I was set apart. Once, at the checkout in Sainsbury's, we'd stood patiently waiting with a heaving trolley. Being only thirteen, rather than assist Mum to load the shopping on the conveyor belt, I'd amused myself looking at the chocolate bars and magazines, wondering whether I could chance asking for a *Big!* or *Smash Hits*, while ignoring my youngest sister's screams to be released from her chair.

A greying man queuing behind us had nudged me sharply, snapping, 'Do what you're paid for and quiet that baby down.' His vexed authoritarian tone made my throat shrink as I stood by awkwardly, unsure of how to respond. My discomfort was lost on the checkout lady, who chipped in to say how lovely it must be for my mother to have an au pair.

'She's my daughter,' Mum bit, laser-beam quickly. 'If I could afford an au pair, love, d'you think I'd be buying basics?'

The checkout woman, recognising her mistake, had winced, wishing she'd kept her mouth shut. But the man. He stepped back, unwilling even to set his eyes on me. I'd had similar moments moons ago; old ladies with sour faces moving away from me and my mum on the bus. Never from a man, though. And I'd never been nudged. It hadn't hurt, but it left an imprint that lasted for years.

Moments like this became routine. I began to dread the family outings, wishing I didn't stand out so we wouldn't get the nasty question marks. Paranoia held me close, dominating every decision. Where am I from? What am I? The passive-aggressive diatribe of how I came to be was asked almost daily. But to explain was impossible, without articulating the truth – illegitimate, disconnected from any cultural bond to my ethnicity. I was ashamed by how these people viewed me, believing their way the right way. Being brown and different was my fault.

It was hard to shut off from the boy who liked to use his stick across my back, shouting the N-word as I legged it home from school. And from the girls who, now we'd advanced to secondary, had become coarser with their insults. I was 'pubic-head' when my Afro roots grew through, because we could only afford to have my hair relaxed twice a year. Instead of embracing the curl, I'd still rather have the three inches of straight at the end of the bulky frizz, to fit and feel comforted by words such as, 'I always think of you as white.' By fourteen, on the single occasion a boy my own age showed interest, the cackling hordes of girls awarded me another fabulous nickname, Divine Brown, Hugh Grant's indiscretion. Any reference to the darkness and difference of me was categorically negative. The only times I became visible, useful, was at the high jump on sports day, and on one occasion (before they knew any better), choir. I was a walking stereotype of all the snippets they'd cobbled from their limited experiences of people of colour.

But in books, and through writing, none of it mattered. I began keeping my diary of the way I wished the day had progressed, starring a far more accomplished and desirable version of myself. My hair flowed fluid and Timotei-shiny down my svelte Topshop-adorned back. Our pebble-dashed, ex-council, end-of-terrace transformed into one of the 1930s detached delights down the tree-lined street I admired on my journey to school. And everyone, from the sixth-former with amazing eyes and cross-body bag that I borderline stalked, to Keanu Reeves and Kurt Cobain, fancied me rotten. Fantasy ruled my waves.

It was a given that when work experience rolled around at fourteen, I would naturally apply to the library. And even in Chelmsford, in this Martian landscape where I'd landed as the oddity, the library still stirred thoughts of home. This library was practically new, however; an enormous two-storey smoked-glass wonder, light years from my East End reading room, yet the sense of peace was identical. There were few things more alluring to me than the thick, slightly grubby scent of well-thumbed pages, and it was a happy discovery that other libraries possessed it. The librarians' downturned mouths, with their raised brows and studious expressions, always felt more as if they were playing a part rather than singling me out. I was familiar with these looks, unfazed. After all those formative days I knew a library's rules; if you appreciate books and are quiet, outside laws are suspended.

But a gawky, silent inconvenience who made the tea and packed the books destined for other Essex libraries was neither my expectation nor the future occupation I'd aspired to for over a decade. She-Ra had long been ruled out, so I began to think of other ways I could do something bookish. Writing never occurred to me.

I opted to stay on at sixth form, but when classmates were gifted blocks of driving lessons, breezing effortlessly through their perfect teen lives which, from the outside, resembled *Beverly Hills 90210*, my insecurities turned to resentment. In English lessons, I would be asked to read aloud any ethnic characters that cropped up between the pages. Little laughs and amused grunts ensued as I stammered my way through the text. The words, 'Eva, you be Tituba,' are branded into my spirit. Lorraine, my (still) best friend (Mauritian–Irish, a rare find back then), would ring in the evening and we'd talk for hours sat on our respective staircases, twiddling phone cords and moaning about our treatment, routinely singled out as the authorities to all things ethnic. Lorraine stuck sixth form for a year. Sick of the people and the books I couldn't identify with, I dropped out a few months after.

Employment took me back to the places I still considered my true home. I worked my way around central London, first in Harrods, where everybody was from elsewhere and, refreshingly, I was considered the local. Often I temped in offices, my favourites being the ones located on or off the Charing Cross Road, because of the bookshops. Glass-fronted giants like Borders and Foyles were appealing because they contained coffee shops (and sometimes piano players), but it was in rummaging through the second-hand bookshops, still with full-on Dickensian awnings and frontages, the jumble-sale racks of well-read random titles, that I began selecting the fiction that appealed to my own palate. Those old and obvious curriculum classics gave way for fresh autonomy over my reading choices. My re-education began with a tatty three-book bundle of Toni Morrison novels, for a fiver. The words warmed again, slowly disarming me of the resentments I still clutched furiously and sparked the recognition that my frustrations were nothing new. My story and experiences were far from unique; for someone like me, they were typical. Later, back in Chelmsford and financially broken, it was the library instead of the bookshops that returned as my educator. And my sanctuary. A place to hide within, keep warm and make a coffee last a century.

These days I am asked what I do far more than what I am, and 'doing things backwards' is the phrase I fall on to respond. Books and reading reignited my love of writing, and at thirty-four I returned to study. And I've found no finer therapy for my soul than from the words of my own pen. Writing helped me explore how truly alien I've often felt, yet it's also taught me that feeling different and less is something I can be free from. There's little more distressing than the idea of my daughters assimilating the same behaviours I spent almost two decades perfecting, shape-shifting for the benefit of others. Approval is no longer necessary. I choose to align with my own self-worth.

Now, when I go to the library, I often have my three daughters in tow. In the sunny and purpose-built children's section there are polka-dot beanbags and child-size sofas and the net at the touch of a button. But I'm always keen to point out the overlooked nooks, the corners I dedicated to the hours of reading on my terms, the choices I selected. Whether I borrowed books in skint times or bought in flusher moments, reading has never been beyond my reach. And in the moments when I felt absolutely burdened, books offered a temporary cure. They still do, only now it's for other things, such as blocking out the high-pitched squabbling of my children, or to calm me after the latest episode of *Question Time*.

My very first library's heavyweight doors have closed for good, replaced by a modernist sensation called The Gate. That old brick building is now an optician's, but just above the new blue signage, the original matte black plaque remains, still with the engraved gold letters, Forest Gate Branch Library.

If it's ever removed, I'd like first dibs.

Uniform

Damian Barr

'And don't you worry about the stamps,' insists Granny Mac as she takes her place at the front of the bus. The 92 stops right outside her front door, so she treats it like her own, always sitting as close to the driver – her driver – as she can. If someone else has the misfortune to be in her seat, they'll get a look, then she'll sit right behind them, resentfully crunching Polos. The instant they ding for their stop she assumes a sort of half-hover and as soon as they're in the aisle she slides in, brushing their still-warm bumprint off the burgundy leatherette with the ironed white hankie she's never without.

Today her seat is unoccupied. She lets me sit by the window as if I've never enjoyed the view of Newarthill giving way to Motherwell, of village turning into town, of knowing every face to only every other face. I'm already taking up more room than I should, so fold my feet under the seat. She looks me up and down then lifts my right arm and tuts. I will turn twelve and hit six feet in the same week. 'That's yer father. And who's the one paying for yer sleeves?' She drops my arm as the brakes hiss and we rumble off.

It takes a quarter of an hour on the 92. 'Same time as a taxi and a fraction of the price,' Granny Mac is fond of saying. I saw her on the bus every Friday morning when she went in to do her big shop at the new Asda – she still grieved for the Fine Fare. The Asda was still new despite being open for years and a dear-hole, but the only place to get my grandpa's whelks. He'd sit for hours on the back step picking them out with a pin because she couldn't abide the reek in her kitchen. Usually her bus passed when I was rushing to Keir Hardie Memorial Primary School with books in my rucksack bumping the bottom of my back. I'd see her and she'd see me. But neither of us ever waved. Displays were not her thing and I was always happy not to draw any more attention.

We pass Keir Hardie now – shut for summer as only a school can be. Day by day that final week we took our last projects down – I'd done the Tudors and, as usual, written too much and drawn too little. By Friday the walls were completely bare except for the high-up tacks that nobody could reach, not even me, tiny coloured scraps of sugar paper pinned behind them. When the doors open again I won't be there waiting to get back to where I know the rules. Fractions frustrate me but even I can work out I've spent over half my life in there. After summer I'll be going up to the big new school I watched being built – six floors of Caramac brick with a sign on top proclaiming *Brannock High School*. I'm the oldest of Granny Mac's sixteen grandchildren and the first to finish primary school, so I better look right for my first-day photo. 'It's a shame you're not going down the road,' sighs Granny Mac for the thousandth time. 'You could have had your uncle's blazer.' Down the road is Taylor High, the Catholic high school where they have to pray every morning.

Nobody is getting on our bus. Summer-holiday sun warms my arm against the window and Granny Mac unbuttons the burgundy-wool cardigan she knitted herself. Her hands are dry from scrubbing the chapel hall every morning, so she folds them under her handbag again as soon as she's done with the fiddly mother-of-pearl buttons.

Newarthill blends in to Carfin and as we pass the Grotto with the big statue of the Virgin Mary looking forgivingly on the traffic, Granny Mac crosses herself and mutters. I wish I knew the words, but my mum's not been back at chapel since the divorce. No sooner are we in Carfin than we're out and heading down the brae past the Craig. It's Fair Fortnight so the Craig is closed. All the men, including my dad, are away to Blackpool or maybe Spain. It's vast and still and silent. Acres of poised black factories and towering chimneys with not a puff. The gates are chained shut.

Now we're in Motherwell, which is where you come for special things – inter-school competitions at the Civic and library books you don't want to get out in the village. Granny Mac opens her handbag and gets out her purse and unclips it. Hundreds of tightly rolled savings stamps spring out like a jack-in-the-box and she pushes them back in. Still there. We pass the Asda and when our destination looms, Granny Mac dings.

I've only ever gone past the Co-operative, which Granny Mac pronounces 'co-opeRAYtive'. It's sandstone and posher than its neighbours and certainly older than the Civic across the road, which is all concrete and windows I can feel Granny Mac itching to wash. Our bus pulls in to the kerb and Granny Mac ushers me off then chides me for not thanking the driver. She adjusts her cardie and smooths her skirt then tugs at my sleeves and tells me to fix my hair – one of the better names I get called is Tumshie, because it sticks up like a turnip top. I can't tame it, have even scorched my scalp with my dad's girlfriend's tongs trying to.

The long brass handles on the Co-operative's doors are not used to the sun. They're warm in my hands. I think again of the Craig and the molten steel that make the sky glow orange every night. That's my dad. He makes the sun set twice. I take a deep breath as I push the door.

Inside there is no music. The light is fluorescent and cold. The air smells polite. Everybody in here knows how to behave.

Granny Mac conquers the shop floor, striding between racks of raincoats whose arms grab at me. Plastic hangers rattle in her wake. We reach the stairs at the back, which point up to school uniforms. Granny Mac pauses to admire the highly polished handrail snaking up and decides not to sully it as we ascend. I am tempted to leave a fingerprint, something to show I've been here, but think better of it.

Upstairs we are greeted by a lady half my Granny's age but still older than my mum.

'Can I help yous?' she asks, the *yous* proof that she's no better than us.

I'm pushed forwards. 'This is ma grandson.'

The woman looks me up and down, measuring me.

'The oldest. He'll be a large already but better start extra-large.'

'Big laddie, eh?' says the lady, approaching me with a tape measure she spools from her sleeve like a magician producing silk hankies. 'You'll have to bend down, son.' I bend. This feels weird in the middle of a shop. A metal tab on the end of her tape feels cold against the back of my neck as she wraps it round, and I must flinch because I get a look.

'Breathe normal,' says the lady. 'Arms up!'

Granny Mac tries to read the tiny notes the lady scribbles on her pad.

'Right, chest.' She stands behind me and feeds the tape around. For one horrific moment it's like she's going to cuddle me.

'Waist?'

I put my hands on my hips.

Granny Mac steps forward and lifts my arms up. 'Stand right,' she snaps. 'Let the lady do her job. Sorry. On you go.'

The disembodied hands appear by my sides and feed the tape around where a belt should go. I look up and try not to swallow.

'Taylor then?' the lady asks, making a final note and walking over to the well-behaved racks of blazers.

'No,' says Granny Mac, straightening up. 'Brannock.'

'Oh.'

'The rest'll be going to Taylor,' says Granny Mac. 'This one's the first.'

'Right,' says the lady brightly, walking around picking things up. 'Large on a shirt and twenty-six-inch waist with a long leg and an XL on the blazer.'

I am handed hanger after hanger and sent into the changing room. The blazer is the big thing and I can't believe the price. This will be the dearest thing I've ever had. I get it all on. The tags itch my neck and my waist. I'm zipping up when the curtain whips back.

'Right,' says Granny Mac. The lady stands behind her, her tape measure draped over her arm.

I catch the end of the curtain and hold it there as I tuck my shirt in. I pull the curtain back and the rings rattle on the rail.

'He'll grow into it,' says Granny Mac with something like pride as she pulls the sleeves of my blazer down over my wrists. The lady nods and walks over, saying, 'PE kit, then, same sizes.' I dismiss the changing-room thoughts.

Arms full, the lady teeters over to the till and lays everything down. I can't believe it's all new and all for me. The old brass till rings and clicks. When it does a final ding, Granny Mac steps forward and puts her handbag on the counter.

'That'll be...' says the lady, naming a number that's months of my mum's Wednesday money, more than anybody ever paid for anything.

Granny Mac pulls her purse out and clicks it opens and out spring the stamps. They skitter across the counter making a tiny scratching noise that I feel rather than hear. I notice some are a bit faded.

'The lot?' asks the lady, stupefied in the presence of years of saving.

'The whooooole lot,' says Granny Mac, closing her purse and plonking it back in her handbag.

The lady bends down to catch the fastest stamps. She returns the escapees to her counter then leans forward and corrals them in her arms. Her lips move silently. She's counting them. I can't believe she'd dare.

'Take yer time, hen,' says Granny Mac. 'The schools don't go back for weeks.' She picks up her handbag and turns to me, folding her arms across her chest. Granny Mac is victorious. Granny Mac is smiling. At me.

Play

Adam Sharp

I'm torturing my dad, Colin. We are in the car. My method of torture is as follows. I make him listen to a cassette tape. On repeat. The tape is an album called *Chorus* by a band named Erasure, a band Colin doesn't much care for. I know this because he tells me so. He says, 'Adam, I don't much care for Erasure.' I make him listen to them anyway. My reason for torturing him is this. He deserves it.

♫

I didn't always want to torture my dad with music. Once, I had been happy to listen to music he liked. In fact, his music saved my life. His music saved my life when my mum wanted me dead.

She missed her chance though, my mum. I had already been hiding in her belly for over six months before she found out. Most mums find out when they miss their period. Not my mum. Years of shooting heroin had already stopped it. The other warning signs of being pregnant – tiredness, dizziness, throwing up – were simply part of her everyday life. She was twenty-one.

Not until her belly began to bulge did she suspect something wasn't right. She visited her doctor and told him to remove the unwanted bulge at once. But her doctor said that she was too far gone – abortion now would be dangerous, and illegal.

My mum didn't let that put her off. She knew of a man. In London. A man who did not care about the law, or danger. A man who would happily take care of her problem, for a price. She sat on the train from Manchester to London, with me in her belly, hoping the man would be successful and swift.

The man was neither swift nor successful. He wasn't there. My mum, Martine, arrived at his office to find it empty. She never discovered whether he had been shut down, or put in prison, or was just taking the day off, but when she got back on the train to Manchester that night, I was still alive.

Martine wasn't about to give up though. She was persistent like that. She upped her daily heroin intake, which was already considerable. By the end of her pregnancy she had to inject it into her groin – all her other veins had collapsed through overuse. She also began punching herself in the belly. When her arms grew tired, she ran into walls. When that didn't work, she threw herself down the stairs. Her belly became black with bruising yet continued to expand.

I had my dad to thank for this, my continued existence. He was comforting me, giving me strength to get through the daily attacks, by playing me music. He had always used music to give him comfort and strength. His records helped him endure his unhappy years in boarding school, where the dorm masters made him touch their willies. When he played me his current favourites – Iggy Pop, David Bowie, Joy Division – he was passing on a tool for survival.

And it worked. I was born healthy and strong. I shouldn't have been. I'd shared my mum's poisonous blood for nine months and I was supposed to be born addicted to heroin. I should have spent my first few weeks fighting for life – shaking, sweating, being sick – as I was weaned off my addiction with morphine or methadone. Martine may then have identified with my struggle and stayed in the hospital with me, giving up the heroin too. We could have bonded over our shared withdrawal experience. Our efforts may have inspired Colin to give up also and the three of us would have stayed together, happy and heroin-free.

I wasn't born addicted though. I had defied my mum again and she didn't want to know me. She wouldn't touch me. She wouldn't look at me. She certainly wasn't about to give up heroin for me. On her second day in hospital, she had Colin smuggle in a hit. The following day she checked herself out so she could return home to her regular supply. Martine kept taking drugs and so did Colin. But, after a few years, he couldn't take any more. He knew he had to stop or he would die. So he ran off to a different city, Newcastle, and got clean for a while.

My mum couldn't look after me on her own, nor did she want to. So her dad, my granddad, took me in, putting off his retirement so he could afford it.

A few more years passed.

I started primary school.

My granddad became my legal guardian.

We moved into a council flat, after our previous house got knocked down.

My mum came to visit us every now and then, but usually she was too busy shooting up, or getting drunk – after she swapped heroin for booze – or being in prison.

And the only time I would see Colin, now using again, was in the odd school holiday. I'd take the train to him in Newcastle and for several days we would go to the park, go toy shopping, watch films. At night he'd read to me and play me his records. I was reunited with the old gang – Iggy Pop, David Bowie, Joy Division. I was happy to listen.

Colin enjoyed all the benefits of being a temporary parent. When I was back home in Manchester, I would build an image of him from only the very best memories. In my daydreams, I never thought of how thin he was, how pale, how his eyes were glazed and bloodshot. I didn't think of the ugly marks down his arms or how he wanted to sleep all the time. Not once. In my dreams he was always awake, always laughing. In my dreams he was strong. He was calm. He was perfect.

But then Mary came along. Mary waddled into Colin's life when he was trying to beat his heroin problem for the second time. Mary was older than Colin, American, and drove a rubbish car. I didn't much care for Mary and told her so. I said, 'Mary, I don't much care for you.'

In truth, I had never much cared for any of Colin's girlfriends, or his female acquaintances, or even the checkout girls who made conversation with him whilst giving him his change. They were all competitors for his time, which, for me, was limited to a few days per school holiday as it was. There was also the fear that one of these evil women would somehow turn him against me – a fear that became a reality when Mary appeared.

I remember when I first met her. I was about eight. I was visiting Colin for the school holidays. Colin wanted Mary and me to bond, so he took us both to Seahouses. During the day, we went on a sightseeing trip that combined two of my favourite things – boats and seals. I spent the entire boat ride ignoring Mary, wondering why Colin was with her. Why would my dad, who I had been certain was both perfect and indestructible, choose such a woman? Maybe he wasn't perfect after all. And if he wasn't perfect, he may not be indestructible. He would die one day. It was the first time

I had considered this. It was all I could think of for the rest of the boat trip. It was all I could think of on the walk back to the bed and breakfast.

Later that night, I went to Colin and Mary's room, which was next to mine. I knocked on the door. I entered.

He wasn't there.

Mary lay on the bed by herself, a mug of coffee in her hand.

'Where's Colin?'

'In the bath.' She blew on her coffee, not looking at me.

'Oh,' I said, and turned to leave.

I couldn't wait any longer though. I needed answers. 'Can I lie on the bed with you?'

'Mm-hmm,' Mary said, in a way that suggested she really wished I wouldn't.

I lay next to her. I had nowhere to rest my head – all the pillows were stuffed under her back – so I leaned on her bloated belly, facing her toes. At least that way she couldn't see my face. Her whole body tensed. She wanted me to get off her, I knew she did, but she didn't say so.

'Is Colin going to die?'

'We all die one day,' she said, sipping her coffee, which made her belly gurgle and grumble.

I tried to say something, but I couldn't speak. I felt sick. Even me? I didn't want to die. And I didn't want Colin to die either.

'He won't die yet,' she said. 'Colin will probably live until he's ninety.'

Ninety? Ninety? Surely he was already nearly ninety? I wanted to hear that he would live for ever, or at least another 200 years or so. I started to cry, my body shaking all over.

Colin didn't see me crying, but Mary must have told him all about it later because he didn't want to know me after that trip.

He went away for four years. Actually, he didn't go anywhere. He stayed where he was – in Newcastle – but he wouldn't let me visit him any more. For four years I didn't get a phone call, a letter, or even a birthday card. Nothing.

What had happened was this. Mary married Colin the first chance she got and told him to break off all contact with me. She also told him to grow a beard, so he looked less boyish. He threw away his razor and listened to her argument for throwing away his son. She suggested that if he wanted to beat his heroin problem, once and for all, he should avoid reminders of his past, his guilt. Seeing me reminded him of the past *and* made him feel guilty – for leaving when I was little. Mary assured Colin it was for the best. She said, 'Colin, it is for the best.' He considered it and agreed, cutting all contact. If I hadn't cried on the bed with Mary he may have decided differently. But my weakness of character had made me, in his eyes, as disposable as his razor.

They moved to a country house outside of Newcastle, Mary and Colin did, and the only reminder of either of them having a previous life was Mary's two dogs. Colin was safe in his little husband–wife cocoon, protected from memory, guilt and crybaby sons.

But after four years it all collapsed. Mary waddled back to America and I got to speak to him again. I was even allowed to stay at his house in the country. I began to dream, as I had when I was younger, of Colin and me building our own cocoon, a father–son version. As it turned out, he now only wanted a pod for one.

This became obvious when I got to his house. I was reminded that I was not at the top of his list of interests – music held that spot. Colin's record-cover images outnumbered photos of me by several thousand to nil. He gave me a chance to be a part of his musical world though. He said I could have one of his albums. I could choose anything I wanted. I could have picked Iggy, Bowie or Joy Division, embracing our shared history. Or I could have chosen one of his latest favourites – Depeche Mode, REM, Primal Scream – and we could have begun an exciting future, discovering new music together.

But I chose Erasure, the tape in his collection he disliked the most. The Erasure album had been an unwanted present from someone with bad taste, someone who didn't understand music should be serious and dark, who didn't understand that Colin's collection had no place for such poppy twaddle.

Erasure didn't fit in at my school back home in Manchester any better than they had fitted into Colin's music collection. For a class project, on a topic of our choice, I picked Erasure. My presentation consisted of me explaining to the class why they were the greatest band on the planet, and then giving proof by playing their three best songs on a tape player. The class weren't convinced. They were all boys – we were at an all-boys school, so they had to be – and when my presentation finished they just sat there, staring. Apart from Scott Brierley, who couldn't stop laughing for some reason.

'Right,' Mr Sweetman had said, leaning back in his chair, his pen in his mouth and his hands on the back of his head. You could see the sweat patches under his armpits. 'Any questions?'

'Yeah,' Scott Brierley said, still laughing. 'What the fuck was that?'

'That's not a proper question, Brierley,' Mr Sweetman said. He didn't tell Scott Brierley off for saying fuck, like all the other teachers would have. Mr Sweetman didn't care about swearing, or the rules. He often had the top button of his shirt undone. And his sleeves rolled up.

'OK,' Scott Brierley said, looking serious as he formulated a proper question. 'Why did you not mention that they're massive benders?'

I turned to Mr Sweetman, who said, 'Answer him then, Sharpy.'

'What do you mean?' I asked Scott Brierley.

'I mean, they're obviously homos. So why didn't you put that in your little speech?'

He didn't know what he was talking about. Vince Clarke, the keyboard player, was a bit funny-looking, but all the women must love the singer, Andy Bell, who probably had loads of girlfriends. Being a ladies' man, they called it. I'd heard people say that about Colin.

'Andy Bell is a ladies' man,' I said.

'A lady boy, more like,' Scott Brierley said, and the rest of the class laughed. Christopher Keville pretended to sneeze and shouted 'poof' at the same time.

'I'd never listen to shit like Erasure in a million years,' Scott Brierley said. 'But my uncle knows all about them. He says they're definitely a pair of benders. And anyone that listens to them is a bender too.'

I looked to Mr Sweetman again, who was swirling his pen around in his mouth and nodding, like he agreed with Scott Brierley's uncle.

I considered what Scott Brierley had said. Now that I thought about it, Andy Bell never referred to women in his songs. He usually just sang something that could describe a man or a woman, like 'you' or 'darling' or 'lover'. And in one of their live videos he did wear a blue sparkly cowboy hat, covered in sequins. He also wore matching cowboy chaps with no trousers on underneath, showing his bum cheeks. That did seem a bit odd. Maybe Scott Brierley's uncle was right. And maybe Colin thought the same thing – that listening to Erasure might make me gay. Colin always seemed proud of how easily he could make women smile, and do other things, and clearly hoped I would make women smile, and do other things, just as easily one day. He really wouldn't much like the thought of me being gay. He would hate it even.

♫

Thanks to some heavy traffic earlier, we are now listening to my Erasure album for the third time. We are just over halfway through. Colin grips the steering wheel with both hands, leaning over it while staring at the sky, as if praying for someone, something, to end his ordeal. He now carries the guilt from running away when I was little *and* from breaking contact for four years. The guilt prevents him from speaking up, from ending the ordeal himself.

The sixth track, 'Love to Hate You', repeats its dramatic chorus one last time and then fades to silence. We aren't too far from his house and there is no traffic now. We probably just about have enough time to make it to the end of the album again. But then he finally speaks up. He can't take it any more. He pauses the tape and suggests we listen to something else. 'How about some Iggy or Bowie, Ads?' he says. He is reaching out. His eyes say, *You remember Iggy Pop, don't you, Adam? I played him to you when you were in your mother's womb, fighting to make it out alive. It saved your life.* His eyes say, *You remember David Bowie, don't you, son? We listened to him when you used to stay with me. We were happy then. We can be again. Just give it a chance.* His eyes, soft and pleading, know things can be different. *You can forgive,* they say.

I look at him closely and I see it too – a different path. I can see us putting on Iggy or Bowie, singing along and playing air guitar for the rest of our days. Together. I see us in our own father–son band – him on vocals, me on bass. Happy. I see us sharing albums, sharing passions, sharing our lives. I see a future for us after all. A future with no more guilt, no more resentment, where our music will always play, our song will always be sung. I see it. I can forgive. *Just take the Erasure tape out of the player,* his eyes say. *Put something new on. Let's start again.*

But before I can agree, I look down from his eyes and into his thick brown beard. I think of how much I like the next song, 'Turns the Love to Anger'. I think of my mum and how things may have been different for her if she had just run off to a different city, like he did. And I think of being on the bed with Mary, crying, knowing for the first time that Colin would die. My dad will die and I'll be left alone, again. I lean forward. My finger skips over the eject button. I press play.

A Pear in a Tin of Peaches

Lisa Blower

Imagine if you will: I am six years old. I have big blue eyes, the sort that tell my stories whether I like it or not. A blonde kiss-curl strokes the left of my forehead, and I am tall for my age, garrulous. Here I am talking to the apple trees in my back garden in Baddeley Green, Stoke-on-Trent. Cookers mainly. I call them Bonksik, Jumba and Jonty. I am telling them the story of the two girls. The one who has the posh pram and the other who pushes a tin cart with a wonky wheel that falls off and rolls into the pond.

'What happens next, Nan?'

Nan doesn't tell me the next bit. Nan's too busy writing to Mr Del Monte to tell him that she's just found a pear in her tin of peaches. 'When you buy peaches you expect peaches,' she wrote to the global fruit merchant. 'And a pear don't make a peach.' He sent her a 50p voucher for a tin of pears. She sent it back and told him, 'I didn't want pears. I wanted peaches.' He never replied.

Fresh peaches came in a punnet of six. Stoke-on-Trent is made up of six towns: 'Six hearts, beating disharmoniously,' says Linden West, which makes the place, somehow, placeless.

Baddeley Green. That's pretty placeless. A westward thoroughfare to Leek, on to Buxton, and we lived on the main road, two doors up from Bill's Butchers, where my sister filched a pot of salmon paste, and two doors down from the newsagent's, where I'd befuddle Nigel with my many birthdays (Nigel, who fashioned wooden partitions in his spare time – we had one behind our front door – would give you a block of Dairy Milk on your birthday). We were a two-up-two-down semi overlooking trees; galley kitchen, side alley and downstairs bathroom, with no central heating, two buck rabbits and a twin-tub. We were lucky enough to have a garden – my first memory is of my sister taking her first steps towards me in the garden, my second making escape routes in the sandpit – but we also played in the backs, which were just that: the backs of houses. Where the dogs cocked their legs and the lads snaffled fags, where footballs got booted – *Cost kick a bo agen a wo an yed it till it bosts?* – and Jacqui W. would flash her front bottom for a pear drop. I remember we once found some dead gerbils rotting inside a pack of Quavers. Old man Mole would shuffle up to us *good-for-nothings*, brandishing his stick – 'You should all be in bloody work!' We were always ten pence short of a 99, high on sherbet, and no one was ever allowed chewing gum because of what happened to that little girl. *Chew, chew chewing gum, don't chew chewing gum. That's what brought me to my grave.*

I couldn't find the grave last time I looked, and that irked me. We used to go roller-booting round the crem with my nan. She'd take us from one grave photograph to the next to the next; ritual visitations to check on those whose young lives had been snatched by motorbikes, illness and, of course, chewing gum. I should've known exactly where it was, because I could always see the top of my nan's head, cleaning Granddad's grave with a Brillo and a squirt of bleach. The flowers she laid on him were always plastic, like on most graves in Milton Crematorium: cost-effective, annual-respects-paid-plastic with the colours bleached out.

'Ta-ra then,' Nan would say, then tell us that when she died she'd be going on top of Granddad, 'for the first time in years'. And not to forget to have engraved: *Too pretty to die.* 'I was that beautiful I could've been murdered,' she used to say, with grave honesty.

Honesty ruled the roost, family, and my childhood was all the peachier for it. My dad was an overhead linesman on the Midlands Electricity Board – he moonlighted on weekends to buy new settees and French dressers. We used to buy him tools for his box at Christmas. My mum was a housewife who worked in Burtons on Saturdays. We'd spend Saturday mornings doing the dying fly with Sally James, drinking Ribena in milk (Nesquik was 'too dear'), with runny-egg oatcakes, and we might go play up the fields/down the wreck/round the backs with whoever knocked on the door and asked if you were coming out.

True, there were times when everyone else seemed to be out at Alton Towers except me, and Sally Midwinter (oh, what happened to you, Sally Midwinter?) once sent me a birthday card that said, *I do not like you or your house it smells,* as I never had the right trainers (partly why I could never get my run-up right), only Clarks, and wore hand-knitted ballet boleros in the wrong pink. I wasn't the carnival queen but played Mary Poppins; I was in the Elves, Frobisher and the netball team. I was knee-high to a grasshopper and saw a lot of folk down there too. But at school I was taught to look up to people. Mrs Galley. Mrs Kaczmar. Miss Wade. We'd learn about the kings and queens, the Second World War, and practise long division.

↑ North

South ↓

Understanding that we were always somewhere in between, hiding behind the settee from the milkman and, if we weren't careful, passed by.

Passing by our front window were the protests. Stop this. Save that. We'd sit in our wellies in the gutter sucking on rhubarb sticks dipped in cups of sugar. Some of us got to get up from the gutter. Others just didn't know how. Many gave it their best shot and ended up back down there. Because 244,800 miners had been employed in the Staffordshire collieries in 1984. There were still kilns in use across 298 factories and 70,000 pottery workers. Today there are fewer than 7,000 people employed in the factories, forty-seven kilns cold as the grave.

Back to those crematoriums, then; back to a post-war Hanley, where my nan could fall out with the shop steward, walk across the road to another factory, start working there by the afternoon shift. She was a dipper and she married a placer, and after they were married and after the Germans bombed their chip shop, and after my granddad had returned home, burned in the liberation of Rome, they lived with my nan's mother Martha – or Patty as everyone called her – in a two-up-two-down with tin bath and outside loo, two children by then too. Peaches, plural.

Nan's father was a plural too. He had a second family with Phoebe up Stone Road. Nan said that one day she was walking down the street and this girl was coming towards her and it was like looking straight in a mirror. She went home and told Patty, and Patty told her that her father had always been a beggar for second helpings. He never did know what he had at home.

I didn't know Patty, but she saved my mother's life. She had pneumonia when she was six and Patty sat with her through the night making bread-and-milk poultices. My mum and Patty shared a bedroom until my mum was sixteen, around the time my mum won a competition to meet the Beatles. Which she did. At the Savoy. In London. Nan went with her. The first and only time she went to London, and she saw nothing but the Savoy Hotel reception and the carriage they sat in on the train.

My mum wasn't trained but sent to work at fifteen. She wanted to go to art school but she ended up painting the plate rims on a pot bank with gold leaf. Remember, she had pneumonia? Well, the paint fumes affected her lungs, so she went to work in Hanley Baths.

I learned to swim up Hanley Baths. Top of Lichfield Street and the bus wouldn't make it up the hill, so we'd have to run. I learned to run in Hanley Park. Nan would take me on the swings. Then she'd show me where her brother Ron hid out; a coward gone absent without leave. She'd take him jam sandwiches wrapped in greaseproof paper and got the local bobby to turn a blind eye. It would be nice if the jam was apricot, but I don't know for sure. She would show me the exact bush he hid in. By that time, I was toddling, so went and hid in it too. 'You can't find me,' I'd say.

What my nan would say to me: 'Do you want a piece of jam for your tea?'

After we'd been for Sunday dinner. To their house up Rosevale Street. To their bungalow in Barratt Gardens when my granddad, with forty years of pot-bank smoke fogging up his lungs, could no longer manage the stairs. The kitchen would smell of Bisto. The rest of the house would smell of Pledge. Another new hearthrug from Stoke Market would be in front of the electric bar fire; blazing away, chucking out no heat. We'd have hot milk poured onto treacle-thick Camp coffee; marrowfat peas and Mr Del Monte's fruit cocktail with evaporated milk, me and my sister fighting over the single cherry.

I google this: *Why is there only one cherry in a tin of fruit cocktail?*

I quote: 'Cherries are more expensive than peaches and pears.'

I thought glacé cherries *were* cherries. That's what Sally Midwinter told me.

Then we emigrated to Shrewsbury, fifty-three miles down the A53.

When we first moved to Shrewsbury, some of the mums told their children to stay away from me and my sister because we had Scouse accents. Then I went for tea at a friend's house and we had spaghetti bolognese. I started to cry because I didn't know how to eat it.

I didn't know I was different. I didn't think fifty-three miles would make a difference, yet girls called me common and some called me poor. I knew poor souls in Stoke. My mum will talk of families she grew up with who were dirt poor, as she talks of my dad's family as poor as crows. My dad had grown up not a stone's throw from where we had moved to in Shrewsbury, in the tin houses on the Rad Valley council estate. I used to take the dog for a walk past where Dad used to live. The houses were owned now. It never looked poor to me.

Poor means having few or no possessions, deficient, in need, scant. Then I learned some bigger words: underprivileged, disadvantaged, inferior, second-rate. I like the fact that poor sits between poop and pop in the dictionary. A lot of people, I realised, those who'd called me poor, those who choose not to see the poor, were either up their own arses or full of hot air.

What my nan said when I went to university: 'With too much education comes too much choice. That's all that's up with you girls today.'

I got really interested in women's writings at university, feminist agendas and working-class matriarchs. D. H. Lawrence and Nell Dunn. I talked to my nan about it. She said they were too busy working to go in for all that women's stuff. She forgets that she helped to make ammunitions during the war. That she did more for the women on the estate than most and, most importantly, brought up a daughter who enables and encourages beyond what I can ever pay back.

'Aren't you ambitious?' my mum's cousin, now having told her I'd given up my job to return to university and was midway through a PhD on female autobiographical practices: I was particularly interested in why working-class women didn't think their lives worthy of the pen, so persisted in telling them in my fiction. 'And that's your job?' she asked. She would still send me typed letters in the post – gossip she'd overheard on the bus. *I thought you'd like them for your stories*, she wrote. She called those stories 'the *titpips*'. I never corrected her.

Because you never quite know when you've swallowed a pip, and here's another one: when we got flashed at in Milton Park by the witch's hat. Nan squealed then told him to put that bloody pigeon where the children can't see it. Since most granddads I knew kept and flew pigeons from their allotments or converted coal sheds, I carried on climbing to the top of the witch's hat to see if I could watch them fly. Pigeons, said my nan, were filthy, and that's why London was full of them. 'You never see a London pigeon up here,' she'd say. But then the man burst into tears and she sat him down on the swings and listened. I have no idea of their exchange, just that he was a pitiful soul. 'A bit poorly,' is what she said.

I thought Nan was always poorly, she went to the doctor's so much. Turns out it's what she called the bingo. She was at the doctor's so much you'd have had to hire Pickfords to transport her files.

Only in old age did she get ill, diagnosed with breast cancer at eighty-six. She told me, 'If I dwell on it, it'll make me ill,' so she put all the pills in the cupboard drawer along with her blood-pressure tablets, haemorrhoid cream and hearing aids. 'That's the first time I've ever been touched by a black man,' she told the consultant who first checked her breasts. 'Shame it's not spread in the other breast too.' My mum said that a small part of her died, but I don't think my nan had ever been more alive.

She'd remind us she was still alive. 'I'm just phoning to use my voice,' she'd say, me now at work. 'I haven't spoken to a soul all day. I'm still here, you know.' I'd ask if Uncle J. had been. He didn't count. It was us she wanted. My mum. Me. My sister. All that women's stuff she'd never gone in for. She couldn't get her pips out quick enough.

'I'll leave you that in my will,' she'd say, but there never was one because there wasn't enough.

I have a couple of her sherry glasses. A silver toffee hammer. A photograph of her in her twenties, which is like looking in a mirror. Her engagement ring bought up in Blackpool, barely a carat in gold.

There are gold pears and peaches called Summer Gold. Three thousand varieties of pears, in fact, and two thousand varieties of peaches, most of them grown in the States. Nan always called us Little America as we privatised this and privatised that, but blamed China mostly. MADE IN TAIWAN, she said, had brought Stoke to its knees.

Taiwan isn't China, I know, but then peaches and pears belong to the same Rosaceae family, which is one of the six most economically important crop plant families. See? Six families, six towns *can* live harmoniously. Yet when I googled this, I also found people arguing about whether nectarines were derivatives of peaches, as some botanists argued that peaches are also plums. In which case, it shouldn't have mattered that there was a pear in a tin of peaches if they are one and the same.

I think about all that long division:
$\leftarrow$ I left being a peach when I moved to Shrewsbury.
In Shrewsbury I became a bruised pear and wanted to go back $\rightarrow$
$=$ If I'm ½ there ½ here, do I still belong in the same tin?

I don't have the answer. I'm not sure why I need to be reconciling this anyway when peach and pear, just six centimetres apart in the dictionary, share the same page. So, I ask Mr Del Monte. Mr Del Monte, he says yes ✓.

And yes, she is six years old already. Big blue eyes, so tall for her age, so pretty, so me. She has the same name as my nan, my porcelain babe, and stands talking to the apple trees. She calls them Rigger, Olga and Iggy One. She is telling them the story of the two girls. The one who has the posh pram and the other who pushes a tin cart with a wonky wheel that falls off and rolls into the pond.

'What happens next, Mummy?'

That's who I am. Until I become Nan.

I open my mouth.

She beats me to it. 'Granddad will mend it with his toolbox,' she says, and as I slice up some fruit for her and her friends, I think how peaches and pears were both discovered in China, how I met my husband in China, how she is fine bone china, that time has its place and we are all things made but above all, put simply, *us*.

A Brief History of Industrial Action, Vauxhall Motors, Ellesmere Port

Lynne Voyce

As a child, I knew my parents hated the Conservative Party, because every time either Bruce Forsyth or Jimmy Tarbuck came on TV, they'd switch over. 'Can't stand him; he's a Connie,' they'd say, and that was explanation enough. These days, that may seem an extreme reaction to other people's democratic rights, but in the dark depths of the early eighties, the battle for workers' rights had not yet been fought and lost. And a family like ours was at something close to war with the Tories. Their general, Margaret Thatcher, a spindle-fingered bogeywoman in pussy-bow blouses, part Child Catcher, part Grand High Witch, was the stuff of my nightmares. Her strategy was attrition warfare, in which she relentlessly attacked the worker, until they had nothing left; their only choice was to surrender. A war like this is always won by those who have the most.

But still, even knowing this, the fight went on and – in our house – strikes were the crusades. My father was a mere foot soldier. Every few months, at the directive of the union, Dad got on his 250 Honda and went the eleven miles to Prenton Park for the vote. A strike was inevitable. There were no secret ballots in those days; each worker would a raise a hand for or against strike action, and a steward with a pencil and paper would walk the terraces and count. Under the judgemental, beady eye of a shop steward, and in full view of your comrades, it was pretty tough to defy a call to stop production.

To complicate matters further, even if those on the production line decided to keep working – Dad put gearboxes in Bedford vans – the skilled workers, who voted separately, could still call a strike. Those fabled fitters and electricians often held the factory to ransom.

There was always a dreadful pall over the house when Dad was on strike. Although, as kids, we were relieved that the silent pantomime of 'letting your father sleep because he is on nights' didn't need to be performed daily: we could flush the toilet and turn the TV up. But there was a price to pay for being able to freely make noise: that price was hunger. Strike pay from the union was never forthcoming; this was a source of much bitterness, as union fees had been paid for twenty years. And the bitterness always grew when the cupboards were bare after the two-week mark, when the strike really 'bit'. Indeed, there were times in week five or six when we barely ate, resorting to flour-and-water pancakes with salt to fill us up. Thank God Mum's cleaning job was in a café; her wages barely covered the rent, but the leftovers were handy. If we were lucky, dinner might be a slice of apple pie with a chocolate teacake for afterwards. We loved it, but there were many days when she came home with an empty basket. There were no savings to fall back on, and in a small industrial town, when the factory was 'out', everyone was in the same boat, so there was nothing to share.

I do remember one particular act of charity, though. In this instance, the dispute had reached seven weeks and, as is the way with poverty, it was the monotony of life – the endless diet of potato and egg – that had weakened our spirits. On a Friday evening, when the last seed potato from the back garden had been dug up, sliced and dry-fried, there was a knock on the door: a bold, musical knock. Standing on the step in a Harris Tweed sports jacket and beige slacks was our neighbour Mr Dooley – a man who had never worked a day in his life but still had a colour television and a Vauxhall Viva. Under his arm was a white-paper parcel. 'This is for you and the family, Bill,' he said, 'don't give in to the bastards.'

Minutes later, with empty tummies, and hearts full of hope, the four of us stood in wonder around the kitchen table as the parcel was unwrapped. In all its fleshy glory, coiled like a pink, pepper-flecked snake, was a Cumberland sausage and next to it a sapphire-skinned black pudding; both lay on a stack of best back bacon, deep pink and edged with ivory fat, like the illustrations on the Second World War rationing posters we'd seen at school: Eat for Victory. God knows where it all came from – other than being heaven sent – after all, this was Merseyside in the eighties. It may have 'fell off the back of a lorry' or even been passed on by the butcher himself as a means of support. That evening we all ate hearty.

In fact, many of my memories of strike action are ones of people pulling together: men playing football in the street with the kids, because they had naff all else to do, or the women placing unwanted tins from long-forgotten Christmas hampers on a communal table, so others could pick up their cast-offs and put down their own. Mum would put down a jar of mincemeat, for example, and pick up a tin of gooseberries.

As a family – perhaps even as a community – we didn't think we were 'sticking it to the bosses'. I know my father didn't. Rather, we felt poor, depressed and manipulated by all sides. Dad was a man stuck between the managers and the union. If a strike was called, whether you had voted for it or not, there was absolutely no way you would break it: to be a scab was a terrible shame on you and those you loved. But there was one time he spoke to me, when we'd not eaten properly for weeks, when he'd explained that for all the hardship, he had to stand his ground. A dispute had sprung up when it was decided that the table by the factory drinks machine was to be removed, and the chairs around it; this was where the workers took their break. I'd thought it silly to strike over a table and chairs and said so. 'First it's the table and chairs,' he'd said, sagely, 'then it's the break. They won't care, as long as they're making money.' I understood. And subsequent years, with the introduction of zero-hours contracts and docking staff wages for keeping a hospital appointment, have proved him right.

But there was one strike that bit harder than the others; it tore the flesh from our optimism and resolve, and left us permanently wounded. It was called in late autumn but lasted until winter; yet another winter of discontent for us. Christmas came: the tinsel tree stood in the corner, faded paper chains hung on pictures, and the brass candle carousel on the mantelpiece, little winged cherubs with horns, spun above the flame of a candle stub. But there wasn't so much a feeling of celebration as there was a sense that we were doomed. There was simply no money.

At least my brother was working; at weekends, early mornings and after school, he'd rig up a market stall and sell handbags with a man called Tony. Of course, even at the market takings were down, but my brother earned enough to buy us a small turkey. And my sister, married and living away by then, sent a bottle of sherry and a tin of biscuits.

I was used to sparkling Christmases, full of presents to open: Matey bubble bath; Sindy accessories; and the latest walking doll or talking teddy bear. So, on 25 December, when I tumbled downstairs at the customary time of 5 a.m., I couldn't hide my dissatisfaction when all that was there was a sage-green Raleigh Shopper with one wrapped parcel in the basket. What I should have felt was humble elation, but there was hardly anything to tear the paper off: there were no surprises. Mum had got the bike on the weekly from the Janet Fraser catalogue. It won't have cost much shy of a week's wages. But I wanted to drown in a sea of cheap festive paper and disappointment made me cruel. 'Is that all?' I said instantly, then sulkily opened the single present in the basket: a copy of Robert Louis Stevenson's *Kidnapped*. Mum looked crestfallen. It was not my finest hour as a human being.

I know my mother cried that morning; and I also know there was a ball of indignant shame and rage in my father's stomach, the sickening effects of which stayed with him for days.

The siege finally ended a few weeks later. Hungered and depressed, my mother complained there was neither money for the rent, nor the bills. It was then my father made up his mind: it was time to leave Vauxhall and look for something else.

It can't have been an easy decision: unemployment was over 3 million, and Merseyside was hit particularly hard. In our street there were only two men who weren't unemployed or striking, and one of them was a window cleaner, who'd heard 'I'll pay you next week' so often that winter, he'd practically given up asking for payment.

To call what my father did then 'voluntary redundancy' is one of the great misnomers of the eighties: he'd had no choice. The union kept redundancy pay low too, in order to keep the workforce at work and fighting; still, with no savings, nor anyone around who could help financially, the small payment seemed like the only option. So, the morning after my mother's desperate plea about having to pay the rent, following a sleepless night, Dad rang the factory and asked for his 'cards' to be made ready: he was leaving Vauxhall for good.

His mates on the production line couldn't believe it; he 'was part of the furniture', having been there since the plant opened in '62. But over the following years, most of them left too. Battle weary, probably. Their payouts were bigger than Dad's, though, and some even took Thatcher up on their 'right to buy', refurbing their square red brick council houses with double glazing and porches.

The months following Dad's decision were ones of hope, despair and pretty much no money – but we were used to that. The only difference was the Thursday arrival (or non-arrival) of the dole cheque to tide us over for the following week. If the cheque was late, we went back to flour-and-water pancakes.

After six months, dad took a part-time job at what was then Chester College, as a night porter. The dole cheques stopped, and we were all managing on part-time money – both Mum's and Dad's, but there was a feeling of a new beginning. Hopefully, the 'war' was over. Dad had a smart blue uniform and a big set of keys. He was even trained in first aid and conflict de-escalation. He'd patrol the buildings and grounds with his torch a couple of nights a week, dealing with drunken, keyless trainee teachers, and on at least one occasion, chasing a black-clad cat burglar off the roof of the science block. Eventually Dad became full-time, and that was the rest of his working life: a little lame from the smoking, a little deaf from the production line, and a little battle-scarred from a war in which there was only ever going to be one winner.

The Things We Ate

Kit de Waal

Broken biscuits from her factory bag with shards of dusty icing and a scratchy fight for the custard creams. Half a fig roll no one wanted. Toffee apples from her factory bag with sticky wooden sticks and brown paper stuck to the brown sugar, to the brown apple inside. Squashed potato crisps from her factory bag with little blue shakes of salt, split open and useless, which we opened anyway, like we'd bought them from new.

White bread, old bread, West Indian bread with jewels of pork fat, soda bread from Nana's Irish oven, brown bread at a posh girl's house, mouldy bread with the mould cut out, butties, sarnies, toast, bread pudding black with treacle and sultanas, butter on the dry, burned crust.

Sliceable, fry-able, pink and trembly Spam, steak and kidney pies cooked in a tin that opened with an exciting key. Tinned pork in see-through jelly. Red, molten corned-beef hash, sardines – skin, flesh and vertebrae – and six pigs' trotters in lemony water, the lungs of a chicken, the neck of a lamb. Ribs.

Johnny cakes sweet as biscuits sopping up the saltfish juice. Leaden lumps of dumplings, rice and rice again, and cold rice that turned to maggots in washing-up water, yam and sweet potato and Irish potato and old potato and baked potatoes, big as your face, their hot, leathery jackets full of beans and margarine. And chips! And chips! And chips! And red sauce when we had the money and vinegar when we didn't.

Our oven door left open for warmth and steam on the kitchen window and plates that never matched and spoons for everything and, once in a blue moon, blancmange and once a summer ice cream with Guinness, but cake every Christmas. The meticulous division of a golden egg in April.

Pains in your belly on a Sunday when the gravy ran off the plate. Pains from Monday to Friday when it didn't. And Saturday's cauldron of St Kitts soup, dangerous bubbles, whole carrots, mysterious meat.

And cocoa with sugar and unexpected, unaccountable heart-lifting chocolate shortbread biscuits after a winter's night shift from a silent father who thought of his children on his long walk home.

Night

Elaine Williams

Walking home through a city curled up in bed, the night chill cutting through my jacket and freezing my sweat-drenched T-shirt, anxiety kicked in. This wasn't the first time that I'd broken the 'home before midnight' unofficial curfew. The Mexican standoff with my dad as I crept in the front door was becoming routine. He'd pounce out of the darkened hallway and suddenly the lights were on and the gloves were off.

One night, he'd stood stern, in wait in the kitchen.

'Wha' time yuh call dis?'

The kitchen lights glared, interrogation-ready.

'Fram eight a clack yuh leave dis house, an' a jus' now you a come een?'

Silence.

Silence was my weapon of choice. It hadn't started out that way. No; in the beginning, silence was something me and my siblings did because we valued our lives. In my late teens, however, I'd stumbled across its power accidentally, when I observed how much it riled my dad, especially when teamed up with a dead-eyed stare. It was like his kryptonite and, seemingly defenceless, he'd become incensed and yell at me to get out of his face, which would at least put some distance between me, him and the cussing.

'Wheh yuh deh fram evening till now?'

Silence.

I wasn't entirely sure if he wanted answers, but with my sixth sense on hyper-alert, I detected that his questions were not an invite to a father-daughter-how's-your-day-been type of chit-chat.

'Yuh nuh see yuh maddah 'ed need comb?'

My mum was sitting at the kitchen table looking cuddly and super-bright in her plus-sized shocking-pink quilted dressing gown. Damn! In my rush to get out of the house, I'd forgotten to do her hair for bed. My dad had helped her with her nightclothes, but her hair was my job. She propped her left elbow on the table, rested her chin in the palm of her left hand and stared at me, slightly smiling and intrigued, and I was terrified that she could tell what I'd been up to.

When I was twelve, during the six-week summer holidays, she'd had a massive stroke that resulted in paralysis down the right side of her body. She lost the use of her right arm and leg, and her speech was severely affected. The stroke turned our family upside down because it diminished my mum's reign as the undisputed head of our house and demanded that she needed looking after. Despite her disability, you didn't mess with Mum. The wisdom 'never judge a book by its cover' could've been learned with her in mind.

I tried my hardest to focus and control the comb, but my brain was hashish-bleary and my hands had turned to jelly... or was it Mum's hair that had turned rubbery?... Feeling exposed by my parents' gaze, my inner struggle to appear normal became increasingly desperate. My stomach churned and threatened to release an explosion of random alcoholic beverages topped with blackcurrant cordial. My thoughts raced: 'Why are the lights so bright? Why's he still in the kitchen? Is he watching me? Did I just talk out loud? When did Mummy's hair become so amazing?' My focus flashed to Dad's makeshift mousetrap, positioned on the linoleum floor at the foot of the cooker. This was the nightly invite to supper that our resident mice looked forward to. Every morning, the morsel of cheese or bread or cracker or boiled dumpling was gone, a signature scattering of droppings neatly arranged – a 'thank you for supper' note – the trap still in place and the mice missing. Every night my dad would get out the contraption from the cellar shelf and painstakingly set his bait.

'A wha' yuh a do?!' he erupted, unimpressed by my haircare effort. His outburst snapped me back into the room and out of my code of silence. I quickly mumbled, 'I'm plaiting Mummy's hair.' Or that's what I thought I was doing, but it was probably more patting and prodding than plaiting 'cause Mum kept grunting and wincing and turning her head to shoot me disapproving looks.

Dad slowed his pace and reduced his decibels to a menacing whisper.

'Humph! Yuh tink me nuh know seh yuh a tek drugs?'

His monosyllables were like abracadabra and in a flash, I was sober. Images of hot knives and poppers and microdots and dancing to Talking Heads' 'Road to Nowhere'. How the hell did he know?! This was a life-and-death situation. I switched into mortal-combat mode – summoning up my most intense death stare.

'Wha' yuh a look pan mi fah?' He snarled and inched towards me.

My secret weapon didn't seem to be having the usual effect.

'Yuh mussie wan' mi... humph!'

He paused and fixed his killer gaze on me.

Help! System malfunction... something wasn't working.

'Yuh know wha' one mine tell me fi do?' he seethed, and inched towards me some more.

No. But whatever it was, from the look in his eyes I knew it wasn't good. It was never entirely clear just how many minds my dad had, but my one and only mind prayed that all his others were skilled mediators and were standing on guard ready to stop his crazy-ass mind from making him do something we'd all regret.

'Come out!' He ordered me out of the kitchen.

'Mum–my's – hair…' I stammered. By now, I'd ditched my dead-eyed stare; the new look was wide-eyed terror.

He took a clear step. 'Mi seh come out!!!'

Instinctively I knew that wasn't the time to test the 'bark worse than bite' hypothesis. I parked the pink comb skew-whiff in Mum's hair and backed out of the kitchen.

The rush of a passing car swiped the kitchen scene from my memory and jolted me into my present solitary walk home.

With each step, my music-drugs-alcohol high ebbed and waned. The sounds and twinkle from the main road gradually faded, leaving only echoes of the excitement of the town centre. Side-splitting laughter with Shaye (not her real name), both of us saddled with teenage self-consciousness, wanting the world to notice how hilarious we were and see what a good time we were having.

We were roughly the same age, eighteen. Shaye was rootless; a white working-class girl from a side of the city that I knew nothing about, except the deprivation and that it was not an area that black people in 1980s Sheffield really needed to visit. I was a black girl born and raised by the generation of Caribbean parents who arrived in the fifties and sixties, and soon discovered that England was the 'bitch' that Linton later said it was.

We'd met at a Sheffield Youth Theatre summer scheme. The gravitational pull of our misfit spirits towards the familiar was the magnet that drew us to each other. We talked very little about our home lives. I knew there was a stepdad and violence; she knew I had a sick mother and a strict dad. And that was enough. Our friendship wasn't about sharing our real lives, quite the opposite. It functioned as a breathing space in which we reinvented shinier versions of ourselves. She'd told me about the Crucible Youth Theatre; I joined and discovered an alternative universe of drama, drugs, writing, acting, troubled teens and post-punk/new wave music.

Before the youth theatre, my nights out were little more than a flying visit to city-centre clubs bursting with good-looking people in good-looking clothes, flattering disco lights and championship-standard dancers, or heaving house parties that everybody, including my brothers, were allowed to be a part of. I'd have to leave just as the DJ was settling in. And the songs that I loved went unheard by me, and dance moves that my school friends and I had practised were rarely showcased, because my Timex (borrowed from Mum) said it was time to go. I'd make some lame excuse and leave; shamed, but knowing that I ran the risk of a life sentence under house arrest if I got home late.

At eighteen years old, I stopped asking my dad's permission to go out.

It was my gap year before leaving for Essex University, where I'd got a place to study English and linguistics. I was the first one in my family to go to university and my parents were proud, but they still didn't cut me any slack. I was the youngest of ten, and my siblings were spread out – New York, Birmingham and across Sheffield. They'd come and stay and help to ease the pressure between me and Dad, but their visits would end.

The instant I discovered youth theatre, I knew I'd found my place and I was willing to do all-out battle for my liberty.

It was Thursday night, and under the surface of West Street, the Limit nightclub had been host to the usual seemingly incongruent mass of goths, punks, rockabillies and townies, with the occasional natty dread on the sidelines, and us. Dressed in variations of regulation black, the crowd blended into the black-painted interior, which camouflaged dilated pupils sent spinning by the chemical explosion of poppers; teeth grinding, powered by speed; and eyes reddened by cheap booze, hashish and sensimilla. The basement air hung thick with the cloying smell of subterranean debauchery and the DJ locked his dials to one setting only – loud.

A defiant downbeat signalled The Clash's 'Bankrobber'. Difference temporarily disappeared. We peeled our feet off the beer-sticky floor, unified in this anthem for the recalcitrant. Heartened by our mandate, the DJ delivered a bittersweet cocktail of heavy, laboured sounds – a mix that vaporised the early-eighties gloom from our recession-rocked city.

'Gi' us a toke.' Shaye nudged my arm with her elbow.

'You've just 'ad some.' I dismissed her and dragged on the menthol-cigarette-and-black-hash spliff.

'Gi' us a toke', she persisted and made a grab for it. I was too quick.

'Move!' I swatted her hand away.

'Gi' us a toke!' She tried to snatch it again.

'Gerroff, yuh knob 'ed!' I pushed her away and we tussled for the spliff, laughing our heads off. Suddenly, the distinct rumble of thunder, the sound of heavy rain, a shimmering continuous hi-hat, soft sparkling piano and the lazy drawl of Jim Morrison, 'Riders on the Storm'.

'Ooohhh, I love this one!!!' we screamed hysterically and pushed each other to the dance floor to amble, flop, nod and shuffle our way through the Doors.

This way of moving to music was a radical departure from the disco, soul and dub, bump, slide, spin, kick, dip, skank, encoded in my DNA. When me and my school friends danced, our moves were slick, polished, in sync with the rhythm; a cornucopia of steps. In the underground world of the Limit, steps were nowhere to be seen. The dancing was alien, but the dense melancholic cacophony hooked me. Songs and sounds had always been integral to my life – disco, soul, reggae, country and western, two-tone Northern soul, pop, dub; I loved it all. And when the DJ played, nothing mattered but the golden moment I was in.

The B52s 'Rock Lobster' was our cue to scream again and jostle our way back to the dance floor. Then on came Pulp, eye-level with the crowd on the dance-floor-turned-stage. Blue lights, dry ice and Jarvis Cocker's soaring live vocals. We joined in with the few words we knew, oblivious that his small-town yearnings, written for our ears only, would one day scale the heights of the national pop charts. As he sang, we sipped Pernod and black from scratched plastic beakers and got tipsy on life and music.

Bursting from the flood of cheap booze, we ushered each other down the grimy corridor to the girls' toilets where puddles of piss, stray loo roll, cast-off condoms, soggy roaches, fag butts and vomit formed a rancid obstacle course. We took turns holding shut the cubicle door with a foot, as a catch, angled under the narrow gap, to prevent our hands from touching anything.

'Uuuugh! Get a fucking room!' We hurled our usual heckles at whichever messy couple was panting and moaning from behind one of the broken doors.

'Fuck you.' The grunted reply brought our well-rehearsed chorus of 'No thanks!' 'In your dreams!'

And then we turned our attention to the male goths clustered around the mirrors. We entertained ourselves with gibes and wisecracks while they pouted and touched up sweat-smeared make-up, and solemnly preened their big hair.

The musical spell had been all-powerful, and by the time we left, the dance-floor carnage was being cleared. I'd never stayed so late before and my dad's mantra – 'Nevah be di las' fi leave di pahtee' – felt like an omen 'cause when the lights went up it was ugly; and there was no fun being swept out with the debris.

A lonesome meow pulled me back to the present. The pleas for food and warmth softly ricocheted off walls and cars and melted into the night air. I strode on, unmoved; the cat would have to find another after-hours companion.

I wasn't sure what time it was, but empty milk bottles stood on front doorsteps and houses were all fast asleep. The Limit had long closed, Shaye was on her way home in the opposite direction to mine, and I was in serious trouble. I prayed that I could get inside without a front-doorstep scene. Being shouted at indoors was manageable, being cussed on the doorstep in full view of friends and neighbours was breath-stoppingly shameful.

My walk took me deeper into the hush of residential streets. The bite of my heels on concrete caught my ear and sounded overly loud. I tried to reduce the weight of my footsteps, but gave up because the effort slowed me down. Tack, tack, tack, tock, I counted my steps, then got distracted by the moon, the ringing in my ears, snatches of song lyrics, what I was gonna say to my dad and thoughts about how worried my mum would be. Immersed in this internal whirr of mental chatter, buzzing and piercing footsteps, I arrived home.

All lights in the house were off. My heart beat an irregular rhythm as I slid my key into the lock. I prayed that dad's rant wouldn't go on too long. I couldn't wait for the night's memories to take me off to sleep.

I turned my key. It stopped, resisted. Confused I tried again. The key refused to budge. My head started to throb and I longed for the central heating.

My first knock was phrased as an apology. When this got no response, I grew bolder. It felt like the clanging metal letterbox would wake up the entire street and the thought of everyone hearing my pathetic knocking made me stop.

I'd lived in our house in Nether Edge all my life. My family was friendly with the neighbours, a mix of migrants from across the Caribbean, Ireland, Italy and Pakistan, with a sprinkle from Africa, India and Poland. I'd been to school with some of them, and one of my best friends lived a few doors away. I felt exposed. And in my chemically heightened reality, under the watchful eyes of the all-seeing net curtains, everything became a threat. A dog idling past our front gate enjoying its night-time stroll was a rabid beast prowling for human blood. A man on the other side of the road, wobbling his way home, was a burglar or potential attacker. I ducked and crouched behind the bins and, holding my breath, peeped through the hedges watching his every wobble and listening until his footsteps had completely disappeared. It was all too much. Fed up and exhausted, I sobbed. Hot tears comforted cold cheeks, but the heat quickly faded. All I wanted was sleep. I thought about going to Shaye's; she'd left home and was renting a room in a shared house not that far from mine, but it was too embarrassing. And it was late night. Walking home was one thing, but walking away from home, on my own, at that time of night... I wasn't that brave.

Time dragged. My legs ached from crouching. Finally, desperate and unable to cope any longer, I decided to leave the street-lit stage of our front doorstep and seek respite at the back of our house.

My breath drove me out of the front gate, halfway down the steep hill and all the way down the ginnel that accessed the back of the houses on our side of the street. Panic steered me through the hollow-black to the age-old granite steps that led up to our garden. I placed my palms against the rough stone walls that stood like bouncers flanking the ten steps and felt my way up the narrow enclosure to the rusty metal gate. I shoved the gate open, stumbled along the lumpy overgrown path and got scratched passing the wild thorny rosebushes. At last, my foot bumped into the grey stone steps, and the final steep climb up to the back door that opened into our kitchen.

Night draped the house in stillness. Trepidation gripped my throat with its icy hands. My dad had locked me out. He'd upped the ante and I didn't know what it meant or what I was meant to do next, but I knew for sure that knocking on the back door wouldn't be wise.

Careful not to disturb the darkness, I sat on the doorstep, rested my spine against the solid support and tried to hug and rock myself warm. As I skimmed the periphery of sleep, every nocturnal rustle triggered my eyes open. But I had no regrets. Close beneath the surface shock was a profound knowing that assured me it was worth it. This consequence of my unsanctioned hours spent revelling in life was worth it. And so, with cold stone biting through the seat of my pants, and sublime memories of music smoothing the edge of discomfort, I nodded between states of consciousness, convinced that whatever happened in the morning could never spoil the joy of this night out.

Driftwood

Adelle Stripe

Outside his red-brick house, sheets of tarpaulin flap between fallen fence posts, and nettles grow in sheltered corners beneath the elderberry tree. Broken freezers, melted dustbins and a rusting wine rack are heaped by the pebbledash wall. The shed contains a bike with flat tyres, a lawnmower that hasn't seen light in a decade, and cases of damaged crockery from 1996.

Wearing a torn boiler suit, steel-cap wellies and a fleece hat to cover his shiny head, he spends his days carrying seasoned husks of fallen ash, birch, oak and rowan up the farm track with the gales chasing behind him. He drags driftwood from the snake-bend in the river and stacks snapped branches in funeral pyres along the banks.

When the flood waters came, the river coughed up enough debris to cause a fault line of human detritus that extended across the corn fields: doll heads, Vaseline tins, pop bottles, syringes, children's shoes, rusting shot-cases and stained sanitary towels. He sifts through the litter, collects it into bin bags, and hauls fractured trunks towards the house, beyond the latticed blackthorn.

The hamlet where he lives contains seven houses. It has a bus stop (out of use), a bench, a parish council noticeboard, and a road for rat-runners, tractors and joyriders. Along the verges, which are mapped by discarded milkshake cartons and rampant convolvulus, traditionally laid hedges mark the estate boundary. In summer, red kites follow him to the river.

When the wind changes direction, the smell from the sewage works drifts into his garden. It mixes with a heavy scent of brewing malt and diesel exhaust fumes. It is sickly; evocative of childhood bedrooms, a sepia smog that hung over the town, the stench in your hair, clothes and mouth. Live there long enough and you won't notice it.

There's a reason for all this mess. The long days he spends outside, gathering.

'It's cheaper this way,' he says. 'All this for nowt, free hot water. Chopping wood warms you three times; sawing, lifting and burning. Nature's gymnasium...'

The house has a back boiler, no log fire is wasted. His pension would barely cover his heating costs. This is the alternative. Free to those who are fit enough to scavenge.

He doesn't own the house, of course. It's part of the estate, for its workers. Cheap labour in exchange for a roof. No heating, mind, aside from tepid storage heaters. A farm labourer's wage wouldn't pay for the coal.

Over the years he has learned to live with its nip. Ice on the inside of windows, a toilet that freezes up. A pantry colder than the £10 fridge that leaks through the floor each August. Damp sheets. Bare floors. Asthmatic coughs as the sun starts to rise. On the front doorstep, metal buckets filled with ash cool off from last night's fire. Keeping warm is a full-time job.

Not that he wants any pity; it's just how country life is.

You listen to his running commentary as he drags wood along the lane: the useless government, the National League, the loss of everything that once was. But most of all, a nostalgia for how farming used to be. His mother and father, the old ways.

Quiet days are spent in the past, recalling the lost elation of youth. Fights and drinking and women and clubs. Mistakes and heartbreak rubbed out. He takes comfort in the myth of the man he once was.

He moved here twenty-four years ago, following a farming accident. A lord down south needed a man. Three months were spent working in glorious weather, tending to a Friesian herd. One morning the baling machine stopped working. He tried to fix it, to make the bastard work. And it pulled him into its ferocious jaws.

Chomp chomp chomp.

It took half of his foot. Sliced it clean off, and spat it out into the straw.

The doctors said he'd never walk again, but a corset and prosthetic fixed him. He always knew farming was the most dangerous profession. More men killed than in the pits or at sea. It was only a matter of time before something happened to him. Now he walks with an awkward gait, leaning forward, hands clasped behind his back; the only indication of the plastic toes beneath his wellington boot.

Once a month, his friend, Les, chainsaws thick chunks of wood piled up in the garden. Les has a squashed nose, tea-strainer moustache, NHS glasses held together by tape, no teeth. It's a cartoon face that's real. Camouflage to keep the rest of the world at arm's length. He blends into the woodland.

A roll-up hangs from Les's mouth, oily fingerprints mottle the flavoured cigarette paper. Together they chop up piles of wood and talk in the way only countrymen do: stories of lost limbs; escaped heifers on the dual carriageway; floating, bloated bodies;

the pigman who slit his own throat and bled to death in the sty; their friend who sleeps sitting up and hasn't bathed for a year; the pie trade; slurry-pit drownings; petrol prices; tatters stealing gates from the land.

They are the last of a dying breed, carrying tales from way back. Stories that have never been written down, only stored in the imaginations and memories of men who toiled the ground.

His parents lived here long before he did, then moved into sheltered accommodation. Death Valley, as he likes to call it. He's superstitious about that place, the old-people's estate on the other side of town.

'It's where you go to rot,' he says. 'You won't catch me moving down there, I'd rather snuff it in the fields...'

He shakes his head and laughs. He's as much a part of this landscape as the trees and barns and cattle grazing grass. Town is no place for a man like him.

A framed picture of his father, holding a bull on a rope by its ring, gathers dust on the windowsill. It was taken at an agricultural show; his bull was supreme champion that year. In the faded photograph, the Queen shakes his father's hand wearing her white, spotless gloves; he often sold pedigrees to her. That was the gift he had: he could talk to anyone. The gentry valued his cattle (all owned by a local toff), bought semen straws for ten score a shot; his father made them wealthy in return. Rosettes and trophies and hundred-guinea calves. Seven-day weeks to make it work. Never the earnings to save for a house. But free milk, eggs and wood for the stove. A whitewashed pantry of curds out the back. For that, they were grateful.

The afternoon sun beams through the living room, where three radios are stacked on the side. One for football, one for news, the other a digital, which he hasn't quite worked out how to use. He sits on a pile of grubby cushions, wearing a pair of knackered slippers that resemble burst sofas.

When town folk think of country people they imagine a wardrobe of plus fours, tweed hats, expensive coats. The reality for most is this: multiple sweaters (with holes), long johns, odd socks, a fleece jacket with a broken zip, trousers held up by knotted blue twine. And a weathered face, the farmer's tan, which deepens each line in the brow. Or fingers stained yellow with iodine, split nails, and barbwire-scarred skin.

You listen to him slurping tea from an ancient Happy Moo-day mug as he squints at a three-week old supplement from the *Sunday Times*. He's been reading it for as long as he can remember, his favourite section being *STYLE*, and Shelley von Strunckel's horoscopes.

'A good week for Leo,' he shouts. 'Things are on the up. It's a full moon on Friday, best day of the year for luck.'

Beside him, several years' worth of opened envelopes, crumpled lottery tickets and birthday cards spill on to the sooty shelf. Notepads are filled with handwriting only legible to himself. At first glance it could be Cyrillic script. The mantelpiece is cracked from the heat, where the fire burns all day, every day. You sit in front of it on a one-armed rocking chair as the ash crackles and spits.

The view from the upstairs bedroom has barely changed since you lived here. At least it has a carpet now, an improvement on the strips of spongy underlay and random nails that lined the floorboards when you first moved in.

Your old single bed faced the doorway; you warmed the room up with a hairdryer each morning and could see your breath in the air. Baths were even worse; you'd submerge your entire body underwater and leap out into the towel to stop yourself pissing from the chill.

In this bedroom, a record player sat in the corner, and piles of charity-shop vinyl were stacked against the wall. Music was the only way out, some brief relief from the teenage rut. Back then you earned just enough to get by. Call centres. Pubs. Fitting rooms. Tills.

You staggered home in the dark through the woods, washed your tights in the sink. Socks streaked by Daz powder, your hands red raw from scrubbing. Wet clothes were hung on the fire grate, steam-dried at first light by the embers.

Downstairs, he'd be shouting at the television; it was the last thing you heard before drifting to sleep. That, and the widow-makers creaking outside.

It was home for a long time. Still is.

He looked after you here, in this house. Fed you tins of spaghetti hoops on toast, bulk-bought from Netto as a damaged batch. Thirty-pence loaves of white bread. Value packs of watery ham. Own-brand digestives. The occasional Battenberg. That was tea, most nights.

'Always thought you'd be a writer,' he used to say. 'All of them stories you wrote as a kid.'

You felt ashamed that words had abandoned you.

Books gathered dust in a box by the bed.

Out here, the stasis is comforting. From this house, on clear days, you can see cooling towers on the horizon, structures that once belched out steam. They are slowly being dismantled, alongside the pits that surrounded them.

He is preserved in time. Even in retirement he's re-created the daily burden that his body and mind are conditioned to. Slogging is second nature. For as long as he's capable, he will sweat each day until he can no longer lift an axe. The fire in his hearth reminds him he's alive. He dreads the day he can no longer light it.

You walk out into the garden, stepping over the rubble, and walk up a mound of ash, now covered in grass and dandelions.

'Shall I help you sort this mess?'

He pauses as he fills a bucket with damp kindling.

'If you want,' he says. 'Best leave it until later in the year, though. I'll have cleared some of it out by then.'

Three faded bath towels flap in the wind, pegged to a rope that runs from hedge to house. It is propped by a corroded stepladder. He pulls a cloth handkerchief from his boiler suit, blows, and wipes the permanent drip from his nose.

'What about the outhouse? It's full of bin bags, stuff from when you and Mum were together. Mouldy books... a foot spa. As if you've ever used that. You could fill it with seasoned wood.'

'I'll get round to it,' he replies. 'Just haven't had the time.'

'Maybe we could do a tip run,' you ask. 'Clear the beer bottles out. You could do with a new freezer; it's leaking again.'

He rubs his hands and stares out across the fields.

'Might see if I can get one off Emmaus,' he says. 'Can't afford 'em new.'

'The last few you've bought have been used and look what's happened to them.'

You point at the pile of abandoned fridges stacked up next to the shed.

'It's like a bloody scrapyard out here.'

His insistence on paying the lowest amount possible is not only an economic necessity. It's a habit that started when he was a young man and continues into old age. It pains you to see yourself turning into him. Each scrap in his garden symbolic of the person you could become.

Your attempt at restoring some sense of order falls on deaf ears, like it always has done. He'll only clear up when he's ready. And besides, there's work to be done. The fire won't light itself.

A tractor pulls up outside the house, and parks next to the front gate. A clatter sounds from the garden as a pile of pallets are lobbed over the fence. He smiles and nods his head.

'More wood,' he shouts. 'That'll keep me busy.'

Matoose Rowsay

Jenny Knight

It happened every year during muck-spreading season. And every year, Mum smothered our crunchy, air-dried clothes in some choking freebie from one of her elderly district patients to try and disguise it. But pig manure is not a fragrance easily bullied into submission. Lenthéric's Panache didn't touch it, Hartnell's In Love only gave it a fag-breath/Polo-mint twist, and Yardley's Tweed – which should have had it in a headlock, screaming surrender – merely frosted its edges, like egg white and sugar on a glass. More often than not, our already pungent laundry just ended up doubly infused with the sickly, powdery scent of Geriatric. That particular spring – 1978, the year I turned eleven – she'd been given a particularly foul lemon-scented toxin that looked exactly like urine sloshing around in its column of corrugated glass. I hated it so much I forgot about it only with the big news that Aunt Heather was coming to visit.

Aunt Heather lived in a place called Georgia, in the USA, with her millionaire husband, Mac. She had a big white house with pillars and maids, a lake with a little white wooden boat on it, and a brand new, cherry-red Cadillac – all of which I'd only seen in photographs. I didn't know anybody like her. Nobody did.

'My dad says your uncle Russell's a pisshead, your uncle Harry is a jailbird and your uncle Frankie smacks his wife and kids about,' said my school nemesis, Gillian Webb, when she heard. 'So how come your aunt married a millionaire?'

'She was a GI bride, *ac*-tually,' I told her.

'Well, my mum says your aunt Jean was a mouthy old cow, your aunt Violet was a tart and your aunt Blanche was up herself,' continued Gillian, her fat face puckered and narrow-eyed with suspicion. 'But she din't say nothin' about no Heather.'

I'd given her my best Miss Piggy hair flounce at the time, *obviously*. But for once, the mottled infamy of my father's vast tribe of siblings didn't matter. Gillian Webb – whose dad was only one of three, not nine – constantly boasted she was related to Cliff Richard, purely on the basis his real name was Harry Webb, but no one believed her. I, however, really did have an aunt with a mink coat and a Polaroid camera. Proof – and glory – would be mine. I'd had enough of wearing clothes steeped in the smell of old lady and loved-up fox.

'Heard that saying about polishing turds?' my big sister Jane whispered one morning, gurning with disgust as she sniffed her school jumper. It was the first time she'd ever sworn in front of our parents, and it won her a fringe-swinging clip on the ear. For my part, I dropped that wretched bottle as far as I dared – out of the bathroom window onto the hard, lichen-spattered tiles of the outhouse – but it refused to break. Rough materials do that, I've learned since. The finer they are, the quicker to shatter against life's hard surfaces.

Every fibre of me strained to meet Heather; every reference to her visit made my imagination growl with hunger. Dad was collecting them from the airport in an 'automatic', he told Mum, because Heather wouldn't drive 'a manual'. I wasn't sure what that meant, except I'd seen Dad put 'manual labour' on the sort of forms that made his face scrunch up like paper in a fist. 'Automatic', on the other hand, sounded very Shirley Bassey. A world away from the pickup Dad drove, which belonged to the farm. But then, everything belonged to the farm: our house, our phone – and, pretty much all year, except deepest winter, Dad.

I wondered if Heather's kids got told they were 'a breath of fresh air', like posh old people said to me when I read to them while Mum scoured their feet in the summer holidays if Gloria-next-door couldn't look after me. I was quite flattered, until Gillian Webb told me her mum said it meant I was common. Her mum cleaned for posh people, so her mum knew. Posh people had *grannies*, not *nannas*, she said; 'extension' phones in their bedrooms. They didn't have mugs of tea on the table with a meal, and they definitely did not smell of pig shit.

'My mum says you'll never be like them,' she said. 'Not lest there's another war and you get to marry a Yank like your aunt.'

I wanted to ask if Gillian Webb's mum had the same sort of strangling struggle I did when she spoke to them, these people with their off-the-telly voices, but I didn't. It was too confusing. When we went to visit Mum's family up north, *I* got called posh for saying 'barth' not 'bath'. Jane still went to Mum's sister in Lincoln for two or three weeks every summer while Dad did harvest – Mum was one of five, so there were plenty of cousins – but I'd stopped going. I blamed it on not liking cities, street lights, stuffy nights full of central heating, but the truth was I was sick of being called 'mardy' for wanting to read instead of going to the Forum shops to do nothing, or the Malleable Club to watch uncles get drunk. I didn't understand. Not when another time I seemed so celebrated, all 'Ask our mastermind over theer!' for the answer to a quiz, a crossword clue.

But right then, I didn't care about books.

I was too busy hoping Heather would stay with us – I couldn't believe she'd want to stay in Nanna's arctic cottage with its moth-eaten thatch and its mattresses crackling with brown paper to stop the damp. Our brick semi was cold – ice feathered the metal-framed windows and mould spots peppered my bedroom walls all winter – but it couldn't touch the tear-inducing savagery of Nanna's. Still. Adults were incomprehensible things, capable of pulling bizarre stunts like falling asleep on Christmas afternoon, so stay at Nanna's they did.

I heard them before I saw them: Heather's splicing twang and Mac's canyon-deep laugh ricocheting off the pamments and papered-over beams of the cold old cottage. I smelled them too; the burnt wood and boiled fish of Nanna's kitchen subdued by notes of Fabergé hairspray, the pubby smell of tipped cigarettes and an indefinable aroma of difference.

My uncle placed his Stetson on me, lifted me up and tickled my cheeks with his beard until my knees bent almost backwards at the convex bulk of his stomach.

My aunt stroked my face. Her nails were blood red and shone like the crimson paint teachers made at school from gigantic square tins of powder. Her lips were the same colour and she smiled just like Dad, but without the tombstone effect – her teeth shone like the school piano keys. Her hair was a sculpted cloud of chocolate satin, her eyebrows a perfect sideways comma, and things called contact lenses floated in her eyes, their outline rimming her ink-dark irises like a horizon. The diamonds in her ears were stars winking at me, and when she smiled I thought of a peacock spreading its tail. She looked like no one I'd ever met. She was perfect.

'Why din't you want to stay with us?' I burst out, ambushed by hurt. How could she like staying here, with its rustling beds and chamber pots, its one icy tap with a rubber nozzle and the horrible outside privy with that scribble of spider-filled honeysuckle?

Aunt Heather laughed. 'Honey, this is mah home.'

Her accent was like trees swaying in summer.

'But America's your home!'

'Well, baby, you got a point.' She reached for her 'soft pack' of Winston cigarettes. 'But the States is just where Ah live, sweetie-pie. Mah home is here. Wid my mama. Someday y'all gonna git what Ah mean.'

I didn't say so, to be polite, but I didn't think I would.

For two weeks, battling an endless river of relations, my sister and I camped by our aunt's feet. While adults competed for air space in rooms sweating with the layered fug of cigarettes, cigars and unaccustomed heat, we sat in awe of the alien pots and vials that populated my aunt's vanity case: American shampoo, toothpaste, nail polish, lens solutions, all embellished with gold writing, stamping superiority over our drab Co-op own brands. We giggled at 'fanny' and 'diapers', 'pants' and 'trunks'. We pawed albums of tanned American cousins seemingly stapled to photographs by terrifying braces. We fawned over the diamonds encrusted into Heather's watch that glinted like sunlight on snow 'ev'ry which way' we turned it. We twisted the Star of David sapphire that only revealed its opalescent secret if you turned it 'thataways', and wore all at once the pomegranate-seed necklaces and diamond rings that danced under Nanna's fly-specked lampshades and made her low, lumpy ceilings jitter with wobbling lights.

'Now Ah'm gonna fix me a Bourbon,' Uncle Mac would boom at some time after tea every night.

'And Ah'll have a Mateus Rosé, honey!' shrieked my aunt, except she pronounced it 'Mat-oose Row-say'.

It was the most exotic thing I'd ever heard. Dad drank bitter or mild. Mum drank shandy, or maybe a Babycham with a defeated cherry in it at the pub at Christmas. Nanna drank tea, sometimes sherry at weddings. No one drank wine – especially *pink* wine. I was willing to bet even posh people didn't do that.

Then my parents ruined it all.

We'd been admiring, among a handful of Dad's siblings, photos of Aunt Heather and Uncle Mac's 'station wagon', the new red Cadillac, the cute MG shipped over for their youngest daughter's sixteenth birthday so she could drive it to her mysteriously titled 'segregated' school. The row of shyly smiling maids they called 'negras'.

My mother objected. It was offensive, she said, that term. Racist.

My aunt and uncle strongly disagreed – that was life in the Deep South. What did my mother know about it?

A row broke out.

'I am a nurse!' my mother barked before she swept out. 'I happen to believe we all shed the same blood, and I will not have my children's minds poisoned!'

'Too damn right,' Dad said, grabbing my sister and me. 'You might have hell an' all now, Heather, but you han't always bin that way. You should know more 'n most, money's no excuse for downright bloody ignorance!'

My mortification knew no bounds: my parents the only ones to argue with this perfect aunt! How could Heather ever poison my mind? What *did* they know – Mum with her home-made dresses and her Avon dress ring with the blue glass fallen out; Dad with his roll-ups, tatty boiler suit and home-made Christmas-present stilts? And to think I could have been Heather's daughter. What a cruel twist of fate, that I was condemned to a life of lemon-scented pig manure when just a few genes away lay all that. I promised myself

I'd drink Matoose Rowsay and nothing else when I grew up. Even if I hated it.

I consoled myself by taking the Polaroids we'd posed for to school: me and Jane wearing Mac's Stetson, flaunting American-style hairdos (although, sadly, you couldn't smell the Revlon), festooned in Heather's jewels.

'So?' said Gillian Webb. 'My uncle Harry's just waiting for me to be eleven and then he's gonna take me on tour with him.'

I silenced her with a Polaroid of me and Jane in my aunt's mink coats – one dark, one light.

There weren't any more rows, at least. And Heather's mascara didn't run like Mum's when it came to the goodbyes. Tears slipped down her brown cheeks cleanly – no dirty rivulets, no Alice Cooper scariness. Uncle Mac tickled me with his beard and gave me the crossed rifles from his Stetson.

'You come see me, half-pint,' he boomed. 'And Ah'll find you a redneck all of your ownsome.'

I didn't know what a redneck was, but if it was anything like him, I knew when I finally reached my homeland I'd definitely want one.

Colour and sparkle faded from my life after they'd gone, waiting for the garish liberation of the tinsel season. We filled boxes for our American relatives, full of Dairy Milk and Terry's All Gold and the china teacups twined with ivy that my aunt loved so dearly. They sent us American Christmas decorations, Hershey bars, a cookbook bearing recipes for pecan pie and Southern-fried chicken, where ingredients got measured in cups. I took it to school. It was, of course, I said to my friends, because Americans did it all bigger and better than us. Scales were just so *English*.

Then the phone call came.

It was a week before Christmas when one of the maids found him. She'd been on her way to the house early when she'd noticed something blurring the windscreen of the station wagon. He'd been drinking a bottle of Bourbon a day, Heather told Dad, while the court case his estranged mother brought against him over his father's will ravaged his mind.

'Pissed,' Dad said to Mum, and she didn't tell him about swearing in front of us. We knew then it was serious.

'Desperate,' Mum said as she pushed away a plate of egg and bacon. The top of the egg seemed to sink in dismay.

'Even so,' said Dad. 'I couldn't. Never. Not to my girls.'

Mum sighed, picked up her plate and went to the sink, only she kept wiping her face with the backs of her hands more than she seemed to wash anything. When she turned round, there were drips all down her uniform. I wondered if they'd dry before she started clipping all those old feet or doing whatever it was she did with the mysterious Incontinence Pads that filled the boot of her Morris Minor.

'I'd better tell Mother,' said Dad.

I didn't want to tell anyone. I didn't want to say what I'd overheard – that Uncle Mac shot himself in his car with his own handgun; that he'd obviously meant to do it because he'd put the barrel in his mouth, not against his temple, where it could have sheered to one side. Nor did I want to say that he'd been found with two empty bottles of Bourbon, and that Aunt Heather had screamed to Dad how she'd burn all her furs and diamonds and her house full of maids for just one hour with him to tell her why all that courthouse shit mattered more than her or their kids.

Gillian Webb was the first person I saw when I went back to school, though I never knew if she knew or not. No one said anything and it seemed easier to simply follow suit. I didn't know then I was to leave my tiny primary six months later to start a new academic life at the ex-grammar in town, ten miles away. That I'd get to know kids who had nannas, nannies, grannies *and* grandmas – but never feel sure again of exactly where it was I fitted in.

As years passed, my Suffolk accent would wash so frequently in the seas of other voices and other places it would fade until its only colour came from the parrot that waited silently on my shoulder for the cadences of home. I would become chippy long before I slowly, and then quietly, grew proud.

I would live in cities and love central heating; prefer manuals to automatics; get a diamond I'd twist and turn to light its fire. I'd marry, too – though he wouldn't be American, and he definitely wasn't rich. Few people would believe I came from a family so poor the village parson once asked Dad's mother to keep her kids away from the church because the sight of them upset the parishioners. Or that flash displays of cash once impressed me enough to believe a woman's best chance in life was to marry well – and having rows of black maids was fine as long as they smiled.

I would eventually move back to the countryside. I would smile at the smell of pig shit mingling with the scented air of my tumble dryer and tell my kids about my amazing mum, my brilliant dad. And I would always have secret guilt for hiring some other Gillian Webb's mum.

But I never did acquire a taste for Matoose Rowsay.

On Class and the Countryside

Anita Sethi

The huge grey road wound its way up through the hills, further and further up. Out of the M6, the heavy greyness, the cluttered-up world gradually spaced itself out, lifted itself up. Up and up and up we drove, into the high regions of the earth, where the space dived straight into my belly, leaving me winded. The world grew softer, wider, dragged me out of myself and into something larger, layering into the mountains. Suddenly, everything was slightly warmer. Everything was slightly lighter. The world seemed to open itself up, lift itself, lighten up, shrug a weight off its shoulders.

Those roads were taking us to the highest mountain in England, and to the deepest bodies of water.

We were on a journey to the Lake District with Mum. Mum had got a weekend stay in a bungalow in a place called Barbon, subsidised through the nursing association, and for ages beforehand I'd sing about soon going to the Lake District, although technically the Barbon bungalow was in the nearby district of South Lakeland, Cumbria. The nurses at her work had to sign up if they wanted to go, and finally, Mum's turn had come up.

I wonder if I would even have had this early experience of the countryside had it not been for that nurses' subsidy. My earliest memories of nature were visiting the local park in my hometown of Manchester, which had felt like a safe space before I heard about the guns. After hearing that guns belonging to gangs were rumoured to be buried beneath the trees, I could not walk through the park in quite the same way. My childhood home was just two miles from the city centre in the M16 postcode, which criss-crosses Old Trafford, Moss Side and Whalley Range, and at the time my hometown had acquired the nickname 'Gunchester'. It seemed a world away from the Lake District.

There were some trips to parks further afield than our local park, to Lyme Park and Dunham Massey Park. I found a colour photo with my mother, siblings and two cousins, all gazing at a deer, which must have been taken in Lyme Park. This is the closest I came to nature, beyond a school trip to Chester Zoo. For the most part, though, growing up in a single-parent family with a mother who worked multiple jobs, there was not much time or money for many trips away. I rarely ventured out of my home city in early childhood.

But one day we did leave the city behind and venture beyond it; we ventured higher up in the world than I'd ever been before. I don't have a photo of it, but now it's coming out of the dark and into full colour. Before leaving, Mum stuffed all valuables into black bin liners and hid them in the cubbyhole, scared, we all were, of burglars.

We drove away from the city and up through the hills, up and up and up, the roads growing thin and steep and windy and I looked out of the car window and gasped as the grey fell away into an astonishment of green and blue and gold. Then the car swooped down and we were heading towards a lake, a pinprick of blue in the distance that grew larger and larger until it swamped the whole vision. I fixed my eyes on the blue water glinting with jewels on its surface cast by the sunlight, and it seemed as if I was flying towards the lake, flying into the blue.

It was as if a surface had been stripped off the world to reveal its colours beneath.

It was a shock to step out into the world and breathe in, for the air was so much clearer, the light so lucid, the sky vast and blue, reflected in the lakes. I breathed more deeply than I ever had done before and for the first time I could remember, it was a joy to breathe and the oxygen was flowing through the lungs, around the body, lifting the heart, clearing the head. I walked through the grass, which tickled my bare brown legs.

We stayed in a couple of rooms in a bungalow. A strange conception, to have the whole of life spread out on one floor, so sleeping and waking were all on the same level. It was the first time I had slept under the same roof as Mum that wasn't our house curving around a corner of Manchester.

I played outside, picking the flowers, and watching the old couple who pruned the vegetables in the garden next door, not really saying much at all, yet seeming to listen and watch us.

'You don't see many brown folks out here in the countryside,' mumbled the elderly man as he paused from pruning to gaze towards me, squinting his eyes, his face contorting in a frown, then going back to his gardening.

It would be true to say that there were not many brown people to be seen in the countryside, and not many 'common people', either. Over the course of my life I've experienced not only a north–south divide, but class divides within the same region too. When I told someone from Bramhall, Cheshire, whereabouts I lived, nearby the Manchester United football ground in Old Trafford, he shuddered and commented that it was 'not very nice around there'.

One morning I went for a walk with Mum through the mountains, watching how the great expanse of green gave way to the water and watching the wide-open spaces. Mum held my hand as we walked and walked through this new world, stopping to inspect flowers and plants that grew and watch as birds and butterflies fluttered past. We walked through a place filled with so many species I had never known existed. We stopped near a huge tree and I stretched out all my limbs so I was standing firm and proud like the bark of that tree. For the first time I remember, it felt right to be. I felt strong, as if, like that tree, I would be able to withstand any fierce gale that may come battering. The heart was opening; somewhere a tulip that had been trapped in darkness was unfurling itself in the daylight. The heart was growing, becoming as vast and deep as those lakes, as wide as those woods. I walked and walked through the world and the grass brushed my skin and the sweet scents of the flowers filled the lungs and a bright purple butterfly fluttered by so quickly that the heart leapt, and I walked and walked and forgot about myself entirely as the world flooded in and all the bad feelings drained away into the hills, which absorbed them, and Mum's rage seeped away into the lakes, which swallowed it up and washed it away, and I walked and walked and walked, and the skin was renewing itself, each cell was opening up and welcoming in the light, and the skin was shedding itself, the bruised skin, the hurt skin, the thickened, sore skin, shed as the self renewed and strengthened and healed and new skin began to grow. The hard shell that had built up around the self began to melt away amidst all this beauty. Love came flooding in. The world came flooding in, pouring into the emptiness.

I walked through the world and the air filled my lungs until the heart was beating in the ears so I knew that I was alive alive alive and I was no longer just a girl from home but a girl of the lakes, a girl of the hills, a girl of the flowers, spilling filling thrilling the lungs with their scents, a girl from the world I was becoming.

I fell in love with the lakes.

After the bank holiday, we loaded back into the Peugeot and drove back down the mountains, the softness fading away, the car splattered in grey rain.

We got lost on the way back, stuck out in the middle of the mountains. We asked a farmer who was passing by for directions, pointing to Manchester on our map, but it fell between the creases of two pages, between the dark groove in the middle of the faulty road atlas, so that the city was swallowed up, eluding all directions.

The roads swerved through the hills, round bends and past lakes flashing and flickering in the sunlight, and we drove through them for a while, lost, before getting back on the right track and finding the road that took us back down through the mountains and towards Manchester.

It felt strange thinking about our house in Old Trafford without being in it, thinking about it while being so high up, having a distance from it and from everything that had gone on inside it. From up there, near what seemed like the top of the world, I gained a new perspective.

Down down down we drove, away from that place where the light is clear, where the fresh air is abundant, down down down until soon it seemed we were driving into the very heart of a thick blanket of grey clouds. I looked out of the window and the world had vanished beneath the cotton-wool grey as if it had been snuffed out, and even the car headlights made only a thin orange gleam through the fogginess. Back down we drove, back towards our city until soon it had grown dark and the street lights appeared, and we got stuck in a traffic jam, for it was match day and I knew we were close to home again. I felt a lurch of something like excitement mixed with dread to be back in our city for, despite all the goings-on in our house, I must have loved our city, still.

One day soon after our trip, Mum brought the world home for us. It was wrapped in a see-through plastic bag and I saw it before she took it out. It was a bulge in the bag, huge as a pumpkin, though blue, not orange.

'Close your eyes,' she said. She switched off the lights and when we opened our eyes the world was glowing in the corner of the room, spilling its blues into the room, the colours of the land masses bright green or yellow or pink. Then she switched the lights back on again and switched the world off – it was only to be put on on special occasions.

She brought another world back with her too, a flatter, rectangular world. She stuck it up in the living room with Blu Tack and drew some circles around it in blue biro, lines of significant places, as if to remember them even though we were far away from them. Every now and then the world's edges curled precariously, defying their flatness, and it slipped on to the floor.

After the trip to the Lake District, Mum was more gentle, parcelling out her love for us in just the right quantities, not stifling us with it, or starving us of it when it was buried so far down inside her depression that she had none to give.

So full of promise they were, but those days shone in the light precariously.

Those days started to stiffen and gloss over; they moved from being fluid, something we lived in, and froze over. We were trapped in the house once more. I can't remember going to the lakes after that; Mum mustn't have got another subsidised place through the nursing association. I can't remember going to the countryside after that. I think of the world pressed onto the wall, and consider how we move through the world; social mobility and class – how certain places are inaccessible to certain classes, and how important it is to break down such barriers of place. It's vital that children of all classes and cultural backgrounds have ready access to nature and the countryside.

Even from my one trip to the mountains and the lakes, that landscape lived inside. The heart had opened huge enough to be filled with those deep lakes and high mountains; the heart had opened up and fallen in love with the world all over again.

Nothing could take away the great lakes from me; when I closed my eyes, there they swam. There was another world out there, beyond these walls, and another world too, within the mind.

When I had to go swimming in Stretford Leisure Centre and felt the burning shame of self-consciousness, I would imagine that I was wild swimming in a lake, practising my butterfly stroke, and as the cold water crashed against my skin I was a wild thing, I was alive and I was swimming through the world, pressing ahead through the water, and I swam until the heart was beating in the ears, the heart was beating so I knew that I was alive, and I learned to hold my head beneath the surface for seconds and see beneath the surface and survive and carry what I had seen up to the outer world, and I was no longer just a girl from home but a girl of the lakes, a girl of the hills, a girl of the flowers, spilling filling thrilling the lungs with their scents, a girl from the world I was becoming.

Mum sat on a chair by the window in her darkened bedroom, curtains parted, cheeks pressed against the glass. I stood and watched her. The radio clock by her bedside glared out 02:34 in green ghoulish numbers. She stared out into the street. I couldn't see from here where she was looking. When her breath fogged up the window she wiped it away with her face, stroking her cheek against the glass until it was clear again. She did this over and over again, but one time the window fogged up and she didn't wipe it away, so soon a window of white breath rose up in front of her. I thought she must have fallen asleep, so I crept towards her with the irrational intention of trying to lift her into the bed and cover her up so she didn't catch cold. But her eyes were wide open, glazed over, moving.

I touched her arm and she jumped and I instinctively flinched away, expecting a huge thwack across the face, but she lifted me up on to her knee and she held me close to her, tightly, and she rocked me back and forth, back and forth, and started to sing.

The notes floated into the air, clear and bright, bubbles, and I wanted to touch them and keep them safe; something palpable, instead of this fogginess in front of us. She stroked my hair and kissed my cheek.

'What are you looking at in the foggy window, Mum?'

'Oh, I wasn't looking at the fog, I was thinking, just thinking...'

I wiped away the fog, hoping the bad pictures would also be wiped away. It came off clean and cold and squeaky in my hands.

We looked through the window together at the rainy night, empty of all but the dirty gold of the street lights, making the black puddles shine more blackly, glistening. I gazed down at the black puddles and searched their reaches and soon I could see the great lakes inside them; the black water was parting to reveal that glorious blue.

I would draw pictures and paintings for Mum – little bits of inarticulate love – and leave them in places where I knew she'd find them: pictures of houses, when I had just learned the magic of 3D; houses with paths stretching from their doors away over the hills and towards the lakes and off the page into a future we could dream about, if there was space left in the head for dreams; paths stretching into a space off the picture, off the edges of the page, where hope might live.

Stalin on the Mantelpiece

Ruth Behan

I liked the prefab the first time we went there. At that time, I knew I was quite wonderful, especially as I was wearing a complete suit of white fur fabric that Grandma had made.

She and my mother were inspecting the prefab, as it seemed that my mother and father and I were to live there. Mum looked unconvinced but Grandma was encouraging. In the centre of the living room was a square of lino printed to resemble a piece of carpet and this would save a lot of money, she said. A great big space to run around in my fine suit was what I thought.

There was a set of drawers and a cupboard cunningly built into the wall with handles exactly right for climbing up – especially if you ran fast at the wall first. How crazy grown-up people are – they told me I must not do this because the council would not allow it. That's the sort of thing I had to put up with – grown-ups thinking they could overrule my ideas all the time.

A good part of the trouble was really caused by Achy and Smelly, because the two women persisted in the belief that things Achy and Smelly did were in fact done by me. Even when we were on the bus and I pointed out the street where Achy and Smelly lived,

Mum and Grandma continued in this belief and seemed to think it was funny.

Soon after that, we did move to the prefab and enjoy its other wonders – a gas fridge, a table that folded down out of the wall, a wooden draining board, a terrifying toilet and a garden where a bomb had dropped in the war. It had bold concrete paths and a wealth of rockery from broken bricks and concrete. Most people in south London had big rockeries in those days – sometimes the bricks had a blackened and melted look, which was creepy. I could do what I liked with the garden because gardening was bourgeois and gardening tools were a waste of money. Anyway, our father spent all day digging and hod-carrying, so gardening had no appeal for him.

The walls of the prefab were asbestos sheets covered in a gritty paint called distemper, which was also a thing dogs got, so maybe that was why it continually peeled off the walls, very tempting to help it on its way, likewise the covering of the little pulling-down table in the kitchen where we sat to have our meals. The Fablon covering this had a pattern of gay Chianti bottles and cocktail glasses, but if you cut bread on it and didn't use a breadboard, it would cut right through and show the brown stickiness beneath it. But I only harmed it once and then I was sorry because it seemed to be saying something about things that were nice that you could get once you were grown up.

One day I was playing under this table and noticed a very lifelike doll in a nice dress sitting there, so I gave it a shake to see if it would fall over. Or perhaps actually it was Achy and Smelly who did that, because it turns out that was my sister and you must not do that to sisters. Even though I had never been consulted about having a sister, it later turned out she was something of an advantage – not least to keep me company when our mother and father had their rows. The rows were frequent and unpleasant. How annoying it is when you have been given to believe the two parents you live with were admirable people and then you hear them each declaring the other to be thoroughly bad in every way? All Dad's friends and Mum's relatives were very bad people as well, so it seemed.

You can't really play when all this is going on. You just have to be in your bedroom listening to it all and trying to work out when it's safe to come out and work out which of them was winning that time, thinking, 'Oh, she's crying now – that could work – oh yes, he's said he's sorry, that looks hopeful... Oh no, now she's remembered some other bad things he did a while back – now it's all off again; now he is shouting about Your Mother's Effing Tatie Hash!!!' After a miserable hour or two, they would leave off and seemed to calm down and went off to their bedroom to have a lie-down. You must especially not go into the room or knock on the door to ask for anything or they would shout at you in an extremely cross voice. They would not explain this, though. Which was odd, because most generally grown-ups explain things whether you want to hear about it or not.

When they were not having a row, they were cheerful and would laugh and sing. Dad sang about Brave Father Murphy who stirred up the rocks with a Warning Cry, and the Bold Fenian Men, the Yeoman Captain with Fiery Glare and Joe Hill who is Alive as You or Me, and the best one was the rousing '*Avanti o Popolo alla Riscossa Evviva il Socialismo e la Libertà.*' These songs would cheer you up no end – all about bad people and how you had to fight them. The bad people were Parasites, Capitalists, Bourgeois Intellectuals and Effing de Valera.

Our mother would sometimes sing these songs, but also other interesting songs like 'My Tiny Hand is Frozen' and 'They Call me Mimi Though I Know Not Why' and 'I'm Just a Girl Who Can't Say No' and 'Anything You Can Do I Can Do Better'. Dad was a tall handsome red-haired Irish man and Mum was very beautiful. She was also totally fearless in managing the terrifying pressure cooker that had matchsticks for a safety valve and only exploded if you weren't careful. From this unexploded bomb she produced fine stews and boiled bacon and hissing clouds of steam. When the clouds of steam died down you knew it was safe to come out from under the table. Also, rows were never at dinner time. No one with any sense has a row when food is on the table.

There was not much furniture or stuff in the house at that time, most things were a waste of money, but there was no need to worry too much because the Revolution was coming and then everything would be much better.

There was a little stove in the living room to burn coal and stuff on. My sister and I had the job of cleaning that. We had quite a few jobs because if you don't work that means you are a Parasite like the very Fat Man who waters the Workers' Beer.

Dad would come at night and sit over the little stove for such a very long time as if he would never get warm again. He would smoke a cigarette down to the very last bit – holding it like you would to take a pinch of salt. He went all over London armed with only his trusty A to Z, working on various jobs and organising to get better safety conditions.

There were some curious objects did appear and they came as presents from Comrades in faraway places. Dad had been there for a thing called a delegation, and Mum had been to one of the places where she said they had soup with a lot of fat floating on top. There was a green-and-white bedspread woven from scratchy wool, some boxes decorated with little burned-on designs (so many of these that all our relatives had them too). From China came a satin dressing gown for Mum, which had been golden except the colours had run in the wash. I longed to see it in its original state. Above the little stove was a mantelpiece and on this was an inkwell with a pen and the head of Trotsky and a white plaster bust of Stalin. You might be shocked to hear this, but people in those days still spoke about Stalin as Uncle Joe Stalin who had met up with Churchill and helped us win the war.

At times, more Comrades would come round for discussions or socials. The discussions were very interesting to me because they were all about the bad people that had to be got rid of (though not much was said of Effing de Valera and the people who shot James Connolly when he was tied to a chair). Much was made of the Parasites, Capitalists and Bourgeoisie. And as it turned out there were more layers to this. Capitalists were bad and they had everything worked out to be in their favour because they had the Capitalist System. Bourgeois was bad but 'Petty Bourgeois' was even worse. Proletarians were good but some of them had all the wrong ideas so they were 'Lumpen Proletarians'. Likewise, Intellectuals were good but could become 'Bourgeois Intellectuals', which was bad, or 'Effing Intellectuals', which meant they had jobs that didn't involve bricks or concrete or being out in the freezing cold. Some of the Comrades did easy jobs and had posh houses, so might be Effing Intellectuals, but calling them that would be a deadly insult, so they were only called that when they weren't actually there. The discussions often ended in people becoming angry, especially if the people were related to each other. It seemed like the closer related you were, the more the danger of things going wrong and the dreaded 'Bourgeois' insult being used.

However, the socials were jolly affairs, with laughing and music, and grown-ups didn't get up till late on the day after, so my sister and I could drink some of the orange cordial that was left around. Women always drank gin and orange in those days – we had the luxury of drinking the orange without mixing it with water, and savouring the luxurious sweet, tangy taste.

One time, a radiogram appeared for a few weeks and a record of a black man called Leadbelly singing about the Rock Island Line. I was fascinated by this and it seemed to me the best bit of music I ever heard. I pestered my mum to explain it all to me – the man was cleverly tricking someone about what he had on his train. You couldn't really work out if the man was a Capitalist or not, but I loved the music and wondered where you could get more of it from.

The way of getting rid of the Capitalist System was by strikes and Dad was very good at these because he was not a Bourgeois Intellectual. The pay and conditions of the building trade were extremely bad at that time because unions were not allowed then in the building trade. If anyone had any strikes going on, Dad would go and help them, and sometimes take me with him. The men on the building sites treated him with evident respect and did not argue like relatives and Comrades did. They did not say 'Brian' in an exasperated voice like Mum and Grandma did. With them, he seemed very serious and did not burst into mad poems or fragments of old songs like he did at home. Men seemed eager to hear what he had to say. He was put on a blacklist, which made us very poor indeed.

May Day was always a big march in those days – you didn't have the day off like you do now, so marching on May Day was a sign for all the Comrades and Trade Unionists to get together and say things had to be changed. One cold bright spring day, Dad took me to this and carried me on his shoulders amid all the furling embroidered Trade Union banners. At Trafalgar Square, I was amazed to see him climb up to beside the lions and speak to the huge crowd of people who listened to him and cheered afterward. Who would have thought there were such a lot of people who did not think he was silly and funny and only came to England with two pairs of old socks and some black-and-white pudding?

One day my mother told me I was to go to school. She seemed very pleased with the idea but I could not see the need for it at all. She said I would have to go whether I liked it or not because if I didn't, she and Dad would be put in prison. So I thought I had better agree to go, but with foreboding, because how nice could it be if you had to be made to go there or else your relatives were put in prison? How right I was – the teachers in those days did even more shouting than Mum and Dad, and frequently turned violent and beat boys with wooden rulers on their hands and legs. You could never be sure what would set them off, either, and they loved to get the whole lot of us together in the hall and get very angry and tell us off, even if only a few children had done the bad thing. We must be obedient because God said so, but this made no sense because of course there isn't a God, so how could he see us, and anyway I was already being obedient. Then we had to pray with our heads bowed and our eyes shut and this put me in a really bad quandary. If I did do what they told us, I would be a hypocrite and hypocrites were like the Bourgeoisie and the song said 'Let Cowards Flinch and Traitors Sneer'. But what if the teachers noticed I had my eyes open and wasn't saying the words? Who knows what they might do if I went against them? I compromised by bowing my head but keeping my eyes open, but I felt like a traitor to myself and yet still fearful. To comfort myself, I reasoned that if the teachers could see me, they must have their eyes open when they should have them shut, but I thought teachers were capable of anything, so I worried about that very much for the next seven years or so.

Mind you, this was nothing compared with what happened to Angelina Cuthbert. She was one of the children who sometimes smelled of wee. Some days we had to do Agility, which meant taking off most of your clothes and jumping off special things with leather tops onto spiky coconut mats. Or else it would be Music and Movement, which meant running around pretending to be something and then stopping suddenly exactly when the teacher told you to. In order to do this, the teacher told us it was very important to tuck your vest into your knickers; Angelina had an extremely long vest on one day and absolutely would not tuck it into her knickers. After about the third time of telling her off, the teacher grabbed her and I thought she was going to get a big smack, but instead of smacking her, the teacher suddenly hustled her out of the hall. Gradually the dreadful meaning sunk in – poor Angelina had been sent to school with no knickers. To my surprise, it seemed the teachers gave her some knickers from somewhere and did not shout at her, so maybe there were limits to their inhumanity.

After a year or two, I began to get used to school. In time, my sister was also made to go there, so it was seemingly the fate of all children and the only way out of it was to grow up, so I decided to do that as quickly as I could. Pretty soon, adults started to praise me for being 'very grown up' so maybe you could get to be grown up quicker if you tried hard enough.

The Comrades still came round, but not too often. A dog-eared booklet with a sheet of red paper as a cover appeared and seemed to tell of something very bad. Grown-ups discussed it in a serious way, no raised voices, no speeches, no songs, no more gin and orange and beer. Then there were mutterings about the mysterious OGPU, which was more dreadful than any of the other bad people.

One day I came back from school and by the back door was Stalin. Someone had taken him off the mantelpiece and smashed him to bits on the concrete path. I ran to Dad to tell him. He was sitting with his head in his hands, weeping. His face was red and crumpled and he shouted at me angrily in unfamiliar, ugly words. I was frightened but I knew what to do by then – I would have to figure out what had happened to Stalin on my own – yes, that would be more grown up.

What do people do when Superman turns out to be Lex Luthor? My father, to his credit, did not turn to drink – not at that time, anyway, but there was no more singing for a while, no more 'Bandiera Rossa'. Trotsky kept his place on the mantelpiece for a few months, and then began to move about the prefab, eventually ending up on the floor with a big chip out of where the inkwell should have been. Dad bought a typewriter and began writing, and miraculously got money for what he wrote. Mum got some booklets from the Rapid Results College and bought new clothes. Dad's brother got famous by writing and teachers started being extra-nice to me. And best of all, one glorious and wonderful day Dad said we were going to get a dog.

Night of the Hunchback

Paul McVeigh

We're on the landing. Looking down the stairs. It's far too early for us to be in bed, but Alex is minding us and he always puts us to bed as soon as the door closes on Mammy going to work.

'Go on, Dolores,' says Our Gerard.

'No,' says she, 'I'll get shouted at.'

'Ach, go on,' says me, and I scrunch my face like a sponge as if I might wring out some water. 'Just say you're getting a drink, right, and then on the way back from the kitchen say, "Alex, can we can come down and watch the fillim?" But say it like you're about to cry if he says "no".' Alex can't bear it when Wee Dolores cries. When other people do, he looks really disappointed in them or completely disgusted.

I feel sort of guilty because Wee Dolores is about five, my wee sister, and my best friend, and we're as close as is morally possible between siblings. She also knows how much I don't get on with Gerard, so I wouldn't be coaxing her if it wasn't all about me and her, right? Except this is about him. I'll be honest and say I'm seeking approval because he's older, a boy and can't stand me.

'I'll give you some sweets,' says me.

'You haven't got any sweets,' says she, because she knows every single thing about my entire life.

'I have,' says me.

'Show me.' Her arms cross, due to this dramatic plot twist in today's episode of *The Life of Paul and Wee Dolores*, a show we've been making since the day she joined me in consciousness.

I run into our bedroom and recover the 10p-mix-up-sized white paper bag from my pillowcase and return holding it tight in my hand in case Gerard grabs it off me.

'You kept that one quiet, sleekit arse,' says Our Gerard – like I would ever tell him anything.

Wee Dolores is still unsure, doubting me as a punishment for keeping a mixed-up secret from her. In my defence, I didn't tell her as it was part of a non-disclosure agreement when I received the mix-up from a pensioner I think might fancy me and who I kissed on the lips by accident after helping her down some steps.

'OK, look,' I say, opening the bag and putting it under Wee Dolores's nose.

'You'd better give me at least three of those,' says she, 'or I'll start murder.' She walks to the top of the stairs and looks down.

Gerard looks at me like *She's mad, I can't believe she fell for it.* We share a laugh. We've laughed at the same thing about twice in our actual lives, so my laugh doesn't sound like me because I don't know who I am with him.

A hand grabs mine and, before I know it, the bag has gone and so has he. Our bedroom door slams. I run after him but he's holding the door closed from the inside. I can hear him laughing. I knew not to trust him.

'Alex!' I scream at the top of my voice. 'Alex!'

Our bedroom door opens.

'Ye wee yap, ye,' says Gerard. 'I wasn't gonna eat them, I was only jokin'.'

He's shitting himself because Alex might hit him. Me too *and* probably steal my sweets, but it will have been worth it to get Gerard hit.

'What's goin' on up there?' Alex shouts up the stairs.

'Nothin',' Our Gerard shouts and gives me back my sweets and looks *Don't say anything.*

'Who's doin' the shoutin'?' Our Alex shouts, which is funny because, now, it's actually him.

'Paul,' Our Gerard says, looking at me *Now you're in trouble.*

'Alex, Our Gerard wants to know if we're allowed down to watch the TV?' I say, looking at Gerard like *Up your hole with a big jam roll.*

'No, I don't, he's only sayin' that to get me shouted at,' he says, punching me in the arm.

'Alex, Our Gerard just hit me,' I cry, rubbing my arm. 'I hate you, you wee fucker.'

'Alex, Our Paul's cursin',' says he.

'That's cuz you hit him!' says Wee Dolores.

'Right, that's it!' Our Alex comes thumping up the stairs. We run like shite, knocking each other out of the way, dive at the bed and crawl under the covers. The irony being, it's actually Alex's bed because the only other bed at dive level is the bottom bunk, which is blocked by a little ladder.

The covers are being pulled from us but we're holding on to them tight as tight. 'No, Alex!' we scream, so he beats us through the blankets instead.

Our Gerard got the worst of it. He'll hate me now.

'I was going to let yous come down, but not after this,' says Alex. We hear him walkin' away.

'No Alex, we'll be good,' Our Gerard says, uncovering us.

'Ach,' I whinge, 'It's not fair. Bernie lets us stay up.'

'And since yous want to be in bed, yous can get into your own for the rest of the night,' Alex says, the pleasure dripping from his mouth.

'Sure, it's still early,' I say.

'Get up and get into bed, nigh, I'm tellin' yous,' Alex shouts.

Gerard pushes the wee ladder to the end of the bunk beds and gets in the bottom. I let Wee Dolores climb up first and she crawls to the bottom end of the top bunk nearest the bedroom door. I follow her up and get under the covers at the end that hides in the darkest corner of the room.

Alex lets down the blinds; you have to keep them closed at night so that the gunmen can't see in to shoot you. Our blinds are special Venetian ones. Venice is where they have no streets, just rivers. And nice blinds. You have to get special boat-taxis everywhere. We can't afford taxis, so if we lived in Venice, we'd have to swim everywhere.

Alex switches off the big light and closes the door so it goes completely dark.

'Alex?' Our Gerard shouts from below.

The door opens again.

'Wha'?' Alex shouts, even worse than m'Ma does.

'Will you leave the door open and leave the landin' light on?' says Our Gerard, sounding like Bambi.

'No! Go to sleep, nigh,' says Alex.

'But he doesn't like the dark,' Wee Dolores says. 'Mammy allows him to have the light on.'

'Tough shit – Mammy isn't here,' says Alex, 'And no talking either. Straight to sleep or yous'll get beat.' He closes the door. There's a pause and a little strip of light pings under the door as the landing light goes on. We listen to him go downstairs.

Jesus, he's scary. Didn't even thaw at Wee Dolores.

Silence.

The older ones take turns to mind us while Ma goes to work at night. We like it when the girls mind us, as they let us stay up later and watch movies with us on the sofa. Sometimes they buy us wee parties, which consist of a packet of crisps and a juice and, if we're lucky, sweets! And, in return, we let them go out and mind ourselves.

The three older girls live in the room next to us and when Wee Dolores gets bigger she'll have to move in there with them. Older girls do the cleaning, cooking and bring us wee ones up – the usual sort of things daughters do. They're basically other mammies, except they don't hit us. Alex never has to do anything, yet he's the grumpiest. And he *does* hit us. Funny that. Also Da doesn't work. Must be a boy thing.

This is the new improved McVeigh family residence since the Housing Executive came and built extensions on all the houses on our street, giving us an extra bedroom (fancy!) and an indoor toilet (smell us! – well, not literally because that would be disgusting). Before that, in here, me, Dolores and Da shared a double bed while Alex and Gerard had the bunks, and next door had all the big girls plus Ma, two to a bunk bed. I won't ask you to imagine what it was like when Uncle Martin and Aunt Elizabeth moved in for a while and there was eleven of us in a two-bedroom house.

How did Ma and Da manage to have so many babies when they didn't even share a bedroom?

Meanwhile back at the ranch…

There's screaming from the alley at the back of the house where someone is getting a 'community beating' by the IRA for being 'anti-social'.

'I know, let's play I Spy,' says me, to distract Wee Dolores.

'But it's dark,' says she.

'Well, see, what you've got to do is remember what's in the room – it's an even harder game that way. It's called I Spy in the Dark. Or I Can't I Spy.'

I hear her sucking her bottle. She still sucks a bottle even though she's far too old.

'OK,' I say. 'I CAN'T spy with my little eye because it's dark...' She giggles.

'... something beginning with B.'

'Bed,' says she.

'Yes! Brilliant. Your go,' says me.

There's thumping coming up the stairs.

'You've got us into trouble,' says Gerard.

'But he couldn't have heard me,' says me.

Wee Dolores flies up my end, in beside me, and we pull the covers over our heads.

Slow thumping, one step at a time. Angry, but in no hurry. This is not *you're going to get beat* thumping, which normally takes a good run-up.

The windows in the other bedrooms slam, one at a time, and the screaming from out the back sounds like it's in a land far, far away.

We lie still and wait. And wait. Heavy breathing sounds coming from outside the door.

'You can hear it, can't you?' I whisper.

Wee Dolores nods.

Louder moaning.

'Did you hear that?' says Gerard, muffled by the sheets.

I peek my head out of the sheets down the gap between my bunk and the wall. He looks like he's going to throw up.

'It's only Alex messin' about,' I say. 'Alex, is that you?'

A long, loud growl.

Wee Dolores grabs my arm and I grab hers.

'Alex stop messin', you're scarin' Dolores,' says Gerard.

'Let me in!' The voice is deep and growly and scary.

Banging on the door. Thumping on the landing floor.

The strip of light coming under the door pings off.

Wee Dolores screams and near deafens me. We dive back under the covers. A bony avalanche falls on us and it's Gerard, who pokes his way in beside us. I'm squashed right up to the wall while he's squashed against the bars on the other side of Dolores. We grab on to each other and squeeze tight.

'Let me in!' louder this time.

'Go away! Alex, stop messing,' I say.

'I'm comin' in. And I'm goin' to kill yous. And I'm goin' to rip you up. Tear off your skin with my teeth.'

We all scream. We are grabbing, trying to get our legs to grab as well. Like we're all running lying down. We hear the door open and the growling is louder and non-stop. We all scream. Whoever's holding on to my arm is digging their nails into me and it really hurts.

The growling stops, so we go quiet. I open my eyes and slowly, slowly peek out of the covers. Someone or something has opened the blinds a little. In the stripy light, standing at the bottom of the bed, I see a man in a black jumper with a massive hump on his back. I can't see his face.

'I am Quasimodo,' Humpy screams.

The older girls do this. Never Alex.

Gerard and Wee Dolores come out from under the blankets as the hunchback opens his arms and we see his sleeves just hang at the bottom where hands should be. He brings his arm up to his chest and then a light comes out from his stump and shines up onto a face that is all twisted and has massive warts all over it.

The monster jumps at us, climbing the ladder. Wee Dolores screams and keeps on screaming. Gerard joins in. Then so do I. I can't help it.

'It's *Night of the Hunchback*,' Alex growls.

We got it from a movie we watched with m'Da when he came home drunk one night and got us all out of bed to watch. Then we made up our own scarier version when the girls were minding us. Alex is doing an X-rated version.

The covers are being pulled off.

'Stop it, Alex, you're scarin' Dolores,' says Gerard.

But he just won't stop.

I can feel the covers slipping from my fingers even though I'm holding on hard. I panic as the covers come off and then there he is, right there, face to face. He growls. We scream. He puts his hand on his face and pulls at it. His face comes right off and he screams and we scream.

He pisses himself and slaps the light switch, which is right next to my bunk. Why didn't we think of that?

'Mammy!' Wee Dolores starts crying.

'Stop cryin', wee scaredy cat,' says Gerard, when everybody knows there was no one more scared than him.

'Do it again, Alex, do it again,' I say. He's a million times better than the girls.

Alex takes the pillow out of his back.

'I'm tellin' m'Mammy on you,' Wee Dolores says.

'Ach, you weren't scared, were you?' He jumps up and lies on top of us when there's no room at all. We're laughing but it hurts.

That's about the nicest I've ever seen Our Alex be to anybody in his life. He must be drinking. When people have only had a couple they can be dead friendly, like they've drunk some happy potion or are possessed by someone who hasn't grown up in Belfast.

'I'm tellin' me Mammy on you!' This is Wee Dolores's favourite line, being the youngest, and she can get you into serious trouble with Ma. Even Alex runs from Ma's wrath.

'Ach, come on now, Wee Doll.' Alex is trying to coax her but she's huffing. 'That's the last time I'm playing with yous,' he says, like a wee kid, like her. He gets up, goes to the door and stands with his hand on the light switch. 'That's definitely it now. No more playin'. Not with that wee yap.'

'She doesn't mean it, Alex,' says me. 'Do you Dolores?'

'Tell him you don't, do you?' says Gerard.

I laugh and make faces to show her everything's OK. And give her the *C'mon, we have a laugh* look.

'Right, not a word out of yous.' Alex fixes the blinds again, turns off the light and closes the door.

'Alex!' Wee Dolores calls after.

'What?' says he, opening the door.

We all look at her.

'Will you do it again, Alex?' says she, in the cutest wee voice you've ever heard.

He sort of smiles. I think it was a smile; I'm not sure because it's never happened before. He turns the light off again and heads.

'Ach, go on Alex,' says me.

Alex turns and, as he closes the door, sticks his head through the last gap. He doesn't say anything, just looks. Behind him the landing light shines.

'Who's that? Who's that coming up the stairs?' Alex whispers deep, looking scared. We look at each other then back at him.

'Please, don't!' Alex screams for his life. 'Leave me alone, please... no!'

A hand comes over his face and pulls him out the door that closes behind him, leaving us in the dark. We scream getting under the covers.

Out on the landing, screaming, growling, limbs banging against the door.

'It's *The Werewolf*,' I shout. That's an even scarier film we act out. What will he do with this one?

We hear Alex getting eaten alive.

We're next!

Exploding happy scaredness.

Passengers

Shaun Wilson

I'm fifteen and it's five years till the millennium, and some say the end of the world. It's a mild night in October. Above the turning sycamore across the road pile the corrugations and grid work of the cellophane factory, peaking in a long chimney from which underlit, eggy smoke bulges and wisps away like apparitions failing to materialise. I can hear pissheads shouting across the town centre, and I wish I'd had more to drink. It's twenty past nine. Another car coasts by and its driver glances across. I look down, in case it's someone who'll grass me up to my mam, saying I was alone on the streets of Wigton and not at a friend's sleepover. I've been waiting half an hour under the powdery glow of the street lamp, hoping every dazzle of headlights is my brother.

He's really my half-brother on my dad's side, and I only found out about him a few months ago, overhearing a conversation between Mam and her brother, my uncle Danny.

'So I've got a brother, then?'

Mam peered over her shoulder. 'I was waiting for the right time to tell you, Shaun. It's nothing, really. He's only your *half*-brother. Your dad's never had anything to do with him.'

'What's he in prison for?'

'Drugs.'

'He was all right at school,' Danny said. 'A respected lad. He just got in with the wrong crowd.' Danny was a big influence on me, growing up. Cumbria's longest-reigning squash champion, he was a thorn in the side of the national administration, with a reputation for goading referees and intimidating opponents.

'Is he hard?' I asked.

'Yeah, he'll be fairly hard, I reckon. He could pagger when I knew him.'

'He'd be no good for you, Shaun,' Mam said. 'I think it's best if you forget about him. He never stays out for long.'

'What's he called?'

John Cross was reaching the end of his latest sentence, over five years for supplying heroin, and for biting a lump out of someone's face over a debt.

I'm six and I drive around with Dad sometimes when he visits his houses and building sites. We go into the estate agent's and he talks to a lady called Idle Brenda. There are lots of photographs of houses, Dad's as well, and before we go he covers some of the prices and I have to guess how much they are. When I get it wrong he shakes his head and asks me another. He gets mad as well when I put my shoes on the wrong feet. I feel proud in his Mazda sports car with pop-up headlights, and we listen to Dire Straits. 'Brothers in Arms' is my favourite song. It feels like something only we listen to. The baker's is nice and warm and smells of bread in the ovens and the ladies all talk to me. I get embarrassed sometimes when I don't know what to say. Dad knows what to say and how to make them laugh. At one house there's a bull mastiff called Flora and she's friendly and lazy and I don't mind when Dad takes ages there, because I like stroking her and playing hide and seek. I like being with Dad because he's hard and he went to borstal when he was little for fighting. I want to be hard like my dad one day. Dads like having a son so they can talk about fighting and cars and all the things that boys like, and it reminds them of when they were boys and going fishing with their dads. Girls don't know about fighting and you shouldn't tell them about it.

One day we go to a house to see Dad's old girlfriend. She looks nice, but I don't talk to her much. If Dad didn't fall out with his girlfriend he wouldn't have married Mam and I wouldn't be born. I play on the swing in the garden and throw sticks at the conkers. I could climb right up in the tree and get them all if I was allowed. An older boy walks past the garden. He looks at me for a long time and he asks if I have a brother. I tell him I only have a sister called Chloe, who's three and cries a lot. He says brothers are better than sisters and I tell him I think they are as well.

Last week my brother introduced himself. Fresh out of prison, he found me in the upstairs bar of Dad's pub, the Kildare, rehearsing Black Sabbath's 'Paranoid' with my band. He looked like Dad, same spaced incisors, intimidatingly confident, with a home-made tattoo of a tear on his cheek, and others on his hands that looked like dirty marks. I didn't know what to say. I almost started crying. He took me away from my band so he could talk to me in private.

'I've got you a present. It's not for them lot in your band, though – I'm giving it to you.' He gave me a cardboard box. Inside were two book-sized electronic units.

'Fuckinell, I dunno what to say. What are they?'

'Some kind of amplifiers,' he said. 'Don't take them into any shops though – they might want them back.' He had an endearing laugh, one that could've made anything funny. 'Here.' He handed me his fag packet. I took one out and went to give it back. 'Keep them,' he said. 'I've got loads.'

'You sure?'

'Yeah. Listen, have you got any money?'

'About two quid.'

He took a wad of cash from his pocket. 'Here.' He pushed a £10 note into my hand. 'Get yourself some drink.'

I stared at it. 'I can pay you back next week?'

'Don't worry about it.'

All of a sudden I had fags and drink, and a brother as well. The first lesson he taught me was one of principle, after the payphone in the main bar swallowed his fifty-pence piece. He held the receiver to his ear and rattled the hookswitch with his other hand before banging down the receiver.

The barmaid looked over. 'Is everything all right?'

'It swallowed his fifty pence,' I said.

'I don't give a fuck about the fifty pence,' he said. 'If it was someone else's pub I'd take it off the wall and smash it over their fucking head. It's not the money. It's the principle.'

A Mondeo estate brakes hard and grazes the kerb. The passenger window's down.

'Jump in,' says the passenger, a weasel-faced man of around twenty.

I crouch and see the tattooed bulk of John Cross, stacked in the driver's seat in the shadows and slivers of half-light. I get in the back next to a heap of household lamps and hi-fi separates and the car screeches off. He didn't mention anyone else being here. I've been looking forward to seeing him again, imagining things we'll talk about, the lost years we spent apart, and I'm pissed off that some lackey's taking up the passenger seat.

'How's it goin?' I ask.

'All right,' John says, flatly.

Disheartened, I try to match his tone. 'I've been waiting half an hour.'

'Had some business to sort out. Here, give him two of them.'

The lackey rustles about and passes me two small pills.

'What are they?'

'Valium,' John says. 'Tens. They'll chill you out.'

'How much do you want?'

'You don't need money with me.'

'Nice one.' My mood lifts and I swallow them both.

We hit the overlit bypass and John opens up the car. I think about putting on my seat belt, but I don't want to be a pussy. I want to meet the experience head-on.

'Where we going?' I ask.

'Carlisle,' John says.

'Is there a party?'

He doesn't answer and neither does the lackey. After a period of silence the lackey grabs the wheel and wrestles against the road as the car fishtails. I grip the seat in front until we stabilise.

'Fuckinell, John,' the lackey says. 'Watch where you're going!'

'Who you talking to? You little fucking divvy.'

'You were falling asleep, John.'

I fasten my seat belt.

The lackey's on high alert now, studying John, ready to take the wheel as soon as his eyes close, which is happening frequently. I'm grateful for his vigilance, and quietly chuffed that I'm keeping my nerve while he's flapping like a shithouse.

'What's he been taking?' I ask.

'Eh?'

'Why's he falling asleep?'

'He's tired.'

I smile and shake my head.

It's a relief to see the glow of Carlisle as we approach its speed limit. A crash at thirty would be relatively harmless. The wash of sodium light and the demands of the traffic systems appear to stimulate John, and he stays awake. We pass the terraced houses of Wigton Road, a floodlit service station, and corner at Dixon's chimney, past the Royal Mail depot and up towards the city pool. The traffic lights are red and we stop.

Across the intersection, waiting at the traffic light opposite, is a police car.

'Fuck – it's the pigs,' the lackey says.

Their headlights feel watchful, as if awaiting our move.

'Are they after you?' I ask.

'They need an appointment to see me,' John says.

For some reason I find this reassuring.

Even the engine sounds quiet. I realise there's been no music throughout the journey. The lights turn green and we drive towards the police car. As we draw alongside, its blue lights flash on and John puts his foot down. We accelerate down the slope and I'm overtaken by adrenaline, a reluctant fugitive, resigned to the will of the car. Through the rear window I see the police car mount the pavement in a U-turn that seems more pompously ceremonial than rushed. Now I know I'm in a dangerous and unfamiliar world.

We howl past a bus stop, skipping over a mini-roundabout as oncoming cars pull over to make way. I drag myself forward, wrenching at the front seats, as if through sheer determination I can steer us to safety. We corner. It feels like two wheels have left the road. The lackey swears and the stuff on the back seat tumbles against the far door. I thank God the road was clear as we drift back into our lane and accelerate. The lights are red at the end of the road and we accelerate towards them. I prepare for an impact. We brake as we run the lights and turn screeching out of the blind junction. Botchergate is temporarily clear and we make the corner, mounting the kerb with a crash that sounds like the tyre is blown. But we're back on the road and accelerating. The police are no longer in sight, and this gives me no comfort.

We screech to a near halt, turn into a housing estate, and overtake a line of parked cars. The speedo clears 60 mph. I think I'm gonna die. The roads are strange and I don't know what's ahead, but we slow down, and corner onto a wider street. Relief washes over me, and I hope for a minor collision. I envisage police surrounding the car. My secret gratitude after my coward's wish is granted. But we soon reach a speed where one blink could kill us all. It smells like something's burning. I pray for survival, for the chance to tell Mam I'm sorry. We overtake a car as if it's parked and the blare of its horn fades into the red mist of our wake. Boys on the pavement press up against a garden wall as we scream past. Up ahead an oncoming car's in our lane and John hits the horn but doesn't brake. The other car's in the middle of the road. I brace myself for a crash. I'm too flait to scream. We swerve onto the pavement and I don't think there's enough room to pass and there's a crisp thud as our wing mirror shatters. Then we're back on the road, straightening up and accelerating.

'Fuckinell, John,' is all I can say.

We enter another estate and John kills the headlights. We pull up outside a semi-detached house with backlit curtains and I take off my seat belt.

'Where are we?' I ask.

'Get the stuff,' John says, gathering the hi-fi separates off the back seat.

I grab some lamps and we run to the house. In the living room are two men and three women in their twenties drinking lager. One of the men, with pale blue eyes and collapsing cheeks, is smoking heroin off a rectangle of tinfoil. They go quiet. John tells them we just outran the police and no one seems surprised. I'm getting eyeballed until John introduces me as his little brother and tells them to look after me. I feel unspeakably proud, and brave. Blue lights flash in from the street and pulse on the wall. Through a crack in the curtains I see three police cars and a number of officers surrounding the smoking Mondeo, and I remember I'm being chased. Someone tells me to get away from the window.

'What if they come in?'

'They're not getting in here,' says a sturdy woman in a pink velour tracksuit.

'Thank fuck I'm outta that car. I thought we were gonna die.'

Everyone laughs.

I look around but can't see John. 'Where's me brother?'

'Upstairs,' a man in a baseball cap says. 'He's gone for a lie-down.'

The lackey comes back from the kitchen with a can of Foster's. Tracksuit stares at him like he's dog shit on her carpet. 'Ey, radgie, you not getting the boy one?'

'Eh?'

She turns to me. 'What's your name?'

'Shaun.'

'Get la'al Shaun a can, for fuck's sake.'

'Who you talking to?' he mutters, plodding back into the kitchen.

One of the women says something about me to her friend and they start giggling. They're both smiling. One of them's tidy but has a tooth missing.

'What?' I ask.

'She wants to know if you're gonna sit on her knee,' the tidy one says.

'Just ignore them two,' Tracksuit says. 'Get yourself on the sofa.'

I nod at the man in the baseball cap and take a seat at the other side. The pale-eyed man opposite heats his blackened sheet of foil from underneath, liquefying a beetle of heroin that comes to life and crawls down a furrow, giving off fumes he chases with a foil tube held in his mouth. He looks bored but very serious about catching it all and holding it in. It smells sweet, like caramel, not like something harmful. I've found the Holy Grail of rock-and-roll accessories. I'm dying for a go, but I'm too flait to ask. The lackey comes back and hands me a cold can of Foster's.

'Cheers,' I say. 'What's your name again?'

'Flipper.'

'Flipper?'

'Yeah, what you trying to say, like?'

'Nowt.'

He assesses me with amusement. 'You don't look like John. You really his boyo?'

'It's probably me long hair. And he looks more like Dad than me.'

Convinced that John won't be getting back up, I light a crumpled joint I was saving to share with him. It relaxes me and I buzz off the way it works with the Valium. I hand it to Flipper and he nods, takes it, and draws on it like it's the last joint of his life. 'Where'd you get this?' he asks.

'Someone in Wigton. It's just soap bar.'

'Why you smoking that shite?'

'It's all I can get.'

'You might get some skunk tomorrow.'

'Yeah? Am I staying here, like?'

'Where else you gonna go?'

'I don't mind. I'll stay anywhere.' I nod at the man with the heroin. 'Do you smoke that?'

He looks to see if Tracksuit heard. 'Shhh.'

I lean closer. 'You think I can have a go?'

He double-drags the joint and exhales a thin spire of smoke. 'You'll have to ask your brother.'

'I won't say owt if you don't.'

'Aye, but you will, though.'

I shake my head. Really, I'm glad he cares what my brother thinks. It makes me feel looked after. I'm nice and mellow now, tuned in to some kind of astral frequency of empathy and forgiveness. Flipper turns to the other man on the sofa and starts telling him about John's driving. I realise he probably doesn't have a brother of his own, and that's why he knocks about with mine.

The blue lights stop flashing, and no one seems to notice. I think to myself, 'It's just another night for these lot,' and relax into the cushy welcome of the sofa. I don't even know where I am, which part of Carlisle, and I smile and prepare to ask someone, already half-distracted by the luxury of time.

Dear Nobody

Alex Wheatle

3 A Better Place
Self-Esteem
Belief

Dear Nobody,

I hear your wailing every night. My heart senses your pain. My brain stores your memories. I have lived through your agonies. My old friend Loneliness never leaves you alone. The triplets Brutality, Contempt and Insignificance visit you too often. Trust has long ago abandoned you. She has gone to the place where Roots now resides. Hug has never shown her face. Love has never introduced herself. Unworthiness wants to take you out for the day. Low Esteem always wants to party. Empty birthdays of the past fill you. Christmas has always mocked you. Your brother, Rage, now sleeps with you. But I'm coming back, Nobody. So hold on to Hope. I know he's tiny and fragile. I know he's sick. I know you cannot see him in the dark – you have to concentrate hard to hear his voice. But he is there. Nurture him, nurse him. One day he might grow big.

Yes, I'm coming back for you, Nobody. It's been a long road full of wrong signs and deep holes – the odd mountain too. And I have been blind and one-eyed for so long. For many years I didn't want to accept you. I tried to deny you. But you lived in my head. I don't know how you got in. But you did. Yes you did, you and Hope. Most of the time you were both asleep, recovering from the wounds Trauma inflicted upon you. But then you both woke. I pretended I didn't hear you. I tried to wish you away. I broke down when you and Hope were both screaming at me. I was exhausted, spent. You and Hope too. But I remember your words before the fall.

> *Motherless children,*
> *If no one loves you in this world,*
> *Make a start and love yourself.*

Yes, I'm coming for you, Nobody. And when I finally bless my eyes on you, I'll rename you. Yes, you're going to be Somebody.

Yours sincerely,
Your older self

Black Cat Dreaming

Astra Bloom

They asked us to write a story about a dream we'd had. The winner was going to be put on at Christmas. And in this leotard, I was like a girl called Darling.

Snap back.

I am eight, nearly nine. I've never owned a leotard in my life; I got it from our school jumble. In my privates it cuts like a knife, I know it's too tight, but really it is just *so* blackly nice. And my nan's heart stopped like my Timex in the navy month before Christmas, so I won't be putting expensive black leotards on any present lists. And, anyway: *leotard.* I never heard such a wonderful word. I'm almost thinking it's been made up.

Snap back.

It's important you understand I've got my own two cats. The first is black and white, the second is black. Alice is the black and white, she's my Lucky Thirteen. All twelve black and whites were Cindies. All Cindies were killed by idiot lorries on the death road out our front. The cats always wanted to cross; there must have been something very good on the other side. Each time one was lost, my dad bought me another who looked just like her. I crowned her Cindy. Cindy One. Cindy Two, Three, Four, Five...

He, my dad, has no kind words, and a head-of-bees-wife. He had an old-fashioned mother with cancer in her milk – they say he was a wee Scottish baby, sucking when she died, leaving her kitchen door open wide. To all the cold winds. And for an ugly-apron stepmother to come marching in. Only once he said it – once on a rare day – when his lips just slid open, putting pink heat into the frost – *she put him in spider-dark cupboards for all the day if he forgot 'please'* – so I see, I do see why my dad's words are always so freezed.

But. And. I got a pact with me – to love this man over God's green hills and more – for replacing my Cindies. Every cat-killed day I waited by the back door for my dad to come off his shift with a new kitten in a shoebox. Scrap-of-silk straggler, little pearl, a fluff-dragon; I'd dangle the cutie on the slide of my nose, wipe my tears and snot with her soft little paws.

After twelve terrible deaths, when cat number thirteen came to me, I decided she had to be called Alice. Though Cindy was my favourite name, I just couldn't face any more dead Cindies. A new name – and this cat lived and lived – to this lovely purry fatness. I thought, 'So that's how it is: names can kill and names can save.' I was sick, thinking that by trying to keep my Cindies alive I might have killed them, but how could I have known that words did magic?

Anyway. Snap back. Snap back.

I didn't dream much at that time and neither did my Alice – or I think she did, but her dreams were private – so for our school competition I decided to write about our black cat's dreaming. 'Two tramp cats,' my dad had said, when he brought them home in his Old-Spice-smelling holdall one morning. A tramp's cat had birthed kittens at the side of the Old Bath Road and my dad stopped the man from dumping these two in a sack in a bin.

We already had my Alice (after Alice in the *Owl Service* on telly, I think) and our spotted dog, and the miserable rabbit that only sniffed and bit – but Dad still brought one tramp kitten home for me, and one for my little sister Bah. Straight away we named them George and Mildred after the telly that made us laugh. George was mine. He was witch-black wild, full of the suffocating kind of fur, pure rip-you-up fangs; he loved *only* the sideboard – 'cos he could scrunch up behind its back. George's fear was something as sharp and fresh as what I carried. So I gave him what I'd seen being called *respect*. Gentle. Gentle. I'd given the same to Alice, and she came calm-smooth-clever as me, even though they say black-and-whites are usually the most nervy.

So. There was Alice with her mind-your-own-business-dreams, and my dear George's twitching sleeps were too street-gutter-beard-tramp-sink-teeth-someone-put-us-in-a-sack-save-me to put in a dance, but my sister's cat Mildred had these dreams that really flamed me. Mildred, George's sister, was a short-hair; black as sin, too, but skinny and greedy and honest. And she was lucky: all her days Mildred had been protected by her big-haired brother – so all her days she could be too hunty, too sleepy, too watch-the-street, too whatever-she-damn-well-pleased to be, too scared and nervy like my tremble-wild George. *And,* all her nights – *blimey, that Mildred cat, she could dream!*

Mildred's dreams were these dazzling, mad things: millions of bright birds like lanterns lighting the sky, curling rivers stuffed to the brim with talking goldfish, giant saucers of milk for her to roll in. Mildred was Fast and Mildred was Free. It was actually weird to see how I could fit her huge dreams into my horrible, dull red schoolbook. Between the pale tight lines. I did it, though, I wrote her dreaming as well as I could, 'cos I hoped – I knew it – in that leotard – *I could so easily be Mildred* – quick as spit in the wind – it wouldn't be hard – come on, no one was asking me for maths.

Sorry. OK. Just snap back.

You should know that I was the eldest. Really, my sister Bah was still too young and too upset to care for pets, that's how I knew the Mildred facts – it was me, really, who looked after the animals. My sister Bah was amazing, though, she could leap and twist mid-air like the craziest of young ferals. Once I saw her throw herself down the stairs, and even though she wanted to go stiff, fall splat – she didn't, she won't ever. She's a rubber girl, a flying brown tabby – I could never move like that. My sister's cunning is all in her legs and her bend – I have to turn things over inside my head first: my boogie-rhythm *will come*, but only after I think it.

Neither of us can use out-words – not to our mother when she hurts – or before – or after. So we can – what we *can* do – and it's a warm game – is we stick to each other like sticking plaster to a scab; *and,* together we make our mark on the wall next to our bunks. Not for my stories, or her lies, or her drawings of gymnastics – at both of them Bah's bloody fantastic – no, this bed area and this wall is where we tell the truth – record it all. *Mum is a fucking bitch, I hate Mum,* and more. And on. We go to sleep with our cheeks pressed to the writing on the wall. I've gotta say we take some pride, we own it, and though Dad is ordered on bank holidays to paint over it – pink or mauve – we just start our writing over again. Never heard of graffiti or street art. But. This. Is. Where. The. Truth. Starts. This scribbling makes us daring. And this daring gets us dancing – and when I see my little Bah shakin-it I damn well know it's a good thing.

So. So, snap back.

'Dream of the Black Cat' won. Sameera's 'Robot Nan', and

Tracey's 'Lonely Christmas Tree' dream (I don't believe she really dreamt that, I saw the book in the library) were the runners-up.

And the first rehearsal was on a Friday afternoon, the happiest school time in winter.

'Well, young lady! And you are such a quiet girl! We are all impressed by your very imaginative and interesting dream. So. When Mildred comes down from your back wall at midnight and starts to dance – we thought you might like to try that?'

'Yes, that's why I brought my black leotard. I have black plimsolls, but bare feet are better for a cat.'

I knew they'd like Mildred's dance. I quickly go and change, all cocky, thinking about how they'll let me make a pink nose for myself, probably give me soft black triangle ears. (Last year Simon P., a lowly stable donkey in the Bible play, got floppy ears made by retired Miss Platt; he got to keep them, his sister told me. I said she was lying, but I knew she wasn't. I just didn't like her. The size of her smile. The way it went up.)

It's comin-up-to-Christmas-cold-school-hall cold. They've rolled up the gym mats, an ice-shine fairy wood reflects in the lake of what's called the parquet floor.

'Ah, there you are. It's a bit chilly in here, you don't have to wear your leotard if—'

'No,' I say, '*I'm warm.*' The teacher ladies all smile; they have a way of standing straight and thick and slightly waving, in clumps, like long grasses on cliff tops. When they nod with their specs on their heads, their clever eye-wrinkles all alert, I begin to dance my dream scene.

Mildred comes down from the wall – and since our Creative Dancing class at school, I've understood this way to talk. Mildred swirls in her dream. In her dream, giant blood-toothed mice parade the alley behind our house. Mildred is damn fearless. Her pine-needle eyes drop and explode in the long-secret night. She goes prancing between rats, mice and foxes, dodging whiskers sharp as my mum's carving knife. With a click of pink tongue Mildred teases them all, no fleas on her, no worries. No sticking-up hair. She rolls smooth as a marble beneath the full-moon spotlight. When the sharptooths circle her, she cartwheels, back-flips, tail-whips, yeowls her war cry. And then. *Mildred flies*. She is a bat and a golden bird, and she is her magical Mildred self. She flies to a palace on a green and silver hill. She lands on a throne and grows long princess hair. She turns into a bright, clean girl. She stays living there...

I'm just finishing up my dance-dreaming, when I open one eye, see three teachers leaning in, squinting at something, their long strings of beads dangling. The square old one who smells of numbers and wears small adding-box clothes, she almost scratches the back of my thigh with her nose.

They clap, they clap, then, but their whispering is a tower to me. Now I'm not Mildred, it's just me; still as a road-dead cat. Still, not dancing. Eyes on and watching, forget dreaming.

They straighten themselves, put their bosoms back up front of the shop and stroke their necklaces into place. Smiles are strung around me, but it's like I'm wrapped in pricking tinsel.

'Well done! That was lovely. You – you have left quite an impression on Miss Eve.' Miss Eve, my class teacher is wiping her cheek with her sleeve. 'She's very moved... Quite moved, aren't you, Miss Eve?'

No words will jump out of me. What. Did. They. See? What. Have. They. Seen? I do not want to look at my favourite Miss Eve. And she stays being the sun behind a cloud of lace sleeve.

'Dear, can I just ask you? What are those marks?' Old Square speaks.

A chill. Someone's pouring water down my hot danced-off back. Suddenly this is a catch-a-cold-in-your-chest school hall. I need to go change. I sweat-clutch my plimsoll bag. But question marks hang. There's all of their faces. Old Square's a hag. Making me look to see what they have. Long red strips on the back of my thighs. Raspberry-lolly-lipstick-burn-red. Tallies like how many cars in half'n'hour of dread maths.

OK, OK, snap back.

Truth: I've seen marks on my Bah, I just didn't know – well, of course, I'm not stupid – I could have thought – I just didn't fancy looking. I suppose I didn't want to think about my skin; come on, every girl wants to be beautiful, every girl wants to be a clean, pure pedigree-coat thing.

I answer Old Square in my best *I don't know what on earth you are talking about* voice.

'Oh, that's nothing. Cat scratches, probably. One of my cats is wild – he's a tramp's cat.' If Mum hears about this she will call her a Fuckin' Nosy Old Crone.

'I see... Can I ask, is your mother picking you up today?'

'No, she's busy with the baby, Miss,' I lie. 'I walk home on my own.'

After the weekend there is another bloody Monday. I walk to school beneath a grey-beard sky. I've got a nasty stomach ache. Truth: won't even tell it on our pink wall, but I cut up that leotard. It was an embarrassing-small thing, rubbed and dug, probably did my bits lasting damage. Black Cat dance? No thanks. I don't want to be in their stupid show. Was never really *my* dream, anyway.

OK. Snap back for the last time and – well, just scribble this bit out if it's too ugly.

Mildred is all black, but I am a little striped. My markings came from a bamboo cane for garden beans – on top of a mother's handprints, and the flat of a long, bendy knife for roast chicken. Our skin's patterns and happenings are not for telling, but me and Bah remember them on our pink wall. Over and over go our felt-tip pens, they know it all.

I tell Bah when we're older I'll change our unlucky names, I've told her it's a kind of magic I learned about with my Alice cat. We'll have Farrah and Jaclyn, or Delilah, which sounds like a beautiful dark foreigner, and Agnetha like the woman in Abba, who sings 'SOS darling' like an absolute angel... We'll be special or famous, or all the men will want us, but we won't want them, any of them...

I explain to Bah, 'We don't need an idiot school prize, we can dance whenever we want; we're good dancers, *we're the Top Cats!*'

Snakes and Ladders

Malorie Blackman

Were you born on square one?
Or on square ninety-nine?
Do you need extra help,
Or are you doing just fine?
Do you even make it
Into the game?
It's not about love,
It's control, cash and fame.

Don't let them convince you
You've got to be playing,
Make up your own mind
If the price is worth paying.
The game? It is rigged,
And you're not to blame
The ladders are broken
The snakes have your name.

Stop and listen to what I'm saying
Don't throw the dice, cause I ain't playing.
Up the ladder, down the snake
Once on the board, you don't escape.

I'm factory fodder
Well, that's what they told me.
But when learning is power,
No prison can hold me.
Playing the game,
But not by my rules
As players it views us
As sheeple and fools.

Reading is knowledge,
Learning is queen
My mind is the only thing
Left sight unseen.
If life's big game
Is ladders and snakes,
The square you are born on
Is yours to escape.

Stop and listen to what I'm slaying
Don't throw the dice, cause I ain't playing.
Up the ladder, down the snake
Once on the board, you won't escape.

Ladders are smokescreens,
Safety valves, lies.
The snakes copulate
And are breeding like flies.
If you're born on square ninety,
Luck's on your side.
Those on square one?
You may watch with eyes wide.

When the game is against you?
And you can't walk away?
Your style, your own voice
Is the way that you play.
Keep it original,
Style it unique.
Your own way of being.
Your own brand of chic.

Stop and listen to what I'm praying,
Don't throw the dice, I'm no longer playing.
Up the ladder, down the snake
Don't let them tell you, you'll never escape.

Detail

Julie Noble

So I wanted to ask you, what was real?

That night I slouched down Phoebe's garden path in my old clothes and tightly belted jeans, ready to help her as I had promised. We were sorting out the garden for her planned extension. Two weeks earlier, after the first court appearance, the one about the children, I had helped to demolish the old shed.

I had come straight from court, straight from seeing Him with his New Love. New Love had worn a designer suit more suitable for a wedding than a stuffy city courtroom. Smug and untouchable with her cushion of money, my husband's lover had crowed in my hearing: 'I can't wait to get those children.'

Him and Her were accompanied by the solicitor, a well-paid figurehead who may not have known she was lying as she delivered false accusations to the judge about me.

'Justice is for the rich,' a friend had said. It seemed so.

His solicitor knew tactics, sending a spurious report to the court on the eve of the court date. My ex had ordered a privately contracted 'processor' to deliver out of hours a sheaf of already-opened legal papers when he knew I would have the children. The man had blocked my drive and frightened us, but I refused to accept the papers while my kids were present. He had fumed in the street until two neighbours came out to oversee and I got the children out of the way.

Later the man perjured himself to write the report for the court, saying it was me who wanted the children to know everything.

It would have been his word against mine – very dangerous as, if true, that would have been classed as emotional abuse – but my older son had warned me to record any incidents, so I had got the phone out in time. This film proved the man was lying, but left me with a counter-argument to submit. With no legal help that night, I had to prepare my own detailed account.

Alone and scared, in the early hours I typed up sworn statements, trying to meet the stringent requirements, then printed them in triplicate to hand out myself.

Which I did later that day in the courtroom.

Upright I remained, no sign of inner pain. My calmness confused his solicitor but reassured the judge. My children were not removed, though a thorough investigation would ensue.

Afterwards I sought refuge at Phoebe's. She took one look at my face and led me down to her unwanted shed. 'You need to let it out. Here's a hammer.'

'I don't need a hammer.' Part in jest, part using the anger I had repressed, I lifted up one leg and kicked out an entire end panel. Twelve feet long. Gone.

In that kick was the power I should have used to get him out of my bed. In that collapse was the sense of an ending, though not the triumph of winning. The battle had begun. It would go on for months.

As Churchill said: not the end, nor the beginning of the end, but the end of the beginning.

Two weeks after that court date, the interview approached. Too much had changed. Too much was the same.

But I was about to be swept out of all that for five hours of one night.

Slouching down the path to meet you. Unknowing. No make-up on, no perfume. Tired, polite smile. Hand scraping through my scalp not in a show of sexiness to flirt with you, but because life was challenging and that interview was approaching. The constant stress made me scratch my scalp until it was patched with scabs. It still is.

A first date should be like summer flowers. There should be colour in it. My clothes should have been bright, my face highlighted. There should be a boldness in my stride. Scent sprayed over my body and neck, and poured into the cleavage of my chest. At least a hint of which would have been visible, because I would have worn a dress.

In a different life, I'd have been a different woman. I would have shaved my legs, my underarms, those crucial places, just so I would have felt the sensuality of my own naked smoothness against lace. And during our conversation my whole cleaned, primed body would have shivered in anticipation of your touch, the scales of my skin sensitive and tremulous like a butterfly landing on the edge of a fragrant, feather-thin petal.

In a different life, you'd have been a different man.

You wouldn't have been escaping from your own nightmare.

Since your return from war, and before. Your finances a mess and an official inquest ahead and promises to your dead comrade. Promises made before—

That word haunts us both: before.

Before you met me you had a drive out to the hills, where you would have ended it all if you'd had your own gun. You longed for a Glock 17. Three times you told me that detail. That manufacturer's name.

For the truth is in the detail, so I was told after the video interview.

If you're lying, you can't give the finer details. You can talk of a crime and describe it lightly. But you can't dig deep into every second of scratching action. You can't describe in detail how he took his rough hands and sharp nails and held apart your rigid—

And you can't keep repeating it. Intimately.

Nor remember words used as weapons to hurt: 'Frigid.'

Detail. Glock 17. I believed you. Saw the need in you, saw the fear too.

So down I go to a future I still don't know and there you are: big eyes and big hands and a man, so of course I'm wary. You and Phoebe are cosy together on a low bench and I sit at a safe distance and regard you for what Phoebe says you are: a friend who will help do her extension and someone she clearly trusts. She's surprised that I'm surprised to see you.

'Haven't you two met before?'

We regard each other and shake our heads in synchrony. 'No.'

We know we haven't. We know we'd remember. Our brown eyes are the same shade as we stare.

Phoebe brings coffees for the three of us and you two are planning, so I sit and listen. Soon you are joking in a Peter Kay way. Twinkly eyes, cheeky smile. When you show Phoebe a video on your phone, I move across to sit beside her so I can see as well.

At first Phoebe's next to you, leaning low over your shoulder, and I'm hunched alongside, staring wide-eyed at your friend's dodgy, drunken karaoke. We all laugh, but then Phoebe goes to get something from the kitchen and suddenly you and I are alone.

You move closer. Out of nowhere a sentence that floors me.

'You remind me of Emily Brontë.'

Of all the women in all the world, you pick her.

I think of that *Jerry Maguire* film where Dorothy says, 'You had me at hello.'

Well, you had me then, at Emily.

You ask, 'Do you know her?'

I laugh. 'Of course. I've written a book about the Brontës. Didn't you know?'

No, you didn't. You didn't know I wrote. You didn't even know I existed until that night.

'I love their writing, the wildness of it,' I say, and feel a flare of returning life.

You nod. 'I've walked those moors. I love them.'

'Me too. I've been several times.' I can feel my face glowing.

Your eyes are bright with excitement. 'Anne's buried at Scarborough.'

'I know. I've been there.'

You stare right at me – right into me, it seems.

'Of all the people,' I say, still knocked off-balance. 'Of all the women in all the world to pluck out of the ether, you pick a Brontë.'

Phoebe comes back. She's given up on sorting the extension plans and sends me off with you to the shop for wine and cigarettes. She tells me it's because you're on your motorbike and can't carry anything and also because you don't know where the shop is and I do. If there's any other reason than those, I never know.

You start the straight talk in the car. Your questions prompt me; soon words are falling like clothing.

Sometimes it's easier to talk to strangers than to people who've known you for all your life.

They say the truth comes out in the end, but that's a lie.

If you try, you can hide it until you die.

'Be bold,' you say abruptly.

I say I will be.

Because I haven't been.

You know my voice was silenced but you don't know why, so I tell you and I don't even cry and I'm driving you, a man I hardly know, and I'm speaking the secrets of my soul.

Two days after this, I am booked to sit down in a closed, oppressive room with a woman I have never seen before while being monitored by a man I will never remember.

There will be a camera pointing at me – the judgemental lens not even hidden by the dusty curtain – and I will be asked to talk in ever-increasing detail about my past misery.

I did not know then how harrowing that would be.

How the ground we would go over and over would open up to swallow me. Such dirt to be immersed in, smothering my thoughts.

How I would sense the pain in my body and flesh afresh. How I would feel soiled and ploughed inside. How the taste in my mouth would be of him again. Stale, foul. Intense.

How nobody would be holding my hand. How I would clench instead the swabs of squashed tissues drenched by distress and how I would have to keep speaking and keep speaking and keep speaking.

Here's how he lifted my stiffened, coiled body to rearrange the fixed limbs into his desired position. Like manipulating the artist's mannequin I bought him.

That was when he clawed at and parted—

Yes, it hurt. Yes, he knew. I curled up crying afterwards.

The truth is in the detail. Over and over.

Describe those actions I had long kept silent about on parts that are supposed to be private.

Talk of places I can't bear to be touched. Where I can no longer imagine love.

Raw and exposed before people I will never know.

'Harrowing,' the policeman said months later, his gaze shifting away.

But that's all in the future.

Meanwhile, we pull up at the shop and the outpour stops.

In the Spar you bring out the Peter Kay-style banter again, teasing in the same tones Peter used for 'Garlic Bread': 'Shi-raz, Shi-raz. What's that?'

You brag that you never drink, but you stock up on cigarettes. We laugh with the shop assistant about which is the worst vice: my wine versus your cigs. It's nice.

I drive back, looking for a gap in the hedge, because I know something is shifting and I need a chance to clear my head. When I see the distant abbey – solid, spiritual, safe – I park the car in a gateway and we get out and stand looking over a field of still-green wheat.

You never wanted to speak out. Nor did I.

I kept silent during the marriage to protect the children, now I speak out for the same reason.

But it's not easy to return to those years.

The police informed me that it will take months to investigate, and that in the criminal court where the emphasis is solely on evidence and not justice, truth must be provable with dates, words, witnesses and reports.

The solicitor has already said, 'In police terms, it's his word against yours.'

They warn me he will deny everything.

They are right. Not only that, he will quote fantastic phrases provided by professionals. He will tell the court official that I want to 'emotionally castrate' him because I'm jealous and want him back. My 'vengeance' will be his defence. He will say that my description of events is merely the 'pathetic attempts' of a 'bitter woman' desperate to destroy him.

And of course he will talk louder and longer because he is practised at speaking. He is not breaking a concrete wall of silence.

You say that you kept silent at the time of the incident, but now you think your comrade's family need the truth.

But I wonder, do they? How important is truth, after all?

Does truth soothe a tormented soul? Does it defuse a volatile situation?

You thought you got to him in time, but you were wrong, he was almost gone.

You ask me, should you tell his children that as the blood choked in his throat you couldn't make any sense of his last sentences? Those dying words might have been meaningful or they might have been awful, a blur of fear and pain.

You wonder, should you make up something they might want to hear?

You think his family need the reasons why he died, but do you want them to be fighting the 'whys' for the rest of their lives? An ongoing inquest in their minds?

You can only surmise he would have been alive if you'd got properly equipped medical help in time. You can never be 100 per cent certain.

And 100 per cent certain is what the legal system prefers. Reveres.

His family will never stop missing him, but can you stop them reliving it?

And how can you talk so freely, even recklessly to me, when you can't talk to anybody else, not even those closest to you?

Though I could ask myself the same question.

'Be bold,' you say again in the gateway. 'People need to hear your voice.'

You are the second person to say that to me that week.

'Nobody can hear you if you don't speak.'

I swear the land has shifted beneath my feet. I put my hand to your arm – the soft pressure gives a warm surge of connection. I want to say something else – something tectonic, but I stop.

'Phoebe will be wondering where we've got to.'

So we go back to find that Phoebe has gathered friends. Down beneath the fairy lights nestled in the trees, a fire is alight and a guitar has appeared. She knows you can play, so she's been next door and borrowed one from the twenty-something singer who has come along with his parents. Summoned by texts and calls, more friends are at the door.

You and I are suddenly shy of each other.

Phoebe leads you to a chair in the centre and passes the guitar. You begin to tune it, covering your awkwardness by complaining about its strings.

I sit back down at the low bench, nowhere near you, so as not to draw notice. Yet it's obvious to me, as clearly as if there were drums beating, that there is something resonating in the space between us.

You must feel it too, because soon you move your chair to be next to me. Your arm brushes mine and my hand shakes my wine. Daylight is falling from the sky, slipping down like the scarf that drops from my shoulders. I pull it up, quick.

The fire licks at the wood from the old shed and takes hold. Two bright planets come out of the darkness. More people arrive and sit down. We say nothing.

You start singing. A familiar one: 'Half the World Away'. People smile and sing along, but the lyrics speak differently to me. I look up to you and you smile and pat my head like I'm your child or your dog. You go on to play 'Don't Look Back in Anger' and my soul slides towards you.

As the last of the daylight disappears to reveal the secrets of the universe, the fire becomes bolder and ravishes the shed. Night is naked now; even the small, distant stars are visible. You tilt the guitar towards me, your brown eyes gazing into my mine as you sing, and our arms touch again. I sense in my skin a tingling that I had forgotten existed.

For the first time in a very long time, I realise I want to be kissed and held.

Though nothing else.

The weight of his acts crushed into concrete every nerve ending. For years I had no pleasurable sensations left in my skin and my body felt solid as stone. He labelled me 'frigid', though I was loving and giving when I met him. A counsellor told me 'desensitisation' and 'dissociation' were an armour of protection in a traumatic situation. Technical jargon that I looked up and learned from.

I understood it, but it didn't change anything.

That night was the first time my skin had come alive.

Yet anything further was frightening.

Then your girlfriend rings.

I hear you saying, 'At Phoebe's, she got a guitar out,' which jolts me back to reality in an instant. I can't lift my eyes to look at you.

We say our goodbyes and you go, though not without you pressing your number into my phone.

'In case you can get any work for me,' you say, as though you need to explain to onlookers.

I resolve that I will, if only to redefine our meeting into something else.

After you'd gone, Phoebe and her friend were teasing me.

'What was wrong with you? You were like a puppy staring at him with those eyes!'

'He's got a girlfriend.' Phoebe's friend said piously.

'I know.' I was chastened. 'I don't know what came over me.'

Phoebe laughed. 'It was the wine!'

'No it wasn't! It was the stars and the firelight and the music and his eyes.'

'It was the wine!' they both chimed.

'OK, it was the wine.'

Because it was easier to agree than to try and explain that I don't know what happened, but you swept me away.

In a dark, pre-dawn hour, Phoebe's cat climbed on top of my sleeping bag as I slept on the sofa. When I woke at five, my usual time, I was conscious of it lying there. Its body was warm and heavy as it nestled in the folds of fabric, so instead of getting up, I stayed still, thinking.

Thinking sombre thoughts in the early morning is not good. Like soft mud, the sludge sucks you in.

With another day until the interview, I had plenty to do. Paperwork to wade through, a messy house to clear, a difficult past to put behind me and a new life to find. Soon I began to feel overwhelmed.

I listened to the sound of light rain dropping softly onto the ivy leaves outside the open window, the throaty thrum of a wood pigeon purring in the pale dawn, thought back to the magic night, and cried.

But the tears sank into my parched soul and I knew that some part of me was revived.

So after a while I got up, went home and carried on.

Looked up the music you sang for me, and played it on my phone.

Class and Publishing: Who Is Missing from the Numbers?

Dave O'Brien

Class, to paraphrase academic and literary critic Raymond Williams, is one of the two or three most complicated words in the English language. This is, indeed, because of both its history and how it has come to be used by academics, governments, individuals and communities.

On the one hand 'class' is quite a technical term, based on the jobs people do. On the other, it forms a crucial part of the sense of identity many people in Britain hold as part of their everyday lives, as well as their cultural expressions.

This short concluding chapter will try to introduce the 'technical' and the 'identity' ways of thinking about class. It is important to understand both ways of thinking about class *together*. When taken together, identities and technical measurements help us to show *how* occupations such as publishing are highly socially exclusive and begin to explain *why* this is the case.

The technical use of the term 'class' is about understanding how society and the economy are organised. Another way of thinking about how society and the economy are organised is to ask how they are *structured*. This is where technical understandings of class come in. The most widespread and best known of these is the National Statistics Socio-Economic Classification (NS-SEC).

The NS-SEC clusters occupations together into eight groups, from I (higher managerial and professional, which includes doctors, CEOs and lawyers) to VII (routine occupations such as bar staff, care workers and cleaners), with VIII covering those who have never worked and the long-term unemployed.

The NS-SEC groups are based on the way that jobs in each group have similar characteristics. For example, for the professional and managerial jobs, this is the terms of their employment contracts, their pay, the amount of autonomy or control they have in their workplace, and the careers they are part of.

The NS-SEC gives a clear definition of class based on employment and occupation. It allows us to map jobs on to the categories of 'middle class' and 'working class' which are the terms people use in everyday discussions of class. As well as giving a clear definition of class, the NS-SEC means we can be clear about class-based forms of inequality. We can see, through this technical approach to class, how workers in different occupations have differing characteristics.

So far this explanation probably seems very dry, particularly for a subject as emotive as class. Moreover, it is especially dry if class is a crucial part of social inequality, another importantly emotive subject. So we need to think about the other way people understand class, which is as part of their identity.

Social surveys often show a big gap between the numbers of people who would be classified as working class, because their occupation is in the NS-SEC VI–VII categories, and those who describe themselves as working class. Part of this self-description is about describing the feeling of being ordinary, just like everybody else. It is also a self-description that tells us about people's class *origins*.

People's class origins, in technical terms, are about what parents' occupations were when they were growing up. This tells us a great deal about their class origin when we're thinking about the big picture of who is from which occupational NS-SEC starting point. In turn, we know there is a relationship between parental profession and other social resources, such as family wealth or attendance at particular schools and universities. There are also other social patterns associated with occupation, and parental occupation, such as forms of cultural participation and consumption.

As with class, occupational understandings of social origin only take us so far in understanding people's lived experiences and their own sense of identity. Counting the numbers of people with parents who are doctors, compared to the number with parents who are cleaners, can tell us about the patterns of class in society. This type of information, along with understanding the differences, or similarities, between people's origins and their occupational destinations has been a central concern for research on social mobility.

At the same time, and much as with class, social mobility has a broader meaning in the language of the public and politicians, which asks whether society is fair. What are the chances of people making it into prestigious jobs? Or is success solely based on what your parents did for a living, where you went to school or university, and who your contacts are?

It is useful to remember that the answers to these questions are not solely about class either. Class *intersects* with other big social categories, such as gender or ethnicity. Disability and sexuality are also important, as is immigration. Intersectional understandings are most crucial when we ask if particular groups are under- or over-represented in the workforce. This may then help to explain why specific voices and stories are absent from page, stage and screen.

Class origins are a particularly difficult subject for researchers because many people's self-descriptions are subtly different from how their parental occupational *origins* might be classified. This is made even more complicated by how people self-describe their class identity in the context of their jobs, their occupational *destinations*.

In publishing, the core sets of occupations are classified as being professional and managerial jobs. This means they are middle-class occupations, middle-class destinations for the people working in them, irrespective of their social origins and the sometimes low pay and bad working conditions they may encounter.

The fact that publishing is counted as a middle-class occupation might go some way to explaining why we hear so many horror stories of people feeling excluded; people feeling like they don't quite fit with organisational or occupational cultures; and why the statistics on the class origins of people working in publishing are so alarming.

Publishing has a serious class problem, as it is one of the most socially exclusive of all creative industries. According to analysis of the Office for National Statistics' Labour Force Survey 2014, almost half (47 per cent) of all authors, writers and translators in the British workforce were from the most privileged social starting points (NS-SEC I), contrasting with only 10 per cent of those with parents from working-class origins (NS-SEC VI–VIII). For publishing as a whole, including occupations such as editors and journalists, the figures are still highly skewed towards those from middle-class starting points: 43 per cent as opposed to 12 per cent.

This is clearly a major imbalance. It is also an imbalance in the context of the rest of society: the same data set estimated that around 14 per cent of the population were from the higher professional and managerial origins (NS-SEC I). This means that publishing is much,

much more middle class, in terms of the people working in it, than British society as a whole.

Those from working-class origins, according to the ONS, are around 35 per cent of the British labour force, a far greater proportion than the 12 per cent of people from working-class origins working in publishing. It is clear there is an almost total absence of working-class-origin individuals, of whatever gender or ethnicity.

Publishing sees better figures in terms of the gender balance, in ONS data, with women representing over 50 per cent of the publishing workforce (54 per cent). This is seemingly good news about the numbers of women in publishing. It is good news compared to the numbers in the labour force as a whole (51 per cent) and to other creative industries dominated by men, such as architecture (30 per cent women) or film, television, radio and photography (24 per cent women).

What the ONS data doesn't tell us is who has power and control over the industry, as much of the academic work on the specifics of how publishing works shows women are often excluded from the top of creative professions and from prestigious roles exerting power and control over what we see and read – commissioning, for example.

There is a similar, although more worrying, story associated with the ethnicity of the publishing workforce. Publishing is whiter than the general population (93 per cent white vs the general population, which is 90 per cent white). However, this does not tell us who is making the crucial decisions, nor the types of control or creative freedom offered to people. As with gender, we know people of colour are much less likely to be in senior, powerful positions in creative jobs, and we know they are likely to face stereotypes and constraints on their creative freedom when compared to white colleagues.

Moreover, to return to the statistics, the under-representation of people of colour is made more worrying in the context of the dominance in the publishing industry of London, which is a much more diverse city (around 61 per cent white) than the rest of the UK. Thus the lack of diversity is not just unrepresentative of Britain, it is also highly unrepresentative of the city that is home to many of publishing's major players.

One of the things that comes from the statistics is the question of who is missing from these numbers. This is not just about percentages or ratios, as important as they may be for policy or organisational change. It is about the narrowness of the workforce that may have little or no lived experience outside of the white male of middle-class origins. It is about the impact of that on who is permitted to speak, who is allowed to take risks, and who is only offered a clichéd or inaccurate 'gap in the market'. Finally, it is about the lived realities that are overlooked, assumed to be unimportant by commissioners, and never given a chance.

Acknowledgements

All of us who have stories in this book send our thanks to the team at Unbound who helped get them out into the world. Thanks also to the support of the Writer Development Agencies, in particular Claire Malcom and Jonathon Davidson, who have worked tirelessly to see this project through from conception to completion and who will go on supporting new writers at the beginning of their careers.

Thank you to my agent, Jo Unwin, who encouraged me to see *Common People* through even when I should have been doing other things.

Again, thank you to everyone who pledged money, time and good wishes to *Common People*. We truly couldn't have done this without you.

And thanks, as always, to my children Bethany and Luke, everything is for you.

About the Authors

Paul Allen, 'No Lay, No Pay'
When Paul Allen was three, he would watch the gas men lighting the street lamps from his gran's bedroom window. He grew up in relative poverty on a large council estate, which he says 'was actually pretty good, as everybody I knew back then was in the same boat'. He left school at fifteen to be a bricklayer, like his dad before him, and loved it. Paul has played in bands and ridden motorcycles all his life, and freelances, between building jobs, road-testing bikes for a monthly motorcycling magazine. Using that experience, he applied for a degree in journalism at the University of the West of England, swapping on to the creative-writing course, where his tutor has described his writing as 'experienced and emotionally intelligent'.

Damian Barr, 'Uniform'
Damian Barr's memoir *Maggie & Me* was a BBC Radio 4 Book of the Week and the *Sunday Times* Memoir of the Year, and won him Stonewall Writer of the Year. Damian writes columns for the *Big Issue* and *High Life* and hosts his celebrated Literary Salon at the Savoy. *You Will Be Safe Here* is his debut novel. @Damian_Barr

Ruth Behan, 'Stalin on the Mantelpiece'
Ruth Behan was born in 1952 and brought up in south-east London.

Her father, Brian Behan, was very active in organising Trade Union membership in the building trade and her mother's family were Socialists right back to Peterloo. Ruth dropped out of school early due to depression but recovered and worked in the antique trade and also as a care assistant, musician, French polisher and nursery assistant. Returning to education in 1998, she studied counselling skills and then went on to study with the Open University. In the course of this she discovered she was dyslexic and was able to complete her BA/BSc in Childhood and Youth Studies, and other qualifications relevant to Early Years Care and Education. She eventually worked as a Visiting Lecturer in Early Years Studies for Wiltshire College. Ruth now lives in Wiltshire with her partner, who is a songwriter. She teaches fiddle-playing and plays in a folk-rock band called Billy in the Lowground.

Malorie Blackman, 'Snakes and Ladders'

Malorie Blackman has written over seventy books for children and young adults, including the Noughts and Crosses series of novels. Malorie is a scriptwriting graduate of the National Film and Television School. Her work has appeared on TV, with *Pig-Heart Boy* being adapted into a BAFTA-winning TV serial. She co-wrote the *Doctor Who* episode 'Rosa'. In 2008, she was honoured with an OBE for her services to Children's Literature. Malorie was appointed Children's Laureate 2013–15.

Astra Bloom, 'Black Cat Dreaming'

Astra Bloom grew up on the outskirts of London. She worked in catering, education and fashion before moving to Brighton with her family. She has two grown children, two cats, a husband and a labradoodle. Astra suffered a long and debilitating illness which left her housebound for years during which writing was a lifeline.

She received a bursary for a course at New Writing South and one of her poems won the Bare Fiction competition. Astra has since been runner-up in the Brighton prize and won both the Sussex story and Sussex flash fiction prizes. She's been shortlisted by many competitions, including Bridport short story prize and Live Canon International Poetry prize, and was selected to take part in Penguin Random House WriteNow Live event. She has had work published in *Under the Radar*, *Magma* and *Brittle Star*, and forthcoming in *A Wild and Precious Life*, an anthology on the theme of recovery from illness and addiction. Astra had two novels longlisted by the 2017 Mslexia Fiction Award and she is currently polishing these up whilst working on collections of short stories and poetry.

Lisa Blower, 'A Pear in a Tin of Peaches'

Lisa Blower is an award-winning short story writer and the author of *Sitting Ducks*, shortlisted for the Arnold Bennett Prize. She won the *Guardian* short story prize, was shortlisted for the BBC Short Story Award and was longlisted for the *Sunday Times* Short Story Award. Her collection *It's Gone Dark over Bill's Mother's* is out now with Myriad Editions. She lectures in Creative Writing at Bangor University. www.lisablower.com @lisablowerwrite

Jill Dawson, 'The Dark Hole of the Head'

Jill Dawson is the author of ten novels, and editor of six collections of poetry and short stories. Twice nominated for the Women's Prize, she has won awards for poetry, short stories, fiction and screenwriting. Her most recent novel was *The Crime Writer*, about Patricia Highsmith, and her forthcoming book is *The Language of Birds*, inspired by the story of the nanny murdered by Lord Lucan. She lives in the Cambridgeshire Fens with her husband, son and foster daughter.

Kit de Waal, 'The Things We Ate'

Kit de Waal has won numerous awards for her short stories and flash fiction. Her debut novel, *My Name Is Leon*, won the Kerry Group Irish Novel of the Year and was shortlisted for the Costa First Novel Award, the British Book Awards Debut and the Desmond Elliott Prize. In 2016, she founded the Kit de Waal Scholarship at Birkbeck University for a disadvantaged writer to study creative writing. Her new novel, *The Trick to Time,* was published in 2018 and longlisted for the Women's Prize for Fiction. She is the editor of this anthology of working-class writers.

Louise Doughty, 'Any Relation?'

Louise Doughty is the author of nine novels, including *Apple Tree Yard*, which was a number-one bestseller and adapted for BBC television. She has been nominated for the Costa Novel Award, the Orange Prize for Fiction and the EFG *Sunday Times* Short Story Prize, and her work has been translated into thirty languages. Her latest book is *Platform Seven*, due out in 2019.

Jenny Knight, 'Matoose Rowsay'

Born and bred in rural Suffolk – back when no one knew where it was – Jenny Knight was the first in her family to go to university. She has a degree in English Lit & Drama, and after jobs spanning barmaid, temp, roadie, aid worker, proofreader/typesetter, radio producer and prison creative writing tutor, she settled into freelance copywriting and editing in south Norfolk, where she lives with her husband and two sons. A prize-winning writer of short fiction and memoir, her stories have been listed in many competitions, including the Bridport, and appeared in *The Yellow Room*, *Riptide* and *Words with Jam*. She's written two novels and is currently polishing her first narrative non-fiction book.

Stuart Maconie, 'Little Boxes'

Stuart Maconie is a writer, broadcaster and journalist specialising in British social history, landscape, politics and pop culture. He currently hosts shows across the BBC radio networks and is president of the Ramblers, hoping to encourage that august organisation to stay true to its roots in working-class dissent.

Katy Massey, 'Don't Mention Class!'

Katy Massey grew up in Leeds and worked as a freelance journalist in London. She suffered burnout, and returned to education, culminating in a self-funded PhD in creative writing. This allowed her to write her own family's complicated story while researching memoir, and finding out why the lives of some groups of people are much less likely to be recorded, and lauded, than others. Shortly after the birth of her daughter, she was diagnosed with a life-threatening illness, and while recovering from surgery, started working on ways to encourage non-writers to author their life stories, particularly those under-represented in literature. One result of this work is *Tangled Roots*, an anthology of memoir by more than thirty members of mixed-race families, exploring their experiences, history and contribution to British society. She is currently developing *Who Are We Now?*, a collection of memoir responses to the Brexit referendum and a post-European future, while also working on *The Cleansing*, a novel imagining post-Grenfell London after a large-scale attack.

Chris McCrudden, 'Shy Bairns Get Nowt'

Chris McCrudden was born and raised in South Shields and now lives in London. Over the years he's been a butcher's boy, a burlesque dancer and a hand model for a giant V for Victory sign on Canary Wharf. He now splits his time between brand strategy and writing, and is the author of two novels, *Battlestar Suburbia* (2018) and *Battle Beyond the Dolestars* (2019).

Lisa McInerney, 'Working Class: An Escape Manual'

Lisa McInerney is from Galway. Her work has featured in *Winter Papers*, *The Stinging Fly*, *Granta*, the *Guardian* and BBC Radio 4. Her debut novel, *The Glorious Heresies*, won the 2016 Baileys Women's Prize for Fiction and the 2016 Desmond Elliott Prize. Her second novel, *The Blood Miracles*, won the 2018 RSL Encore Award.

Paul McVeigh, 'Night of the Hunchback'

Paul McVeigh's debut novel, *The Good Son*, won the Polari First Novel Prize and the McCrea Literary Award. He has written for radio, stage and television and regularly for the *Irish Times*. His writing has been translated into seven languages. He is associate director of Word Factory and co-founder of London Short Story Festival.

Daljit Nagra, 'Steve'

Daljit Nagra is from a Sikh background and was born and grew up in west London, then Sheffield. He has published four books of poetry, all with Faber & Faber. His poem 'Look We Have Coming to Dover!' won the Forward Prize for Best Individual Poem in 2004. His first collection of the same name won the Forward Prize for Best First Collection in 2007 and the *South Bank Show* Decibel Award in 2008. His subsequent two collections, *Tippoo Sultan's Incredible White-Man Eating Tiger-Toy Machine!!!* and his version of the *Ramayana* were nominated for the T. S. Eliot Prize. In 2014 he was selected as a New Generation Poet by the Poetry Book Society. In 2015 he won a Royal Society Travelling Scholarship. His latest collection is *British Museum*, which was published in 2017.

In 2018 he won the Cholmondeley Award. He is the inaugural Poet in Residence for Radio 4/4 Extra and teaches at Brunel University London.

Julie Noble, 'Detail'

A mother of five, Julie Noble is a lone parent living on a small council estate in north-east Yorkshire. Brought up in Leeds on the border of Chapeltown, Julie was the first in her family to go to university, studying psychology at Lancaster. Two weeks before the final exams, she gave birth to her first child, then graduated with honours. While marrying, having four more children, and divorcing, Julie did various jobs including childminding, banking, television work, bookkeeping and running children's activity clubs. Her writing has won prizes and appeared in *Mslexia*, *Writing Magazine* and *She* magazine. In 2004, she self-published *Talli's Secret* to raise awareness of dyspraxia; her eldest son has the condition.

Dave O'Brien, 'Class and Publishing: Who Is Missing from the Numbers?'

Dr Dave O'Brien is Chancellor's Fellow in Cultural and Creative Industries at University of Edinburgh. He has recently concluded a secondment to the UK Parliament's Digital, Culture, Media and Sport Select Committee and is the co-author of the 2018 *Panic!* report for Create London, Arts Emergency and Barbican. He has published widely on the subject of the sociology and politics of culture, and his next book will be *Culture Is Bad for You? Inequality and the Creative Class*, published by Manchester University Press.

Louise Powell, 'This Place Is Going to the Dogs'

Louise Powell has just completed her PhD in English at Sheffield Hallam University, funded by the North of England Consortium for Arts and Humanities Research. After growing up in receipt of free school meals and attending local comprehensive schools, she was awarded a sixth-form academic scholarship to Teesside High School. She gained a first-class degree in English from Teesside University, and an MA with distinction in Medieval and Renaissance literary studies from Durham University. One of her short comedy sketches, 'Are You Alright?', was performed in 2016 as part of Bolton Octagon Theatre's *Best of Bolton* production, and in 2017 she participated in New Writing North's Significant Ink Professional Development Programme for Screenwriting. She was also shortlisted four times for the Martin Wills Writing Awards for writing on a horse-racing theme.

Emma Purshouse, 'Misspent Youth'

Emma Purshouse left school in the early 1980s at the age of fifteen, initially working on various government schemes interspersed with bouts of extreme unemployment. She gave education another go as a mature student, attaining a BA from Wolverhampton University and an MA in creative writing from Manchester Met.

For the last twelve years Emma has been making a living as a writer and performance poet. Her passion is writing about the working-class communities that she has lived in, often making use of Black Country dialect within her work. In 2017 she won the international Making Waves spoken-word poetry competition judged by Luke Wright. Emma co-runs a successful spoken-word night in the Black Country.

Loretta Ramkissoon, 'Which Floor?'

Loretta Ramkissoon is an Italian–Mauritian Londoner who was brought up by her grandparents on a council estate in Edgware Road. Her love of languages led her to complete a BA in Modern

Languages from UCL and an MA in Translation Studies from Durham University, all whilst working part-time as a shop assistant. She has since been a translator, project manager and copy editor. Though she has been writing stories since she was ten, *Which Floor?* is her first published piece, and she is currently working on her first novel. She speaks five languages and enjoys sunsets and karaoke.

Cathy Rentzenbrink, 'Darts'

Cathy Rentzenbrink is the author of *The Last Act of Love* and *A Manual for Heartache*. Cathy regularly chairs literary events, judges prizes, interviews authors, reviews books and runs writing workshops, and thinks that most lives would be enriched by more reading and writing. She won the Snaith and District Ladies' Darts Championship when she was seventeen but is now sadly out of practice.

Riley Rockford, 'Domus Operandi'

Riley Rockford grew up in East Anglia and spent most of her holidays in Scotland. Now, she loves living in her east London neighbourhood. She manages projects in education and the community, especially relating to writing and/or social justice in some way. At university, she studied literature and culture, focusing on strategic silence, surveillance and standpoint theory. After a break of a few years, she went back to study part-time while working full-time, and after five years graduated with a PhD in creative writing.

Jodie Russian-Red, 'The Funeral and the Wedding'

Jodie Russian-Red is a part-time administrator, part-time writer in Nottingham. Over the past few years she has primarily written for performance art and spoken word and has had writing and performing commissions for Freedom Festival in Hull, The Collection in Lincoln. She was invited to be a featured guest at the spoken word event Women of Words in Hull in 2017. For the last two years she has written a weekly newsletter in the form of a personal memoir blog for the School of Cultures, Languages and Area Studies at the University of Nottingham, where she also holds a completely unrelated day job processing invoices, ordering stationery and monitoring coffee levels.

Anita Sethi, 'On Class and the Countryside'

Anita Sethi was born in and grew up in Manchester, UK. She has been published in several anthologies including the *Seasons* nature writing anthology, *Three Things I'd Tell My Younger Self, Seaside Special, We Mark Your Memory* and the forthcoming *Women on Nature*. She has written for publications including the *Guardian*, the *Observer*, *Granta*, *Times Literary Supplement* and *The Pool*, and appeared on BBC radio. She has been a Writer in Residence in Melbourne, Australia.

Adam Sharp, 'Play'

Adam Sharp is originally from Manchester but has also lived in London, Melbourne, Sydney, Queensland, the Channel Islands, the Canary Islands, Nashville and Newcastle-upon-Tyne. He has had over thirty jobs: some of these include catching footballs, juggling bottles, washing dishes, reviewing music, changing nappies and walking on stilts. He now spends his time working on books and has written four so far. @AdamCSharp

Adelle Stripe, 'Driftwood'

Adelle Stripe is a novelist and poet from Yorkshire. She grew up in a small brewery town and was a Girl Friday for many years before starting university as a mature student. Her debut novel, *Black Teeth and a Brilliant Smile* (2017), is inspired by the life and work of playwright Andrea Dunbar. It received the K. Blundell Award for Fiction and was shortlisted for the Gordon Burn Prize. Her writing has appeared in publications including *The Quietus*, *New Statesman* and the *Guardian*. She is a lecturer in Creative Writing at York St John University and lives in the Calder Valley.

Eva Verde, 'I Am Not Your Tituba'

Eva Verde is a writer from Forest Gate, east London. She is of dual heritage. Identity and class are recurring themes throughout her work. While studying towards an MA in Creative Writing, she is also working on her first novel about a woman's hedonistic rebellion against familial ties and societal pressures. Eva lives in Essex with her husband, three children and elderly black Labrador. Her inclusion in *Common People* is her first time in print.

Lynne Voyce, 'A Brief History of Industrial Action, Vauxhall Motors, Ellesmere Port'

Lynne Voyce grew up on a council estate in Ellesmere Port, a place full of larger-than-life characters, tall tales and the odd dodgy deal. Inspired by her dad buying *The Literary Classics Collection* with some of his redundancy money, she studied English at the University of Leeds, and went on to take a teaching qualification and then a postgraduate degree in educational psychology. Lynne now works in an inner-city comprehensive school in Birmingham. She has published more than fifty individual short stories, won a number of literary competitions, and, in December 2015, published her first story collection, *Kirigami*, with Ink Tears Press. She is currently working on her first novel.

Tony Walsh (aka Longfella), 'Tough'

Tony Walsh FRSA, also known as Longfella, is a professional poet, writer, performer and educator based in Manchester. A former Poet in Residence at Glastonbury Festival, his work has been commissioned by the *Guardian*, the *Observer*, Channel 4 News, the Imperial War Museum, the Lake District National Park and many times by BBC television and radio. Tony's work has been widely anthologised, published in the UK and USA, and is collated into two full collections for adults: *SEX & LOVE & ROCK&ROLL* (2013) and *WORK | LIFE | BALANCE* (2019), both with the fiercely indie Burning Eye Books. He has also collaborated on two picture books for small children with more planned. A passionate educator, Tony leads acclaimed workshops in schools, colleges and universities from Keswick to Kazakhstan, as well as with refugees, asylum seekers, prisoners and socially excluded people in a wide range of settings.

After being raised in council housing and dropping out of the University of Salford in the mid-eighties, Tony was unemployed for eighteen months, worked in a sausage factory, an industrial bakery and on a Post Office counter, where he was tied up at gunpoint, before an eighteen-year career managing inner-city housing and regeneration projects for local authorities. His poem 'This Is the Place' made headlines worldwide when performed at the vigil for victims of the Manchester Arena bomb in May 2017, subsequently raising around £200,000 for local charities. Tony was awarded the honorary degree of Doctor of Letters by his former university in 2018.

Alex Wheatle, 'Dear Nobody'

Alex Wheatle's first novel, *Brixton Rock*, was published to critical acclaim by BlackAmber Books in 1999. He won the London Arts Board Writers Prize in 2000 and was awarded an MBE for services to literature in 2008. His first young adult novel, *Liccle Bit*, was published in 2015 and was longlisted for the Carnegie Medal 2015. His novel *Crongton Knights*, published in 2016, won the *Guardian*'s Children's Fiction Award for 2016 and the Renaissance Quiz Writers' Choice Award, and was shortlisted for the 2017 Bookseller Young Adult prize.

Helen Wilber, 'Underdogs'

Helen Wilber lives in Leicester but was born and raised in Mexborough, South Yorkshire. This is the first time her work has been published, but hopefully not the last. Helen was inspired to start writing after a brief spell working in a library. She mainly writes short stories but has recently been experimenting with different forms, including writing for radio. Helen works full-time and currently writes at weekends and in the evening. When she's not writing, she likes riding her bike and thinking of things to write. @wilber_wall

Elaine Williams, 'Night'

Sheffield-born Elaine Williams has lived in London for three decades. A graduate of the National Film and Television School, she worked in film and TV as a sound recordist, and in the computer games industry as a sound designer. She is a teacher/lecturer/tutor and has worked in secondary, Post16 and adult education; she is currently a specialist teacher in the alternative education sector. Formative to her writing life was her (early noughties) freelance journalism for *Calabash*, a literary magazine that profiled African, Caribbean and Asian writers. She has an MA in Narrative Non-Fiction from City University and is currently working on her first book, a collection inspired by memories of her late father. In 2016, Elaine was shortlisted for the Penguin Random House WriteNow mentoring scheme. In September 2018, she was selected for The London Writers Award professional development programme.

Shaun Wilson, 'Passengers'
Shaun Wilson was born in 1980 and raised in Wigton, Cumbria. In 2011, after fifteen years as a guitarist and lyricist in various rock-and-roll bands, he began learning to write prose. He currently works as a postman and studies towards an MA in creative writing at Northumbria University. In his spare time, he co-edits the university's creative magazine, *Edge*. He was shortlisted for a Northern Writers' Award in 2018 and for a WriteNow mentorship in 2018. @smw_writing

Unbound is the world's first crowdfunding publisher, established in 2011.

We believe that wonderful things can happen when you clear a path for people who share a passion. That's why we've built a platform that brings together readers and authors to crowdfund books they believe in – and give fresh ideas that don't fit the traditional mould the chance they deserve.

This book is in your hands because readers made it possible. Everyone who pledged their support is listed below. Join them by visiting unbound.com and supporting a book today.

Kia Abdullah
Jools Abrams-
　Humphries
Lauren Ace
Martha Adam
Carys Afoko
Haleh Agar
Farah Ahamed
Mediah Ahmed
Holly Ainley
Molly Aitken
Tony Aitman
Emad Akhtar
Hazel Alexander

Ines Alfano
Verity Allan
Joe Allen
Eli Allison
Lulu Allison
Debi Alper
Mellany Ambrose
Sharon Amos
Edie Anderson
Jonny Anderson
Zoe Anderson
Jane Anger
Antonio Arch
Jason Arthur

Will Ashon
Marie Bagley
Scott Bain
Neil Baker
Sam Baker
Alicia Bakewell
Katya Balen
Vivian Bannerman
Nicola Bannock
Zoe Barber
Hazel Barkworth
Anthony Barnett
Janine Barnett-Phillips
Damian Barr

Zena Barrie
Bath Novel Award
Yvonne Battle-Felton
Elizabeth Bazalgette
Rachael Beale
Nichole Beauchamp
Dawn Behan
Ruth Behan
Honoria Beirne
Emily Bell
Jo Bell
Julia Bell
Kevin Bell
Natasha Bell
Paul Benedyk
Bart Bennett
Gaverne Bennett
Lisa Benoist
Amanda Berriman
Lisa Berry
Alice Beverton-Palmer
Jay Bhadricha
Mark Billingham
Helen Bilton
Steve Bilton
Catherine Bjarnason
Nick Black
Melissa Blackburn
Lynne Blackwell
Fanny Blake
Claire Blakemore
Amanda Block
Astra Bloom
Stephanie Boland
Hannah Bond
Alison Bond McNally
Agnes Bookbinder
@BooksandJohn

Stephen Booth
Tracey Booth
Mair Bosworth
John Boyne
David Bradford
Jo Bradshaw
Monica Brady
Celia Brayfield
Nollaig Brennan
Andy Brereton
Laura Brewis
Angela Bridge
Stuart Briggs
David Britten
Richard Bromhall
Iain Broome
Francesca Brown
Pete Brown
Cassie Browne
Catharine Browne
Laura Bryars
Rowan Buchanan
Diane Buck
Anna Bull
Kate Bulpitt
Victoria Burgher
Wendy Burke
Dawn Burnett
Lazlo Burns
Anna Burtt
Virginie Busette
SJ Butler
Aslan Byrne
Colin Byrne
June Caldwell
Mark Calvert
Rosie Eleanor Canning
Anna Carey

Caroline Carpenter
Liz Carr
Maggie Carroll
Sean Carroll
Mark Cartridge
Megan Cartridge
Harriet Castor
Morag Caunt
Cassie Chadderton
Michael and Susan
  Chaplin
Sam Chapman Jones
Stella Chevalier
Lumiere Chieh
Alix Christie
Joe Christie
Neil Clark
Giorgina L R Clarke
Jane Clarke
Paul Michael Clarke
Chris Cleave
Joanne Clement
Helena Close
Garrett Coakley
Dave Coates
Anna Coatman
Ann Coburn
Amanda Coe
Jonathan Coe
Tammy Cohen
Charli Colegate
Jenny Colgan
Bea Colley
Alys Conran
Caitie-Jane Cook
James Cook
Jude Cook
Clare Coombes

John Cooper
Louise Corcoran
Katharine Corr
Isabel Costello
Nick Coveney
Robert Cox
Denis Coyle
Anne Crawford
John Crawford
Joanna Crispin
Kev Crocombe
Maggie Cronin
Julia Croyden
Helen Cullen
Danielle Culling
John Cunningham
Michele D'Acosta
Penny Dakin-Kiley
Dan Dalton
Bucker Dangor
Jonathan Darby
Jane Darroch Riley
A M Dassu
Rishi Dastidar
Rupert Dastur
Ryan Davey
Jonathan Davidson
Peter Davies
Joshua Davis
Laura Davis
Jill Dawson
Becca Day-Preston
Claire de Pourtalès
Dominique De-Light
Jon Dean
Will Dean
Geraldine Deas
Anna Delaney

Deborah Delano
Emily Devane
Alan Devey
Joanna Dingley
Jami Dixon
Claire Doherty
Margaret Dolley
Pete Domican
Caroline Donahue
Helen Donohoe
Kirsty Doole
Maura Dooley
Kay Doragh
Kirsty Dorward
Elisa Doucette
Shaun Dovaston
Ellie Downes
Jonathan Doyle
Kristopher Doyle
Daniel Draper
Adrian Driscoll
Katy Driver
Benjamin Duffield
Kevin Duffy
Susan Duffy
Jane Dugdale
Sharon Duggal
Helena Duk
Katherine Dunn
Emer Dunne
I Dutta
Joely Dutton
Tomek Dzido
Kathryn Eastman
Annie Eaton
Holly Edgar
Kathryn Edwards
Eugene Egan

Ken Elkes
Joanna Ellis
Matt Espley
Ilana Estreich
Fergus Evans
Joe Evans
Lissa Evans
Robyn Evans
Rose Evans
Bernardine Evaristo
Melissa Eveleigh
Penelope Faith
Arnold Thomas
    Fanning
Sarah Farley
Virginia Fassnidge
Rachel J Fenton
Anthony Ferner
Charles Fernyhough
Nathan Filer
Becky Fincham
Arlene Finnigan
Edward Fitzpatrick
Jean Flack
Lucy Flannery
Molly Flatt
Ana Fletcher
Garrie Fletcher
Maggie Fogarty
Jean Forbes
Sheran Forbes
Kt Ford
Jeff Forshaw
Rebecca Fortuin
Tizzie Frankish
D Franklin
Sarah Franklin
Tim Franks

Catherine Fravalo
Tina Freeth
Naomi Frisby
Melissa Fu
Cara Fullbrook
Madeleine Gabriel
Frances Gapper
Sarah Garnham
Michelle Gately
Jeanne Gavenda
Vanessa Gebbie
Aimee-Marie Gedge
Emma Geen
Jonny Geller
Rachel Genn
Fenella Gentleman
Dai George
Martin Geraghty
Friederike Gerken
Ann German
Mog & Pauline
    Giacomelli-Harris
Daniele Gibney
Sirius Gibson
Kate Gilbert
Matthew Gilbert
Ruth Gilligan
Sarah Gilmartin
Sinéad Gleeson
Salena Godden
Clare Goggin
Miranda Gold
Luan Goldie
Clare Golding
Caroline Goldsmith
Sophie Goldsworthy
Andrew Golightly
Katie Goodall

Victoria Goodbody
Anita Goodfellow
Norman Goodman
PM Goodman
Heide Goody
Rich Gordon
Katie Göttlinger
Sharon Goulds
Lucille Grant
Michele Grant
Linda Green
Michelle Green
Amber Greenall-
    Heffernan
Joanne Greenway
Karen Gregory
Sarah Gregory
Meredith Greiling
Tamsin Grey
Hannah Griffiths
Rhiannon Griffiths
Guy Gunaratne
Lisa Hadwin
Daniel Hahn
J H Hall
Nicky Hallam
Patricia Hallam
Michael Handrick
Sharon Hardwick
Alison Hardy
Robin Hargreaves
Gina Harkell
Jac Harmon
Mary-Anne Harrington
Harry Harris
Shelley Harris
Brian Harrison
Ruth Harrison

Tania Harrison
Sally Harrop
Antonia Hart
Francoise Harvey
Simon Hawke
Anthony Hayes
Annie Hayford-Joyner
Sam Haysom
Philip Headford
Abbie Headon
Rob Heal
Mark Hearne, happy
    birthday from
    Marcia Hearne
Hedgehog Poetry
John Herbert
Tania Hershman
Claire Heuchan
Jan Hicks
Jude Higgins
Alice Hiller
Mischa Hiller
Victoria Hobbs
Roo Hocking
Michelle Hodgson
Faye Holder
Lisa Holdsworth
John Holland
Simon Holland Roberts
David Honeybone
Antonia Honeywell
Jon Horne
Gerry Horner
Keith E Hoult
Jo Howard
Katharine Howell
Jenny Hoy
Lesley Hoyles

Nick Hubble
Kerry Hudson
Emma Hughes
Seanín Hughes
Maggie Humm
Catherine Hunt
Roseena Hussain
Charlotte Hutchinson
Tom Hutchinson
Lizzie Huxley-Jones
Louise I'Anson
Christine Ince
Rivka Isaacson
Anietie Isong
Angela Jackson
Helen Jackson
Kellie Jackson
Bethan James
Charley James
Simon James
Robert Alan Jamieson
Kiera Jamison
Christian Jeffery
Alexandra Jellicoe
Ingrid Jendrzejewski
Simon Jerrome
Wally Jiagoo
Marjana Johansson
Denny John
Noel Johnson
Alice Jolly
Ali Jones
Liz Jones
Merith Jones
Sarah Jowett
Avril Joy
Belinda Ju
Zainab Juma

Manveer Singh Kahlon
Meena Kandasamy
Sandy Kaur
Tom Kearney
Kate Kemp
Viv Kemp
David Kendall
Christina Kennedy
Sarah Kennedy
Sue Kennedy
Rachael Kerr
Richard Kerridge
K.L. Kettle
Farhana Khalique
Mobeena Khan
Ansa Khan Khattak
Dan Kieran
Gillian Kilcoyne
Carrie King
Daisy King
Julia Kingsford
Gyda Kjekshus
Simon Kövesi
William Kraemer
Wilhelmina Kraemer-
    Zurné
Dal Kular
Pierre L'Allier
Raj K Lal
Bethany Rose Lamont
Jenny Landreth
Danny Lang
Valerie Langfield
Rebekah Lattin-
    Rawstrone
Claire Laurens
Janice Leagra
Sarah Lee

Diane Leedham
Gayle Letherby
Chantelle Lewis
Sean Linnen
Russ Litten
Lauren Livesey
Amy Lloyd
David Lloyd
Victoria Lloyd-Hughes
Adam Lock
Matt Locke
Kate Lockwood Jefford
Caroline Lodge
Katherine Long
Paul Long
Amy Lord
Suzy Louise
Michael Loveday
Sharmaine Lovegrove
Jo Lovesdancing
Madeline Lucas
My Ly
P K Lynch
Julie Ma
Peter Mackie
Seonaid MacLeod
Margaret Madden
Pietro Magnavacca
Hannah Maguire
Michael Maguire
Rosemary Maguire
Sabrina Mahfouz
Katy Mahood
Tasmin Maitland
Jai Malarkey
Claire Malcolm
Gautam Malkani
Lisa Maltby

Nick Malyan
Rachel Mann
Kate Marcus
Ita Marquess
Anabel Marsh
Ange Martin
Fatima Martin
Pip Martin
Amanda Mason
Robert Mason
Thomas Masterman
Helen Matthews
Nicola Mayell
Melanie McAinsh
Bernadette McAloon
Angela McAndrew
R. E. McAuliffe
Pete McCaldon
Cormac McConnell
Margot McCuaig
Kate McDermott
Polly Fiona McDonald
Amy McElroy
Nollaig McEvilly
Rose McGinty
Peter McGladdery
Rebecca McGlynn
Melanie McGrath
Monica McInerney
Robert McIntosh
Lucie McKnight Hardy
Duncan McLean
David McMenemy
Alan McMonagle
Kate McNaughton
Eileen McNulty-Holmes
Marie-Anne McQuay
Liz Meagher

Rosy Meehan
Glen Mehn
Bob Melling
Ali Mercer
Martin Meteyard
Erinna Mettler
Margaret Meyer
Loretta Milan
Tamar Millen
Cat Mitchell
Fiona Mitchell
Melanie Mitchell
John Mitchinson
Lucy Moffatt
Virginia Moffatt
Sarah Molloy
Damhnait Monaghan
Penny Montague
Nikolas Montaldi
Katy Moran
Sophie Morgan
Sinead Moriarty
Georgina Morley
Emily Morris
Sarah Morris
Anthea Morrison
Peter Mortimer
Nicola Mostyn
Diane Mulholland
Caroline Murphy
Jill Murphy
Mike Murphy
Annie Murray
Kirsty Murray
Simon Musso
Lou Mycroft
Benjamin Myers
Linda Nathan

Carlo Navato
Kate Neilan
Antony Nelson
David Nettleingham
David Nicholls
Kes Nielsen
Jo Norcup
Benedicta Norell
Liz Nugent
Patty O'Boyle
Amanda O'Callaghan
Mark O'Loughlin
Vanessa Fox
    O'Loughlin
Catherine O'Mahony
Grace O'Malley
Mark O'Neill
David O'Reilly
Margaret O'Brien
Rachel Oakes
Rodney Oglesby
Brian Oliver
Mairi Christine Oliver
Phil Olsen
G Oommen
Dr Jennifer Orr
Jeremy Osborne
Elizabeth Ottosson
Lucy Oulton
Charlotte Packer
Rice Parker
Scarlett Parker
Simon Parkin
Monica Parle
Loren Parry
Poppy Peacock
Maxine Peake
AJ Pearce

Jamie Peel
Robert Peett
Alison Percival
Ely Percy
Sarah Perry
Hannah Persaud
Rina Picciotto
Juliet Pickering
Adam Piechocki-Brown
Simon Pinkerton
Chelsey Pippin
Stef Pixner
Eddie Playfair
Carrie Plitt
Justin Pollard
Nicholas Poole
Victoria Pougatch
Dan Powell
Mandy Powell
Andrew Preater
Simon Pressinger
Sharron Preston
Mandy Preville-Findlay
Elizabeth Price
Francis Pryor
Gavin Pugh
Emma Quigley
Joanna Quinn
Linda Quinn
Sadiah Qureshi
Mandy Rabin
Rachey Rach
Alexa Radcliffe-Hart
Leanne Radojkovich
Laura Ramsey
Chris Randall
Hanna Randall
Holly Ranger

Chris Ratcliffe
Peter Raynard
Rebecca
Clare Reddington
Nina Ann Reece
Alex Reeve
Sandra Reid
Kerry-Jo Reilly
Milly Reilly
Barbara Renel
Fran Reynolds
Zelda Rhiando
Emma Rhind-Tutt
Matthew Rich
Hollie Richards
Victoria Richards
Steve Riley
Terri-Leigh Riley
Tim Riley
C Roberts
Jane Roberts
Sarah-Jane Roberts
Imogen Robertson
Frances Robinson
Miriam Robinson
Rachael Robinson
David Roche
Sallyanne Rock
Lisa Rodan
Katie Roden
Molly Rosenberg
Tamsin Rosewell
Iain Rowan
Lisa Ruddy
Reshma Ruia
Lisa Rull
Jonathan Ruppin
Jane Rusbridge

Caitlin Russell
Mark Rutterford
Helen Rye
Camille S
Irina Sabatina
Alison Sakai
Clare Sambrook
Caroline Sanderson
Lou Sarabadzic
Simon Savidge
Nada Savitch
Shannon Savvas
Maggie Sawkins
Cherise Saywell
Elena Schmitz
Rob Schofield
Stephanie Scott
Stefanie Seddon
Claire Sedgwick
Rose Servitova
Ajay Sethi
Becky Sexton
Keith Shackleton
Carl Shanks
Fiona Sharp
Gemma Sharpe
Katy Shaw
Richard Sheehan
Nadia Shireen
Robin Shortt
Nikesh Shukla
Jared Shurin
Julia Silk
Betina Simons
Chris Simpson
Susan Sinclair
Yvonne Singh
Rashmi Sirdeshpande

Amy Slack
Frances Sleigh
Rebecca Smart
Clare Smith
Elizabeth Smith
Ken Smith
Lewis Smith
Michael T A Smith
Polly Smith
Stephanie Smith
Will Smith and Polly
   Atkin
Carolyn Soakell
Sam Solnick
Justine Solomons
Eamon Somers
Jo Somerset
Mickela Sonola
L.M. Sorrell
Malcolm Spatz
Dee Spencer
Sid Spencer
Truda Spruyt
Nicola Spurr
Eliza Squire
Oliver Stapleton
Henriette B. Stavis
Cathryn Steele
Gabriela Steinke
James Stelfox
Martha Stenhouse
Laura Stephens
Karen Stevens
Katherine Alex Stevens
Alison Stewart
Peter Stojanovic
Ashley Stokes
Susan Stokes-Chapman

Degna Stone
Louie Stowell
Shane Strachan
Christopher Stuart
Anne Summerfield
Laura Summers
Nuala Suttill
Becky Swain
Emily Sweet
Kate Swindlehurst
Susie Symes
Daniel Syrovy
Preti Taneja
Helen Taylor
Paul Taylor
Hannah Telfer
Carrie Thompson
Dick Thompson
Gillian Thompson
Jackie Thompson
Patrick Thompson
Pen Thompson
Sandy Thomson
Lorna Thorpe
Ali Thurm
Monica Timms
Lisa Tippings
Louise Tizzard
Gemma Todd
Pippa Tolfts
John Tomaney
Rose Tomaszewska
Tramp Press
Helen Trevorrow
Catriona Troth
Alexandra Trott
Carol Troy
Jennifer Tubbs

Cyan Turan
David Turner
Antonia Turnip
Wendy Tuxworth
Harriet Tyce
Tor Udall
Jo Unwin
Julia Unwin
Tracey Upchurch
Wouter van Dijke
Sandra van Lente
Laure Van Rensburg
Janet Vaughan
Anna Vaught
Sally Vince
Annie Vincent
Hannah Vincent
Paul Vincent
Peter Viner-Brown
Alice Violett
Jo W
Jonathan Wakeham
Alex Walker
Sue Walker
Chris Walsh
Judi Walsh
Andy Warmington
Ruth Waterton
Alex Watson
Colin Watts
Cat Weatherill
Lara Weisweiller-Wu
Tom Wells
Annice White
ML White
Michael Whitworth
Li Whybrow
Erica Whyman

Rachel Wickert
Philip Widdop
Susan Wilde
Louise Wilkin
Andrea Wilkinson
Andrew Wille
Carol Williams
Helen Williams
Kathryn Williams
Catherine Williamson
Emily Willsher
Louise Wilson
Laura Windley
Terri & Howard
    Windling-Gayton
Lucie Winter
Lesley Wood
Ravensara Woodley
    Cadey
Denyse Woods
Rebecca Wright
Hannah Wroblewski
Josef Wyczynski
Natasha Wynne
Helen Young
Missie Young
Stephanie Young
Thomas Young
Shahed Yousaf
Martina Zandonella
Rupert Ziziros